THREADS

THREADS

GENDER, LABOR, AND POWER
IN THE GLOBAL APPAREL INDUSTRY

JANE L. COLLINS

THE UNIVERSITY OF CHICAGO PRESS   CHICAGO AND LONDON

The University of Chicago Press, Chicago 60637
The University of Chicago Press, Ltd., London
© 2003 by Jane L. Collins
All rights reserved. Published 2003
Printed in the United States of America

12 11 10 09 08 07 06 05   3 4 5

ISBN: 0-226-11370-1 (cloth)
ISBN: 0-226-11372-8 (paper)

Library of Congress Cataloging-in-Publication Data

Collins, Jane Lou, 1954–
     Threads : gender, labor, and power in the global apparel industry / Jane L.
Collins.
        p. cm.
     Includes bibliographical references and index.
     ISBN 0-226-11370-1 (cloth : alk. paper) — ISBN 0-226-11372-8 (pbk. : alk.
paper)
     1. Women clothing workers—Virginia—Martinsville. 2. Knit goods industry—
Virginia—Martinsville—Employees. 3. Clothing workers—Virginia—
Martinsville. 4. Clothing trade—United States. 5. Consumers—United States—
Attitudes. 6. Women clothing workers—Mexico—Aguascalientes. 7. Knit goods
industry—Mexico—Aguascalientes—Employees. 8. Clothing workers—
Mexico—Aguascalientes. 9. Globalization—Economic aspects—United States—
Case studies. 10. Globalization—Economic aspects—Mexico—Case studies. 11.
International business enterprises—United States—Case studies. 12. Liz
Claiborne Inc. I. Title: Gender, labor, and power in the global apparel industry.
II. Title.

HD6073.C62U537 2003
331.7′687—dc21
                                                                        2002045579

If we grant the existence of such connections, how are we to conceive of them? Can we grasp a common process that generates and organizes them? Is it possible to envision such a common dynamic and yet maintain a sense of its distinctive unfolding in time and space?

—ERIC WOLF, *EUROPE AND THE PEOPLE WITHOUT HISTORY*

Feminine and masculine gender identity run like pink and blue threads through the areas of paid work . . . and citizenship.

—NANCY FRASER, *UNRULY PRACTICES*

Scissors
have gone
everywhere,
they've explored
the world . . .

—PABLO NERUDA, "ODE TO A PAIR OF SCISSORS"

CONTENTS

PREFACE

This book is based on a multisited ethnography of the global garment industry, focusing on four locations: a knitting mill in southern Virginia, the
New Jersey corporate headquarters of a successful apparel firm with a global
production strategy, and two apparel factories in Aguascalientes, Mexico.
It traces the flows of resources and power between these sites in the late
1990s, a period when the industry was experiencing intense competitive
pressure. The essential question that underlies the endeavor is what it
means to be a worker in an industry with a global labor market and how
participating in such a labor market affects the social relations of work, the
organization of production, the opportunities for negotiating with employers, and the forms of resistance that make sense.

Given the composition of the apparel workforce, this is a profoundly
gendered question. Textile production was the most important industry in
the first Industrial Revolution, and women were key players in the movement of work from home to factory. Today the apparel and textile industries
are leading the way in developing a truly global production process, and
once again women and gender are central to the story. This book tries to
work against the gender-neutral, or sometimes simply male, categories of
traditional economic analysis to shape our understanding of new global processes of industrialization and deindustrialization.

I brought to this project both my childhood in Virginia and nearly thirty
years of research in Latin America. At the time I was growing up (the 1950s
and 1960s), Latin America seemed much farther away from Virginia than it
does today. People working in factories like the Martinsville plant described
in this book had a hard time seeing any connection between their lives and
the lives of women in places like Mexico. In contrast, in 1999—the year I
carried out most of the fieldwork for this project—there was no Virginia
worker who didn't have an opinion on the relation between her livelihood
and that of women in southern countries. Some workers understood their

relationship to be one of competition. They suggested that Mexican women drew jobs with their cheaper labor the way they themselves had attracted jobs from the northern United States in earlier decades. Some joked that they were thinking of moving to Mexico to get work. Many said they wanted to go there to see where their jobs went and what the conditions were.[1]

In a similar way, Mexican apparel workers now grapple with the paradoxes of global connection. I was struck by the words of one young woman who took part in a strike at her factory in December 2001 that was supported by North American college students. She said:

> We produce things; they wear what we produce. . . . They say that they didn't like learning how we produce their sweatshirts, that they didn't like knowing that . . . our little sisters sewed them in the maquiladoras . . . the mistreatment, the low salaries. And of course we didn't like it either, because we had to leave our games and school to go to work, but for us there was no alternative. We agreed on this, that we didn't like a situation where differences existed because some had money and power and others had nothing but their hands and their ability to work. But we were and are together, and that is what's important. It is a new world where we can know what happens on one side and the other in a few seconds, and this unites us."[2]

For this worker, the daily irony of sewing blue jeans that she could never afford was coupled with an understanding of the usefulness of labor solidarity across borders.

In this book I ask, and try to answer, questions about how competition in the apparel industry shapes the organization of work, and about how workers experience these changes in work organization. I do this using two methods. The first—a version of commodity chain analysis, traces the economic linkages that run between Wall Street and Madison Avenue, the factories that make garments, the stores that sell them, and the consumers who buy them. Using this method, I attempt to draw out hidden connections and to clarify the ways actions taken in one part of the commodity chain reverberate in other locations. A second method makes comparisons across cases. I examine differences in the workings of two companies that

---

1. See William M. Adler, *Mollie's Job: A Story of Life and Work on the Global Assembly Line* (New York: Scribner, 2000).

2. Worker at Kukdong factory (now Mexmode), Atlixco, Puebla, Mexico, cited in Huberto Juárez Núñez, *Rebelión en el Greenfield* (Puebla: Benemérita Universidad Autónoma de Puebla and American Federation of Labor–Congress of Industrial Organizations, 2002), 128. My translation.

produce different kinds of apparel, and I compare one firm's United States factories with its operations in Mexico. These analytical techniques help answer some focused questions about how apparel work is changing.

But the significance of the ethnographic material presented here is broader than that. In so much recent writing, globalization appears faceless and inevitable, a vast, abstract process that few of us understand and none of us control. I hope the stories in this book will help us think through current debates about globalization and sweatshops, putting some names and faces on the actors. In this way the book raises questions—if not fully answering them—regarding what we as a society, or as global citizens, want to do about the apparel industry's current practices.

As I was finishing this book, I happened to reread Jane Schneider's work on the fairy tale of Rumpelstiltskin. Schneider reads this familiar tale in relation to the emergence of industrial linen manufacture in early modern Europe. In the story, a father locks his daughter in a room and insists she must spin straw into gold. The young woman despairs at the impossible task. A demon or spirit appears and offers to help with the work, but at the price of her firstborn child. Schneider probes versions of the Rumpelstiltskin tale for the ambivalence they convey about early industrialization. She argues that they reflect the profound contradictions that peasant women of that period experienced—better chances of wealth and marriage, but jeopardy to their children, as well as greed and litigiousness in social relations: "The producers crystallized their ambivalence toward the promotion of linen in tales of misfits like Rumpelstiltskin, who were nasty and yet helpful at the same time."[3]

The current era of globalization needs its own tales of ambivalence. Or perhaps those of an earlier age still apply. In the late twentieth century, state industrialization programs drew young women into the burgeoning factories of export processing zones and set them to work at seemingly impossible tasks. Foreign capital organized the work, but for a price. Like Rumpelstiltskin, the corporations that subcontract apparel production across the globe are ambiguous figures, promising help in creating wealth but asking nations to mortgage their futures in other ways. Assessing the nature and effects of these bargains is part of my task.

Remembering the folktales from an earlier period of industrialization helps remind us that while globalization presents us with many new possi-

3. Jane Schneider, "Rumpelstiltskin's Bargain: Folklore and the Merchant Capitalist Intensification of Linen Manufacture in Early Modern Europe," in *Cloth and Human Experience*, ed. Annette B. Weiner and Jane Schneider (Washington, D.C.: Smithsonian Institution Press, 1989), pp. 207–8.

bilities and problems, the central dilemmas are not new. To address them, we need to return to big questions about what development means: Is it the simple increase of wealth, or does it entail fostering social well-being? We need to pay attention to how power is distributed in new transnational arrangements, to examine who gains and who loses, and to ask who has a voice. These are not new questions; they are older dilemmas of social justice returning in new forms.

ACKNOWLEDGMENTS

I thank the National Science Foundation and the University of Wisconsin Graduate School for funding the research for this book. Greta Krippner and Deniz Ozesmi-Yildiz provided expert research assistance, and Greta traveled to Aguascalientes in 2000 to carry out the field research there. Molly McGrath generously shared notes from her visits to Mexican apparel factories as a member of a delegation sent by United Students Against Sweatshops. My University of Wisconsin colleagues Stephen Bunker, Myra Marx Ferree, Gay Seidman, and Jonathan Zeitlin provided thoughtful feedback on various versions of the manuscript, as did colleagues from other institutions, including Caitrin Lynch and Laurie Green. Anthropologist Micaela di Leonardo not only offered extraordinarily useful and engaged commentary but challenged me to make the book readable to a popular audience. If I have come anywhere close to achieving that goal, it is because of her assistance. My thoughts on the apparel industry in Mexico were sharpened by conversations with economist Huberto Juárez Núñez of the Universidad Autónoma de Puebla during his visits to Madison in 2001 and 2002. Thanks to Jocelyn Olcott, Michaeline Crichlow, Rex Honey, Ann Orloff, and Micaela di Leonardo for speaking invitations that provided opportunities for feedback on my ideas.

Liz Claiborne Incorporated and Tultex Corporation were extraordinarily gracious and receptive to my inquiries. At Liz Claiborne, I especially thank Robert Zane, Margaret Schneider, David Baron, Donald Baum, and Daryl Brown. At the former Tultex Corporation, I received assistance from Kim Adkins, Jack Gardner, Jeff Judkins, Debbie Lewis, Henry Moore, Barbara Prillamon, Jerry Robertson, John Smith, Gene Teague, and Sheila Webb. In Martinsville and the surrounding area, I also thank Carol Sheerer and Anthony Coles of UNITE and a large contingent of Tultex workers including, but not limited to, Joe Compton, Anthony Hairston, Vicky Hooker, Geraldine Horton, Terry Lockhart, Sandra Mikles, Glenda Scales, and Sammy

Schoefield. In Mexico City, Greta Krippner and I thank Graham Anderton of Aztex Trading Company and Omar Dominguez Vega of CANAIVE (the National Apparel Industry Chamber of Commerce). In Aguascalientes we received help from Sergio Aguire, Luis Patrón, and Heriberto Malcampo of Burlmex and Carlos Ramos of Confitek, as well as Juan Antonio Huerta Morín, the director of the Aguascalientes branch of CANAIVE.

Thanks to Alda Blanco, Michaeline Crichlow, Aimee Dechter, Patricia Hodson, Nancy Kaiser, and Susan Sterett for fun, food, friendship, and support, and to Mariamne Whatley not only for friendship but for helping me carve out the time to complete the manuscript. Thanks also to family members Bonnie Tunney and Annabelle Collins for being there, and to the Painter family of Charlottesville and McGaheysville, Virginia, for their interest and encouragement and for clipping news articles on the apparel industry from the local press. Finally, my son Robert Painter traveled with me to field sites, provided encouragement (and distraction), and came up with the book's title, all of which I deeply appreciate.

1

TRACING THE THREADS
OF A GLOBAL INDUSTRY

*If, as Marx defined them, commodities are the containers
of hidden social relationships, certainly these social relationships are all the more concealed by the movement of
production to the Third World.*

—SUSAN WILLIS, *A PRIMER FOR DAILY LIFE*[1]

Workers in a Global Labor Market

In the United States in the late 1990s and the early years of the twenty-
first century, sweatshops were national news. The press reported that a
factory in El Monte, California, making clothing for major corporations held
immigrant Thai workers in slavery.[2] It covered the arrest of a garment shop
manager in New York City's Chinatown whose employees were laboring
twenty-hour shifts, seven days a week.[3] News stories from Seattle, New York,
and Washington, D.C., showed streets filled with people protesting corporate profit derived from sweatshops. Student, labor, and religious groups
organized boycotts of name brands associated with sweatshop conditions.
The papers reported on sit-ins at administration buildings on college campuses, where students demanded that clothing bearing their schools' logos

---

1. Susan Willis, *A Primer for Daily Life* (New York: Routledge, 1991), 52.
2. Julie Su, "El Monte Thai Garment Workers: Slave Sweatshops," in *No Sweat: Fashion,
Free Trade and the Rights of Garment Workers,* ed. Andrew Ross (New York: Verso, 1997),
143–50.
3. Jimmy Breslin, "In Sweatshops, Plundered Lives," *Newsday,* April 11, 2001. A2.

be produced under humane working conditions. The abysmal workplaces and poor wages that drew so much attention were not just a problem of factories on far-off shores; they were occurring in the United States as well. Contradicting the industrialized world's belief that its economies were different, a proliferation of sweatshops in developing nations appeared to coincide with the increased number and declining conditions of such factories in the United States and Europe as well.[4]

This trend, which linked the fate of workers in industrialized and developing countries, had been documented by several academic observers. As early as 1983, an anthropologist studying garment factories in Mexico noted that the expansion of the industry there paralleled "the resurgence of so-called sweatshops in metropolitan countries."[5] Seventeen years later, the incidence of sweatshops in Los Angeles had grown to alarming proportions. In writing about the growth of sweated labor in that city, sociologists Edna Bonacich and Richard Appelbaum argued that it needed to be understood as part of the restructuring of global capitalism and as linked to the increased exploitation of workers in the Third World.[6] These accounts stressed that the livelihoods of immigrant workers in U.S. cities, of rural workers in economically threatened factories of the southern United States, and of women and men laboring in export processing zones of developing nations were all linked to the fate of the same rapidly changing industries, an insight that challenges the boundaries of our time-honored concepts of "national" or "community" development.

That the growth of sweatshops in the United States and their growth

4. In the United States, the General Accounting Office defines a sweatshop as an employer that violates more than one federal or state labor law (United States General Accounting Office, *Garment Industry: Efforts to Address the Prevalence and Conditions of Sweatshops,* GAO HEHS-95-29, November 1994). According to federal and state government, there was an increase in labor law violations over the 1990s. A Department of Labor survey of registered garment firms in Los Angeles in 2000 showed that only one in three was in compliance with Federal minimum wage and overtime law (U.S. Department of Labor, Employment Standards Administration, Press Release USDL-112, August 25, 2000). An investigation of registered New Jersey shops that same year showed that more than half were in violation of labor laws (U.S. Department of Labor, Employment Standards Administration, Press Release NY-206, October 26, 2000). The Department of Labor estimates that nationwide 40 to 60 percent of registered establishments violate wage and overtime provisions of the Fair Labor Standards Act and that thousands of these shops have serious safety violations that threaten the health and lives of their workers (U.S. Department of Labor, *"No Sweat" Initiative Fact Sheet,* 1996, www.dol.gov/dol/esa/forum/fact.htm).

5. María Patricia Fernández-Kelly, *For We Are Sold, I and My People: Women and Industry in Mexico's Frontier* (Albany: State University of New York Press, 1983), 80.

6. Edna Bonacich and Richard Appelbaum, *Behind the Label: Inequality in the Los Angeles Apparel Industry* (Berkeley: University of California Press, 2000), 7.

abroad were interrelated was brought home to me in a vivid way as I conducted research for this book in a southern Virginia knitting mill in 1999. At a meeting of local 1994 of the garment workers' union UNITE, visibly angry workers described managers' attempts to increase the variety and complexity of tasks they were expected to perform under piece rate. They complained of ineffective grievance procedures and of union leaders so afraid of plant closure that they would not pressure management on the issue. One young African American man recalled the day in 1993 when 120 workers from the plant traveled to Washington, D.C. They visited members of Congress to encourage them to support legislation banning imports from sweatshops in the developing world. "We went to Washington to protest sweatshops," he said. "But third-floor knitting is a sweatshop now." Both the workers' collective trip to Washington and this man's assessment of his job situation reflected an understanding that the forces that caused firms to establish low-wage enclaves of garment production overseas were also undermining the conditions and security of jobs in Virginia.

Just one year later, a worker at a Mexican apparel factory told a similar story of intensification of the routines of work. She said that her employer, a Korean company that produced athletic apparel for some of the world's biggest brands, had raised workers' quotas from 3,000 to 3,600 pieces a week. Managers marked each worker's progress toward the quota on a graph above the person's station. The pressure to make these quotas while doing work that met quality standards was causing burnout within a very short time. This inspector said, "I could work here for perhaps two years before being exhausted, but the sewing operators get more pressure on them, so they can't stay as long." She explained the relation of the speedup to the global scope of the apparel labor market. "When people slow down or complain," she said, "the manager tells us that the workers in their Indonesian plant get paid much less and work harder."[7]

In response to situations like these, many people have called for transnational organizing. Bruce Raynor, the president of UNITE, argues that "the connections between the international unions and American unions need to be close" and that "eventually you may have to organize and negotiate on a world-wide basis."[8] William Greider, Kim Moody, and other popular writers have criticized analyses that pit the interests of older, more prosper-

---

7. From an interview conducted by University of Wisconsin undergraduate student Molly McGrath, at Kukdong factory, Atlixco, Puebla, Mexico, in December 2000.

8. "A Changing of the Guard at UNITE," *Women's Wear Daily*, June 26, 2001, 8.

ous workers in the United States against those of newly recruited, poorer workers in the developing world, arguing that the fates of workers at the top and the bottom of the ladder are interrelated.[9] Such organizing efforts are made difficult, however, by the real competition among groups of workers to secure and retain the rapidly shifting jobs of the "new economy." Transnational organizing that transcends protectionist impulses requires a clear understanding of the economic forces that sometimes link workers' interests and sometimes divide them, a willingness to consider long-run as well as short-run impacts, and a politically grounded analysis of the ways firms use and benefit from competition among workers.

Too often, calls for transnational labor solidarity treat workers as generic beings, without gender or ethnicity. When the newspapers report job loss in the United States, we tend to think of white men in hard hats receiving the pink slips. When we hear about the movement of jobs to Mexico or China, we tend to think of new industries with new male workers. In some cases this is a true picture, but as Jefferson Cowie has noted, the fact that women are often the first to be hired into assembly work and are often the most disposable workers in the chain of production "places them at the heart of the story of both industrialization and deindustrialization."[10] Not only are women workers in the majority in the world's new export assembly zones, but ideologies of gender and ethnicity are crucial to the political strategies through which employers recruit and administer a low-cost, efficient, and orderly labor force. In the global labor market, women continue to be paid according to prevailing gender ideologies that assume they live with husbands or fathers who help support them. They continue to be exhorted to be "good girls" whose productivity sustains both the family and the nation.[11] These ideologies and practices are central to the construction of the labor market and the organization of work wherever it takes place.

Apparel workers participate in an industry whose labor market has become interconnected—where workers in different parts of the world find themselves competing to perform the same operations for the same firms. Such a claim is not merely hyperbolic. By the turn of the twenty-first century, the vast majority of apparel firms could effectively locate, or subcon-

9. William Greider, *One World, Ready or Not: The Manic Logic of Global Capitalism* (New York: Simon and Schuster, 1997); Kim Moody, *Workers in a Lean World: Unions in the International Economy* (New York: Verso, 1997).

10. Jefferson Cowie, *Capital Moves: RCA's Seventy Year Quest for Cheap Labor* (New York: New Press, 1999), 197.

11. See Caitrin Lynch, "The 'Good Girls' of Sri Lankan Modernity: Moral Orders of Nationalism and Capitalism," *Identities* 6, no. 1 (1999): 55–89.

tract, their production in just about any part of the world. As one industry executive told a trade press publication in 1999, "There's no difference in manufacturing in North Carolina or El Salvador: it's the same everything except the cost of labor."[12]

Scholarly attempts to account for such global connection have been characterized by what Karel Williams has called "the slow death through a thousand qualifications about the global, the local and their interpenetration."[13] The ink spilled on this problem is not just a compulsion to repeat platitudes, however; it is a reflection of the awkwardness of our paradigms and concepts when we try to grasp phenomena of broad scope as they play themselves out in local environments. There is no single framework that allows us to integrate an understanding of labor struggles as they unfold on the ground with the financial imperative for firms to deliver not just higher rates of return, but consistently rising share prices. As apparel firms seek what David Harvey has called their "spatial fix,"[14] they are looking for cheap and controllable labor, but they must incorporate that consideration within a complex equation that includes transport costs, speed of delivery, distribution channels, import rules, fashion cycles, branding strategies, profit levels, and share prices. For workers in the industry, the equation includes the structure of local labor markets, social reproductive needs and choices, gender roles, racial hierarchies, job characteristics, and the evaluation of those characteristics within locally evolved moral economies of work. The shop floor is where these two equations intersect. All of this takes place within the context of national and international governance and the institutions that coordinate labor and business.

The art critic and essayist John Berger has written about the problems of grappling with complex entities and our difficulty, in the late modern period, in telling any story sequentially as if it were simply unfolding in time. "This is because," he observed, "we are too aware of what is continually traversing the storyline laterally. That is to say, instead of being aware of a point as an infinitely small part of a straight line, we are aware of it as an infinitely small part of an infinite number of lines, as the center of a star of lines."[15] The apparel labor market is at the center of a star of lines that traverse Wall Street and Madison Avenue, Mexico City, Ciudad Juárez,

12. "Women's Wear Makers Look Ahead to 2005," *Apparel Industry Magazine*, November 1999.

13. Karel Williams, "From Shareholder Value to Present-Day Capitalism," *Economy and Society* 29, no. 1 (2000): 5.

14. David Harvey, *The Limits to Capital* (1982; New York: Verso, 1999), 215–16.

15. John Berger, *The Look of Things* (New York: Viking Press, 1974), 40.

Djakarta, Hong Kong, and Shanghai. Choosing sites for investigation and telling meaningful stories about dynamics requires both a theory of global economic change and a grasp of the "commodity chain" through which clothing is produced and distributed. Studying it requires us to track the social relations of apparel production as these are restructured by local and global forces and enacted by employers and workers within their disparate and shared frameworks of meaning and power.

The Apparel Industry as Part of a Global Economy

Much social science writing about the global economy recalls the story of the blind men and the elephant. For whoever is investigating the trunk, it is all trunks, and for whoever has the tail, it is all tails. This is the point made by Walden Bello in his critique of Naomi Klein's *No Logo*.[16] Klein's book is a fascinating exposé of the ways that large firms use branded marketing strategies to create new markets, drive out competitors, and change the rules of the game in corporate competition. She also shows how "the branding of everything" changes consumer culture and factory working conditions. But as Bello points out, Klein's analysis does not hold true for every kind of manufacturing, and it is not an accurate portrayal of the global economy as a whole. While it does a good job of describing the dynamics of industries that sell consumer products and services, its insights do not apply to high technology and knowledge-intensive industries or to the production of inputs (like steel or oil) or machinery. More significantly, it ignores the role of finance and new forms of financial speculation in driving investment decisions.

A study of the apparel industry provides a very specific piece of the elephant, or the globalization picture. Like the consumer products industries Klein describes, apparel is what Gary Gereffi has called a buyer-driven commodity chain. This means that retailers and merchandisers play the leading role in setting up production networks. The dynamics of the apparel industry are different from those of producer-driven chains like automobiles, aircraft, and machinery. In these industries, the administrative headquarters of the producing firm organizes the production chain's backward and forward linkages.[17] This is a significant distinction because it tells us

16. Walden Bello, "*No Logo*: A Brilliant but Flawed Portrait of Contemporary Capitalism," *Z Magazine*, April 2001; Naomi Klein, *No Logo: Taking Aim at the Brand Bullies* (New York: Picador, 1999).
17. Gary Gereffi, "The Organization of Buyer-Driven Global Commodity Chains: How U.S. Retailers Shape Overseas Production Networks," in *Commodity Chains and Global Capi-*

where the greatest power lies within the industry and which actors are shaping trends.

Another distinctive feature of the apparel industry is its historically low levels of concentration. That is, it has been made up of many small firms that were often family owned. As late as 1987, the U.S. Office of Technology Assessment noted that the industry came close to representing a situation of "perfect competition" because of the large number of small companies it encompassed.[18] This situation began to change in the 1990s as "concentration became a fact of life in the once fragmented . . . industry."[19] Corporate mergers and an expansion of productive capacity through subcontracting fueled a trend toward fewer and larger firms over the decade.

One of the reasons the apparel industry has historically been congenial to small-scale entrepreneurs is that they did not need to make large investments to start a shop. Because garment work involves manipulating limp fabrics, its operations are not easily mechanized. Most of the recent technological developments in the industry have been in nonsewing operations such as design, cutting, warehouse management, and distribution.[20] The sewing itself is not all that different from what it was one hundred years ago. Entrepreneurs wishing to set up an apparel factory have needed only to rent a space and buy sewing machines, which they could often obtain secondhand from larger firms. This has made the industry especially attractive to immigrant entrepreneurs, who could get started with only small loans and tap kin and community networks to recruit workers.[21] The simplicity of its technology has meant that the industry remains very labor intensive. While labor costs average slightly less than one-third of total manufacturing expenditures, they are still the most significant production cost.[22] It is this heavy reliance on labor as a factor of production that has driven

talism, ed. Gary Gereffi and Miguel Korzeniewicz (Westport, Conn.: Praeger, 1994), 95–122.

18. Kitty Dickerson, *Textiles and Apparel in the Global Economy,* 2d ed. (Englewood Cliffs, N.J.: Merrill, 1995), 290.

19. Richard Appelbaum and Gary Gereffi, "Power and Profits in the Apparel Commodity Chain," in *Global Production: The Apparel Industry in the Pacific Rim,* ed. Edna Bonacich, Lucie Cheng, Norma Chinchilla, Nora Hamilton, and Paul Ong (Philadelphia: Temple University Press, 1994), 47.

20. Peter Dicken, *Global Shift: Transforming the World Economy,* 3d ed. (New York: Guilford, 1998), 297.

21. See Roger D. Waldinger, *Through the Eye of the Needle: Immigrants and Enterprise in New York's Garment Trades* (New York: New York University Press, 1986).

22. Fariborz Ghadar, William H. Davidson, and Charles S. Feigenoff, *U.S. Industrial Competitiveness: The Case of the Textile and Apparel Industries* (Lexington, Mass.: D. C. Heath, 1987), x; Dicken, *Global Shift,* 295.

apparel industry firms to seek cheap labor throughout the developing world.

Because of its labor intensity and low capital requirements, the apparel industry is one of the most broadly distributed across the globe, in both industrialized and developing nations. Counting only officially recognized workers, the industry employs 6 million people around the world, plus an additional 13 million in the manufacture of textiles. In the early 1980s, apparel and textiles taken together represented the largest manufacturing sector in the United States, employing 1.9 million workers, or 10 percent of the manufacturing workforce.[23]

Within the United States, the apparel industry has the most diverse workforce of any manufacturing sector. It is the largest employer of women and minority workers. In 1984, women made up 81 percent of the apparel workforce, while 27 percent of workers in the industry were minorities.[24] Noting that average hourly earnings in the garment industry were only about 60 percent of the average wage in manufacturing, one industry analyst has asked, "Is it more than coincidental that the manufacturing sector with the highest proportion of women and minority workers is the one with the lowest wages?"[25] Not surprisingly, as U.S. apparel firms have shifted more and more operations out of the country, the loss of jobs has disproportionately affected women and minorities, as well as inhabitants of rural communities.[26]

Apparel is the most important merchandise category for department stores, mass merchandisers, and specialty stores in the United States. As a consumer good, apparel is pervasive (everyone needs it), but it has what economists call "low demand elasticity." That is, as personal income rises, a smaller percentage of income is spent on basic clothing. Historically, the way the industry addressed this dilemma was to stimulate demand through fashion change. This process intensified and took new shape in the 1990s

23. For numbers of textile and apparel workers internationally, see Dicken, *Global Shift,* 283. For U.S. figures, see Ghadar, Davidson, and Feigenoff, *U.S. Industrial Competitiveness,* x. According to the Labor Department, employment in textiles and apparel peaked in 1973 at 2.45 million jobs (United States Department of Labor, Bureau of Labor Statistics, *Employment Hours and Earnings, U.S. 1990–94,* vol. 1, Bulletin 2445 (Washington, D.C.: Government Printing Office, 1994). By June 2002 that number had declined to 520,000 in apparel and 434,000 in textiles (Joanna Ramey, "More Industry Job Losses in May," *Women's Wear Daily,* June 10, 2002, 3).

24. Ghadar, Davidson, and Feigenoff, *U.S. Industrial Competitiveness,* x.

25. Dickerson, *Textiles and Apparel in the Global Economy,* 303.

26. Karen S. Hamrick, Stephen A. MacDonald, and Leslie A. Meyer, "International Trade Agreements Bring Adjustment to the Textile and Apparel Industries," *Rural Conditions and Trends* (publication of U.S. Department of Agriculture) 11, no. 1 (2000): 31–41.

with the development of new forms of branded marketing. The emergence of huge branded marketers, who sold garments under high-visibility labels while subcontracting all or most of the production, has become one of the most important features of competition in the industry in the past two decades.[27]

Apparel is thus not the whole elephant, but is a very important component of the global economy. It is a large industry that has always been broadly distributed across the globe, but the organization of its commodity chains (what is produced where, by whom, and for whom) has changed dramatically in recent years. It is an industry where control, if not ownership, has been wrested from small entrepreneurs and lies in the hands of a shrinking number of highly capitalized corporate giants. As a labor-intensive industry, it employs millions of workers under widely varying conditions. A large proportion of those employees are women and people of color throughout the world. The fate of many households is thus linked to its dynamics, and their health and well-being to the working conditions it provides.

The Politics of Production in a Globally Integrated Labor Market

Increasingly, the expansion of global labor markets has heightened a fundamental paradox: that firms and their employees are geographically constrained in different ways. Geographers have expressed the situation as follows: "Not all capitals are equally mobile, and not all working people are equally immobile, but in general capital is more mobile than labor. Locations that, for capital, are a temporary space for profitable production, are for workers and their friends and families places in which to live; places in which they have considerable individual and collective cultural investment; places to which they are often deeply attached."[28] Or, "The spatial mobility of capital is pitted against the geographic solidarity of labor. Capital can make positive use, in a way labor cannot, of distance and differentiation."[29]

A New York City financier has made the same point in a slightly different way: "Now capital has wings . . . capital can deal with twenty labor markets

27. See Klein, *No Logo;* Gereffi, "Organization of Buyer Driven Commodity Chains."

28. Huw Beynon and Ray Hudson, "Place and Space in Contemporary Europe: Some Lessons and Reflections," *Antipode* 25, no. 3 (1993): 183.

29. Doreen Massey, *Spatial Divisions of Labor: Social Structures and the Geography of Production,* 2d ed. (1984; New York: Routledge, 1995), 57.

at once and pick and choose among them. Labor is fixed in one place. So power has shifted."[30]

As the financier suggests, this differential geographic mobility has altered the power relation between employers and workers. It allows employers to scan the global landscape and to pick and choose workers at a wage level and under conditions that employers find amenable. But just as significantly, it creates a situation in which all workers, wherever they are located, know that their jobs can be moved at any moment. This gives rise to a form of labor control that Michael Burawoy has called hegemonic despotism. He defines hegemonic despotism as a situation where the "arbitrary tyranny of the overseer over the individual worker" is replaced by the "'rational' tyranny of capital mobility over the collective worker. . . . The fear of being fired is replaced by the fear of capital flight, plant closure, transfer of operations and plant disinvestment."[31] The ability to move their production operations allows firms to pit workers in different locations against each other, dampening wage negotiations, undermining unionization, and fostering concessionary bargaining in which employees must give up benefits in order to retain their jobs.

A report prepared for the U.S. Trade Deficit Review Commission in 2000, which examined a random sample of over four hundred union certification votes conducted in 1998–99, provides an extraordinary example of how this works. According to this survey, more than half of all employers threatened to shut down operations during the period preceding the vote. In easily mobile industries such as apparel, threats occurred in 100 percent of cases. Not surprisingly, the success of certification campaigns was significantly lower in plants where closure was threatened.[32]

Many economic policymakers have commented approvingly on the role of worker insecurity in reducing wage demands. In 1997, U.S. Federal Reserve chair Alan Greenspan linked the nation's "sustainable economic expansion" to "atypical restraint on compensation increases [that] appears to be mainly the consequence of greater worker insecurity."[33] A fellow Federal Reserve Board member, Laurence H. Meyer, elaborated: "According to this theory, corporate restructuring, globalization and technological

---

30. Robert Johnson, cited in Greider, *One World, Ready or Not,* 24.

31. Michael Burawoy, *The Politics of Production* (London: Verso, 1985), 150.

32. Kate Bronfenbrenner, "Uneasy Terrain: The Impact of Capital Mobility on Workers, Wages and Union Organizing," report submitted to the U.S. Trade Deficit Review Commission, September 6, 2000.

33. Prepared statement of Alan Greenspan, chair, Board of Governors of the Federal Reserve System, before the House Banking and Financial Services Committee, *Federal News Service,* March 5, 1997, 2, cited in Bronfenbrenner, "Uneasy Terrain," 3.

change have increased workers' insecurity about their jobs. As a result, workers have been willing to accept some restraint on real wages in order to increase their prospects of remaining employed."[34]

Both of these quotations point to the causal link between corporate mobility and workers' unwillingness or inability to fight for increased wages. The result, of course, was that the real wages of American workers remained stagnant or declined through the long economic expansion of the 1990s.[35]

Hegemonic despotism is an important part of what it means to be a worker in a global labor market, but it is not the whole story. We do not yet fully understand what participating in such a geographically dispersed "community" of workers entails. We have good accounts of dislocation and economic harm to communities that lose jobs and of the ways corporate mobility undermines union movements.[36] We have more than two decades' worth of ethnographies of factory work in new zones of capitalist investment. But conflicts of interest and intersections of interest among workers in different locations and at different points along the commodity chain remain unclear. As Chandra Talpade Mohanty has argued, much of this writing presents the story of "oppressed Third World woman workers" in a stereotyped way while ignoring the potential for "imagined community" and political alliance among First World and Third World women.[37]

The firms that relocate or subcontract their production do not approach the developing world as a homogeneous sea of cheap labor but seek to take advantage of many types of variability across localities. The specific attributes of places and their people matter to multinational corporations. As David Harvey has noted, "The free flow of capital across the surface of the

---

34. Prepared statement of Laurence Meyer, member, Board of Governors of the Federal Reserve System, before the House Banking and Financial Services Committee, *Federal News Service*, July 23, 1997,10, cited in Bronfenbrenner, "Uneasy Terrain,"4.

35. Lawrence Mishel, Jared Bernstein, and John Schmitt, *The State of Working America 2000–01* (Washington, D.C.: Economic Policy Institute, 2000).

36. On job loss, see Barry Bluestone and Bennett Harrison, *The Deindustrialization of America: Plant Closings, Community Abandonment and the Dismantling of Basic Industry* (New York: Basic Books, 1982), and Kathryn Marie Dudley, *The End of the Line: Lost Jobs, New Lives in Postindustrial America* (Chicago: University of Chicago Press, 1994); on union issues see Moody, *Workers in a Lean World;* Andrew Herod, ed., *Organizing the Landscape: Geographical Perspectives on Labor Unionism* (Minneapolis: University of Minnesota Press, 1998).

37. Mohanty applies the term "imagined community" to issues of transnational feminist solidarity (Chandra Talpade Mohanty, "Cartographies of Struggle: Third World Women and the Politics of Feminism," in *Third World Women and the Politics of Feminism,* ed. Chandra Talpade Mohanty, Ann Russo, and Lourdes Torres (Bloomington: Indiana University Press, 1991), 1–50. She draws the concept from Benedict Anderson, *Imagined Communities: Reflections on the Origin and Spread of Nationalism* (London: Verso, 1983).

globe . . . places strong emphasis upon the particular qualities of the spaces to which that capital might be attracted. The shrinkage of space that brings diverse communities across the globe into competition with each other implies . . . a heightened sense of awareness of what makes a place special and gives it a competitive advantage."[38]

Firms that move their operations engage in "regime shopping" for advantages in tax law, incentives, and environmental and labor regulation.[39] They may have specific requirements for infrastructure and transport, or they may be primarily concerned with access to local markets. At the same time, firms seek out specific kinds of labor pools whose relevant characteristics include wage levels, but also skills, turnover levels, the overall availability of labor, unionization, and worker militancy. Firms perceive the gender or ethnic composition of the workforce to be relevant to these other features and thus may frame their quest for labor in gendered or racial-ethnic terms. Managers' perceptions of an appropriate fit between type of worker and kind of work may contradict existing local beliefs, opening new possibilities for labor market participation or, alternatively, engendering resistance. At other times, a firm's perceptions of a properly structured labor force may correspond to local custom and thus reinforce and deepen existing divisions of labor.[40]

As firms locate and "localize" their operations in new parts of the world, corporate strategies come in contact with the livelihood strategies of families and individuals. As firms experience pressures to obtain profit levels predetermined by Wall Street and to produce garments whose quality and timeliness build a brand image developed on Madison Avenue, they construct labor practices exercised upon women and men whose needs and desires are determined in different spheres. Labor recruitment and control thus become the site of negotiation and struggle, as midlevel managers seek to implement policies and procedures, working through local institutions and cultures. In this way "the production of material goods is bound up with the making of new social relations and with the forging of new meanings with regard to those relations." It entails, as Burawoy reminds us, a fragile balance between control and consent.[41]

38. David Harvey, *The Condition of Post-modernity* (Cambridge: Blackwell, 1989), 271.

39. Tony Elger and Paul K. Edwards, "Introduction," in *The Global Economy, Nation-States and the Regulation of Labour*, ed. Paul K. Edwards and Tony Elger (London: Mansell, 1999).

40. Fernández-Kelly, *For We Are Sold, I and My People;* Susan Tiano, *Patriarchy on the Line: Labor, Gender and Ideology in the Mexican Maquila Industry* (Philadelphia: Temple University Press, 1994).

41. Burawoy, *Politics of Production,* 11.

Labor markets are deeply rooted in local institutions and practices. The labor contract is a social contract, which contains tacit expectations and is based on trust.[42] Employment relations are never simply market transactions; workers and employers struggle over the terms and conditions of labor. They draw on rhetorical strategies, habits, and traditions that are familiar to both groups, if not endorsed by them. They forge provisional agreements about what constitutes justice, what is a fair distribution of rewards and efforts, and how the parties should behave toward one another. These moral economies of the workplace provide the grounds on which one group makes claims on another and the language for framing those claims.[43] They are not closed and immutable systems but open, communicative frameworks susceptible to innovations of many kinds.[44]

But what happens to moral economies and their rhetorical frameworks when the labor market in question becomes global? In situations where employers and workers share a history and culture, tacit expectations can often remain unarticulated. But in situations of transnational investment, assumptions about labor practices must be confronted from the very beginning. Because apparel firms often seek out "greenfields" locations, where workers have little or no labor market experience, the norms and practices of the workplace have little historical precedent and must be actively constructed. Many firms prefer to employ workers with fewer labor market options and little exposure to organizing traditions. As one Mexican manager expressed it, "entre más antiguas, más inconformes son" (the more experienced they are, the less compliant).[45]

Feminist ethnographers have produced many accounts of the initial encounters between multinational firms and young women entering the labor market in export processing zones of the developing world.[46] These authors

42. See Jamie Peck, *Work-Place: The Social Regulation of Labor Markets* (New York: Guilford Press, 1996).

43. James C. Scott, *The Moral Economy of the Peasant: Rebellion and Subsistence in Southeast Asia* (New Haven: Yale University Press, 1976); E. P. Thompson, "The Moral Economy of the English Crowd in the 18th Century," *Past and Present* 50 (1971): 76–136.

44. Gareth Stedman Jones, *Languages of Class: Studies in English Working Class History, 1832–1982* (New York: Cambridge University Press, 1983).

45. Cited in Cowie, *Capital Moves*, 161.

46. To name but a few, Wendy Chapkis and Cynthia Enloe, *Of Common Cloth: Women in the Global Textile Industry* (Washington, D.C.: Transnational Institute, 1983); Fernández-Kelly, *For We Are Sold, I and My People*; Ching Kwan Lee, *Gender and the South China Miracle: Two Worlds of Factory Women* (Berkeley: University of California Press, 1998); Aihwa Ong, *Spirits of Resistance and Capitalist Discipline: Factory Women in Malaysia* (Albany: State University of New York Press, 1987); Devon Peña, *The Terror of the Machine: Technology, Work, Gender and Ecology on the U.S.-Mexico Border* (Austin: Center for Mexican-American Studies, 1997); Helen Safa, "Runaway Shops and Female Employment: The Search for Cheap

have documented the strategies that firms instituted, beginning in the 1970s, of recruiting mostly young, unmarried women without children and firing them when they married, gave birth, or simply reached a certain age.[47] They described the ways young women found wage work liberating, opening new possibilities for autonomy and self-sufficiency; the ways they found it difficult and demeaning; and their strategies for gaining new skills and autonomy within the factories. Ethnographers found resistance in unexpected places, such as episodes of "spirit possession," struggles over meals and holidays, or support for female managers. They also traced important shifts in both managerial strategies and workers' responses over time. As more and more companies moved into export processing zones, labor markets tightened and firms found it necessary to diversify their workforces by hiring men as well as married women with children. Of equal importance, as workers in these regions gained labor market experience, they became both more skilled at their jobs and more savvy about the ways they could exercise their collective power.

The larger rhetorical battles that accompany globalization shape these site-specific struggles for recognition, rights, and remuneration in the workplace. Within this broader frame, neoliberal discourses argue that poor working conditions in industries like apparel can be tolerated because they are a stepping-stone to something better; they are a rung on the ladder of development. Labor-intensive industries tap the only resource that many poor nations have—their "cheap" labor. They generate economic growth that will eventually trickle down to all sectors of society. According to this view, labor conditions will naturally improve over time as a result of economic growth. The problem for poor nations is that they are getting "[not] too much globalization, but too little"; and for this reason, when student groups, unions, and churches wage campaigns against sweatshops, they are harming the very people they intend to help.[48]

Labor," in *Women's Work,* ed. Eleanor Leacock and Helen Safa (South Hadley, Mass.: Bergin and Garvey, 1986); Janet Salaff, *Working Daughters of Hong Kong: Filial Piety or Power in the Family?* (London: Cambridge University Press, 1981); Leslie Salzinger, "From High Heels to Swathed Bodies: Gender Meanings under Production in Mexico's Export-Processing Industry," *Feminist Studies* 23, no. 3 (1997): 549–74; Tiano, *Patriarchy on the Line;* Diane Wolf, *Factory Daughters: Gender, Household Dynamics and Rural Industrialization in Java* (Berkeley: University of California Press, 1992); Melissa Wright, "Crossing the Factory Frontier: Gender, Place and Power in the Mexican *Maquiladora,*" *Antipode* 29, no. 3 (1996): 278–302.

47. There are clear parallels here to the "Lowell system" of labor recruitment, which drew young farm girls to textile factories in New England in the nineteenth century. See Thomas Dublin, *Women at Work* (New York: Columbia University Press, 1979).

48. Thomas L. Friedman, "Protesting for Whom?" *New York Times,* April 24, 2001, A19;

The "global justice" or "antiglobalization" critiques of this perspective argue that the protection of labor and the environment cannot be left to market forces. They echo Karl Polanyi's fear that labor markets, left to their own devices, will thoroughly deplete workers and destroy the social basis through which labor is reproduced.[49] These critics argue that neoliberal policies force workers in different parts of the world to compete based on how little they demand—on who will work longer hours, for less pay, with fewest health and safety rules and the least in the way of job security and provision for times of sickness and old age. Often glossed as "the race to the bottom," this kind of competition pushes the social reproductive needs of workers to their lowest limit and is not sustainable in any long run. It undermines the kinds of achievements in education and health that form a strong basis for democratic institutions. Proponents of this view point out that improved labor conditions did not emerge simply as a result of economic growth in the industrialized countries. Rather, workers "fought their way out—marched for economic justice, built unions, voted and finally forced the Gilded Age to become the New Deal."[50]

These discourses draw stark contrasts, and the press frequently presents their social visions in all-or-nothing terms. Yet within each camp practitioners work to craft new social arrangements that are more complex than the arguments would allow. Globalization critics experiment with "fair trade" arrangements, investing their own capital to set up socially responsible market relations. Neoliberal gurus like George Soros and dyed-in-the-wool economists like Jagdish Bhagwati argue that globalization needs regulation and redistributive policies to mitigate its effects and to reconcile market forces with social and economic goals.[51]

One of the central lessons that can be drawn from the case studies presented in this book is that just and humane working conditions do not emerge automatically as a by-product of economic growth or from the production of "advanced" goods. If global production arrangements are to be fair, they will have to be *made fair,* either through mindful social regulation or as a result of the same kinds of social struggle that brought labor rules and collective bargaining to the industrialized nations. Another key finding

Nicholas D. Kristof and Sheryl WuDinn, "Two Cheers for Sweatshops," *New York Times Magazine,* September 24, 2000, 6–7.

49. Karl Polanyi, *The Great Transformation* (New York: Rinehart, 1944).

50. Tom Hayden and Charles Kernaghan, "Pennies an Hour, and No Way Up," *New York Times,* July 7, 2002, A27.

51. George Soros, *George Soros on Globalization* (New York: Public Affairs, 2002); Jagdish Bhagwati, *Free Trade Today* (Princeton: Princeton University Press, 2002).

is that new global sourcing arrangements make workers' efforts toward those ends more difficult. They do so by separating workers from their employers in space and through layers of subcontracting. These arrangements "deterritorialize" workplace community in ways that make it more difficult for moral economies of work to emerge. A third finding that emerges from the cases is that gender relations also complicate workers' attempts to struggle for change. This is in part because unions have excluded women from their affairs and have suppressed their voices. There is another process at work, however. Managers in the apparel industry have historically relied on gendered ideologies of sewing work to devalue women's skill and lower their wages. In the context of global apparel production, managers have redeployed these ideologies in new ways to justify hiring inexperienced young women in regions without strong labor markets. In order to craft more just and humane labor relations, workers will need to establish new forms of "deterritorialized" community and to overcome these legacies of gender. And in fact they are doing so.

Studying Global Processes: Notes on Method

Moody has observed that deepening internationalization places workers in competition with one another at the same time that it binds them together "in common international production systems, often under a single employer."[52] While the relocation of firms breaks apart certain kinds of communities, it creates others. The difficulty, given our existing array of conceptual tools, is that these communities, and the social processes that construct them, do not operate within the geographic boundaries we have come to expect.

Many researchers have noted that place-bound analytical categories impede our comprehension of emerging global processes. Greider has argued that "the growth of transnational corporate investments, the steady dispersal of production elements across many nations, has nearly obliterated the traditional understanding of trade."[53] We no longer confront a situation where nations buy and sell things to each other; we now face one in which multinational companies export and import among their own subsidiaries. The proportion of world trade consisting of such intrafirm transactions rose from 20–30 percent in the 1960s to 40–50 percent in the late 1980s and early 1990s. In 1990, more than half of all U.S. exports and imports by

52. Moody, *Workers in a Lean World,* 36.
53. Greider, *One World, Ready or Not,* 22.

value were simply the result of transfers of goods and services within global corporations.[54]

It is not only national accounts data that are organized by place, however. This is also the way we tend to think about effects on human lives. Decades of community studies and community development planning have taught us to look at the effect of job loss on geographically bounded spaces. We tend to ask if the movement of factories to sites in the developing world is good or bad for a nation or region. This kind of industrial relocation, however, frequently divides nations into new camps of conflicting interests—those who benefit from the move and those who lose. In the 1980s and 1990s, such dynamics split the firms of the U.S. apparel industry into two camps. Companies with a commitment to producing apparel in the United States lobbied the government for protectionist policies, while companies whose corporate strategies emphasized producing or subcontracting abroad for import to the United States favored free trade provisions. In developing nations, globalization has created a divergence of interest between organized labor movements and industry groups that compete for new foreign investment based on low-cost unorganized labor. New forms of corporate mobility have also created conflicts between older, more prosperous workers of the global North and newly recruited poorer workers of the global South.

Developing new concepts to encompass activities that cross territorial boundaries is challenging. It requires us to abandon traditional notions of community, region, and nation-state and to replace these "spaces of place" with what Manuel Castells has called "spaces of flows." John Ruggie has suggested that historical precedents can help give concreteness to such thinking. He argues that medieval trade fairs organized economic transactions that transcended existing political boundaries, required new forms of regulation, and expanded participants' cognitive horizons. Giovanni Arrighi has associated "spaces of place" with government institutions and statecraft and "spaces of flows" with functionally specific business organizations that transect and transcend national boundaries. He argues that while such thinking challenges our perceptual habits, its novelty can be exaggerated.[55]

54. Giovanni Arrighi, The Long Twentieth Century: Money, Power and the Origins of Our Times (New York: Verso, 1994), 72.

55. Manuel Castells, The Informational City (Oxford: Blackwell, 1989), and Castells, The Rise of Network Society, vol. 1 (Oxford: Blackwell, 1996); John Ruggie, "Territoriality and Beyond: Problematizing Modernity in International Relations," International Organization 47, no. 1 (1993): 173; Arrighi, Long Twentieth Century, 23, 81.

To think globally does not necessarily mean to think generally or abstractly; it means to understand interconnected processes. It requires us to develop new ways of conceptualizing the links between Hong Kong bankers and North Carolina textile mill workers, designers in New York City, and Mexican seamstresses. As Neil Smith has said, "It is all very well and good that $500 million can be whizzed around the world at the push of a button, but it must come from somewhere and be en route to somewhere."[56] Or in Peter Dicken's words, "Every component in the production chain, . . . every economic activity is, quite literally, 'grounded' in specific locations. Such grounding is both physical, in the form of sunk costs, and less tangible, in the form of localized social relationships."[57]

One approach that has sought to grasp how "spaces of flows" operate is the study of commodity chains, which seeks to capture the "disaggregation of stages of production and consumption across national boundaries under the organization . . . of densely networked firms or enterprises."[58] Commodity chains encompass networks of labor and production processes whose result is a finished commodity.[59] Constructing models of these chains helps us conceptualize international linkages that we have previously assumed to be discretely contained within national and local units.[60] Tracing these processes allows us to ask questions about which nodes in a chain control others, how profits are distributed among nodes, and how this is related to monopoly and competition. It tells a story that has business organizations at its center, that locates those enterprises within the competitive conditions of a particular industry, and that interrogates their logic and practice. While the analysis of commodity chains is often associated with scholars working within a world systems or political economic perspective, it has served as a methodological schema, or heuristic device, for researchers of diverse theoretical orientations.[61]

56. Neil Smith, *Uneven Development: Nature, Capital and the Production of Space* (London: Blackwell, 1990).

57. Dicken, *Global Shift*, 11.

58. Gary Gereffi, Miguel Korzeniewicz, and Roberto P. Korzeniewicz, "Introduction," in Gereffi and Korzeniewicz, *Commodity Chains and Global Capitalism*, 1.

59. Terence Hopkins and Immanuel Wallerstein, "Commodity Chains in the World Economy prior to 1800," *Review* 10, no. 1 (1986): 157–70, 159.

60. Gereffi, Korzeniewicz, and Korzeniewicz, "Introduction," 2.

61. Business analysts refer to the "supply channel" approach, which includes "all the firms and relationships that get a product to market" (Frederick H. Abernathy, John T. Dunlop, Janice H. Hammond, and David Weil, *A Stitch in Time: Lean Retailing and the Transformation of Manufacturing; Lessons from the Apparel and Textile Industries* [New York: Oxford University Press, 1999], 2). Some economists have referred to similar methods

One reason the apparel industry has attracted the attention of students, activists, and consumer movements in recent years is that the apparel commodity chain is relatively transparent and easy to trace. Our shirts, shoes, and coats are marked with information about where they are produced. Though we many not comprehend silicon chips or semiconductors, most of us have a basic understanding of how apparel is made. Sweet Honey in the Rock can trace the journey of a shirt from cotton field to the rack at Sears in the space of a single song.[62] This transparency and tangibility invite us to trace connections between producers and consumers and to ask how the item in question came to us and how it came to be.

Social movements have recognized that it is difficult to organize people around abstract issues of poverty in the developing world. But to tell people that poor children made their carpets or their sweaters gives them a sense of tangible connection and responsibility. This idea galvanized new consumer movements in the United States in the 1990s, which organized around ensuring that apparel bearing collegiate logos was not manufactured in sweatshops, that carpets from the Near East and South Asia were not made with child labor, and that Nike workers were not forced to inhale dangerous chemicals in putting together shoes. There is a compelling directness to this approach, and it draws on a long tradition of consumer boycotts and movements calling for corporate responsibility.[63] Like recent accounts that track investment dollars as they circulate around the world or follow jobs as they are relocated from global North to global South, tracing the journey of a shirt appears to offer a mnemonic—a way to visualize and organize the complex relationships and processes associated with globalization.[64]

Despite its seeming transparency, studying the apparel commodity chain presents numerous challenges. Marx defined commodities as the containers

---

as a "value chain approach" (Michael Porter, *The Competitive Advantage of Nations* [New York: Free Press, 1990]). French planners have adopted the term *filière,* literally "thread."

62. "Are My Hands Clean?" *Sweet Honey in the Rock: Live at Carnegie Hall,* released by Flying Fish Records, 1987.

63. In *Out to Work: A History of Wage Earning Women in the United States* (New York: Oxford University Press, 1982), Alice Kessler-Harris quotes an activist from 1834: "I do not see how these grinding evils of small pay and unjust treatment from employers can be remedied except by holding up to the public gaze and reflection the names and places of business of those who are living on the tears, pain and toil of the daughters of Free America" (79).

64. Barbara Garson, *Money Makes the World Go Around: One Investor Tracks Her Cash through the Global Economy, from Brooklyn to Bangkok and Back* (New York: Viking, 2001); William Adler, *Mollie's Job: A Story of Life and Work on the Global Assembly Line* (New York: Scribner, 2000); Cowie, *Capital Moves.*

of hidden social relationships, and as Susan Willis has said, these relation-ships are all the more concealed by the movement of production to the Third World.[65] Understanding these hidden ties is hard, particularly given the ascendancy of narratives of the free market. Attention to market forces often diverts us from considering the political forces shaping the regional labor market or the ways that labor entering that market may be unfree. It distracts us from the bold and sometimes brilliant moves through which multinational corporations have been able to reshape trade rules and inter-national financial arrangements to suit their agendas. We need theoretical and methodological tools that will challenge our commonsense understand-ings of transactions that are too easily characterized as market forces play-ing themselves out. Conceptualizing a commodity chain can help us recon-struct transactions and relationships that may otherwise remain hidden.

Critics of a commodity chain perspective have argued that it oversimpli-fies each step of the process and particularly the financially motivated ma-trix of choices faced by complex multinational firms.[66] Construing a set of activities as a "node" in the chain reduces concrete geographical and histor-ical instances to their role in a single global production process. While using the concept of a chain or thread to organize our understanding of connec-tions, we need to resist reifying it in ways that obscure these more complex determinations.

Theorists of globalization have complained that "virtually all the statisti-cal data on production, trade, investment and the like are aggregated into national 'boxes' and that this level of aggregation is less and less useful since national boundaries no longer 'contain' production processes in the way they once did."[67] Tracing the global division of labor by which a com-modity is produced and brought to market presents data problems as well, since many of our accounting measures were designed in an era of "shallow global integration," or connection through arm's-length trade, rather than "deep integration," or connection through cross-border production.[68] Par-ticularly when firms subcontract production, their investments, losses, and profits from globally dispersed production may be anything but transparent.

Understanding how a firm is linked to other enterprises, when and where it subcontracts, and how it fits within a commodity chain is important to workers as well as industry analysts. Speaking of the newly emerging work-

65. Karl Marx, *Capital*, vol. 1 (1886; New York: Vintage, 1954; Willis, Primer *for Daily Life*, 52.
66. Williams, "From Shareholder Value to Present-Day Capitalism," 6.
67. Dicken, *Global Shift*, 7.
68. Ibid., 5.

ers' centers representing immigrant workers in many U.S. cities, Miriam Ching Yoon Louie has emphasized the local and strategic character of their activism, working within specific economic and cultural contexts to solve particular kinds of problems. She ironically refers to this approach as using "just-in-time" methods to organize "small batches" of immigrant workers.[69] Her language here refers to the new practices of "flexible specialization" that swept through business and management schools in the 1980s and 1990s. It suggests that the workers' organizations she writes about are learning to gear their strategies to an understanding of the competitive pressures that their employers experience because of their location within specific commodity chains.

To understand what has been happening within the apparel industry over the past two decades, we need to think dialectically, moving between the activities of Wall Street or Geneva and those of Djakarta or Aguascalientes. To do this successfully, we need to avoid reifying large-scale processes. Many accounts invoke globalization as an abstract and inevitable force—as a ghostly actor that appears to have a will and an agenda without having a face or an address. But talking about globalization as an abstract force lets real actors off the hook. Globalization is not a ghost, and it is not like gravity. It is made up of decisions and actions, struggles and negotiations carried out in a large number of specific places where people live and work. Bruno Latour has asked,

> What . . . is the size of IBM, or the Red Army, or the French Ministry of Education, or the world market? To be sure, these are all actors of great size, since they mobilize hundreds of thousands or even millions of agents. . . . However, if we wander about inside IBM, if we follow the chains of command of the Red Army, if we inquire in the corridors of the Ministry of Education, if we study the process of selling and buying a bar of soap, we never leave the local level. We are always in interaction with four or five people.[70]

While scale matters, and important aggregation effects come into play all along the commodity chain, individuals with faces and histories manage these processes. The workings of the chain bring benefits to some groups of people and loss to others. Latour remarks that the organization of American big business described by the historian Alfred Chandler is not the Orga-

69. Miriam Ching Yoon Louie, *Sweatshop Warriors* (Boston: South End Press, 2001), 217.

70. Bruno Latour, *We Have Never Been Modern* (Cambridge: Harvard University Press, 1993), 120–21.

nization described by Kafka. Chandler, who did so much to advance our understanding of the importance of economies of scale and scope in business, did so by recounting the breakthroughs of named individuals working for particular firms seeking to solve concrete problems.

The approach I take in this book puts names and faces on actors all along the commodity chain. I have accepted George Marcus's challenge to conduct "multisited ethnography," using the commodity chain as a "tracking strategy." Marcus has argued that we can enlarge ethnography's paradigmatic "local, close-up perspective" by discovering "new paths of connection and association" while retaining its concern with agency and everyday practices.[71] By moving between four sites where apparel production is constituted, I attempt to examine agency in the boardroom and on the factory floor, to raise questions about easy distinctions between local and global, and to show how the fates of people in dispersed geographic locations are bound together by the social relationships in which they participate.

A Tale of Two Companies: Overview of the Case Studies

In this study, I have tried to trace the connections between the women and men who make clothing in small communities of the United States and Mexico and the men and women who organize that work from corporate headquarters. Rather than describing the plight of apparel workers and locating it within a context of abstract global forces, I have attempted to show how competitive conditions and political forces shape the goals of managers, the opportunities for workers, and the interaction between them in these specific places.

My account is based on case study research conducted in 1999 and 2000 at two clothing firms, one producing low-end "commodity" apparel and the other producing a broad range of garments from "moderate" to "designer bridge" lines. The first firm, Tultex Corporation, had its headquarters in southern Virginia. The company began production in the 1930s and operated as a family business until the 1980s. In the early 1990s it employed nearly 6,600 people in its eight plants in southern Virginia and northern North Carolina as well as in one plant in Jamaica and another in Mexico. By the middle of that decade it had begun to combine its direct production with subcontracting, mostly in Mexico. The largest factory in Tultex's com-

---

71. George Marcus, "Ethnography in/of the World System: The Emergence of Multi-sited Ethnography," *Annual Review of Anthropology* 24 (1995): 95, 98.

plex, located in Martinsville, Virginia, was organized by the Amalgamated Clothing and Textile Workers Union in 1994[72] after two decades of unsuccessful campaigns. The union vote was the largest victory for the ACTWU since its J. P. Stevens drive (memorialized by the film *Norma Rae*) in the late 1970s.

Tultex had $650 million in sales in 1998, placing it among the top thirty U.S. apparel producers. It appeared to be on a path to modernization and growth. But the firm, facing the brutal competitive pressures of the 1990s and having made a series of arguably bad decisions, declared bankruptcy in December 1999. I had originally planned to study Tultex's transition from an "old paradigm" paternalist firm to one that was initiating a variety of "new paradigm" procedures—from collaboration with the union on work teams and flexible production to incorporation of global subcontracting. In the end those changes were insufficient, were abandoned, or did not come soon enough. Thus the story of Tultex can be read as a case of a traditionally organized firm that could not weather the harsh competitive conditions of the 1990s.

The second case study firm, Liz Claiborne Incorporated, has its headquarters in North Bergen, New Jersey. The designer Liz Claiborne and her husband, Arthur Ortenberg, started the company in 1975. It had $2.2 billion in annual sales in 1999, based on more than 130 million units of apparel and 30 million accessory items under twelve divisions, making it the third largest apparel firm in the United States. Liz Claiborne produces none of its clothing directly, subcontracting production to a network of 262 factories in thirty-two countries. It was one of the first apparel firms to develop expertise in global sourcing, working with procurement agents in Taiwan and Hong Kong from its earliest years. Industry analysts see the firm as an innovator in organizing global production, and the trade press considers its supplier certification programs and procedures of "statistical process control" to be state of the art. Liz Claiborne is an example of a "branded marketer," trading primarily on the reputation of its portfolio of more than twenty-six brand names, which are sold in a wide variety of retail settings. It emerged from the difficult era of the 1990s as an industry leader and is an excellent example of a "new paradigm" apparel firm, which has found a way to organize global production for consistent profits. If this research project could be characterized as a tale of two companies, it clearly shows that the

---

72. The Amalgamated Clothing and Textile Workers' Union (ACTWU) merged with the International Ladies' Garment Workers' Union (ILGWU) in 1995 to form the Union of Needletrades, Industrial and Textile Workers (UNITE).

1990s were the best of times or the worst of times depending on how a firm was positioned within the global economy.

During field research, I interviewed corporate officials and managers in Martinsville, Virginia, and North Bergen, New Jersey, reviewed financial and human resource documents, and visited production facilities. This included factories operated by Tultex in Martinsville, Virginia, as well as plants in Aguascalientes, Mexico, producing for each of the companies.[73] I interviewed workers as well as union organizers and officials, and I attended both general membership and board meetings of UNITE Local 1994. In addition, I spoke to community development officials and trade board representatives in the primary research sites and conducted a comprehensive review of the apparel trade press and of articles on apparel in the economic press during 1990–2001. Out of these materials I have pieced together a story of change in the apparel industry over the 1990s and the way it conditioned the shop floor struggles of workers in the United States and Mexico.

Examining the cases of Tultex and Liz Claiborne allows us to consider several important questions. Comparing the way Tultex organized production in Martinsville, Virginia, with its operations in Aguascalientes, Mexico (arrow 1 on table 1.1), is helpful in understanding how geographic distance and subcontracting as a form of economic organization affect the firm's relation to the places where its production is carried out. It lets us investigate the distinct "localization strategies"—or forms of social economic embeddedness–through which production is realized in the two regions.

Although a late twentieth-century apparel firm could choose to locate its production operations anywhere in the world, once it selected a site, it had to effectively engage local institutions in order to recruit, control, and reproduce its labor force. In every place where global production touches down, it is instantiated differently. It works through local institutions and establishes the necessary organization to get the work done. The close-knit, yet oppressive, social relations of paternalism in the southern Virginia town where Tultex began its production contrasted sharply with the deterritorialized, arm's-length relations the firm constructed with workers in Aguascalientes. As David Harvey has emphasized, social geographies are not merely reflections of capital's needs but are the locus of powerful contradictions.[74] Working through the contrasts between the labor regimes of Martinsville

---

73. Greta Krippner, a doctoral student in the Department of Sociology at the University of Wisconsin, conducted field research in Mexico for this project.

74. Harvey, *Limits to Capital*, 403.

Table 1.1. Comparing the case study firms

	Geographic location	
Characteristics of the firm	United States	Mexico
Basic apparel Midsize firm "Old paradigm" (vertically integrated, no brand)	1 **Tultex**, Martinsville ↔	**Confitek** (producing for Tultex in Aguasca- lientes) ↕ 2
Fashion apparel Large firm "New paradigm" (branded marketer, no factories)	**Liz Claiborne headquarters** in New Jersey	**Burlmex** (producing for Liz Claiborne in Aguas- calientes)

and Aguascalientes reveals important tensions in deterritorialized labor regimes that are at the same time potential points of emergence for new social
movements.

Comparing the factories producing for Liz Claiborne and Tultex in Aguascalientes (table 1.1, arrow 2) provides a different kind of insight. Researchers have advanced many strong hypotheses about the ways work changed
in the last decades of the twentieth century and the early years of the
twenty-first. They have predicted the conditions under which firms will
invest in physical and social infrastructure, seek to develop their workers'
skills, and create flexible new work regimens that increase workers' autonomy. Their theories suggest that firms will make such investments when
they produce small batches of a high-value product, and where the style
of that product is subject to rapid change. Many researchers have claimed
that the "high-end" or fashion segment of the apparel industry provides a
good example of such a situation. Based on these predictions, we would
expect that Liz Claiborne, which produces fashion apparel, and Tultex Corporation, which produces low-end or "commodity" apparel, would establish
very different types of production facilities in Mexico. We would expect Liz
Claiborne to develop a more flexible production process, and to be more
reliant on skilled labor, than its counterpart producing basic sweatshirts.
The case studies reveal that the factories operated by the two firms are
surprisingly similar and that the differences that do exist are not those
that theory would predict. Liz Claiborne's formidable size and substantial
resources have enabled it to develop a production process that achieves
quality through strict control over operations rather than relying on more
skilled and autonomous labor. The Burlmex factory, where Claiborne pro-

duces in Aguascalientes, provides an example of the deepening and extension of the early twentieth-century principles of Frederick Taylor to contexts in the developing world.[75]

At times in the chapters that follow I adopt the strategy of telling the
story as a straight line—providing a map of the apparel commodity chain
and the way it links managers, workers, and consumers in diverse sites. At
other times I pause to consider distinct locations and the "star of lines"
radiating out from them. In this way I am hoping to provide an account
that combines the insights of political economy with those provided by
ethnographic investigation in order to break open the black box of the commodity and expose the social relations it contains. Constructing such an
account requires that "our minds," in Chandra Mohanty's words, be "as able
to move as capital is."[76] It requires us to develop positioned understand-
ings that recognize both the unequal power and the agency (and fallibility)
of actors at each distinct location. In the end, I believe that the stories
of workers and managers in Martinsville, North Bergen, and Aguascalientes will elucidate the dynamics of the apparel industry, on one hand,
and the complexities of workers' lives, on the other. I hope that such an
account will be useful both to those interested in constructing new, more
humane forms of work organization and to those struggling to create effective practices of international labor solidarity.

75. Alain Lipietz has described an investment pattern that he calls "primitive" or
"bloody" Taylorization. Under such a regime, he argues, companies transfer fragmented
and repetitive assembly jobs to states with high rates of exploitation and reimport the
products. The logic of the system, he says, is to extract value from labor without any
attempt to reproduce the labor force in the long term. He argues that such regimes are
politically supported through centralized political measures to hold down living standards,
repression of independent labor unions, establishment of company unions, and other
means (*Mirages and Miracles* [New York: Verso, 1987], 74–78). The vast majority of apparel
firms that globalize their operations could be considered to fall under this rubric. The point
here is that Liz Claiborne's production process has found new ways to systematize apparel
assembly, drawing on principles first elaborated by Frederick Winslow Taylor in 1911 in
his book *The Principles of Scientific Management* (New York: Norton 1967).

76. Chandra Talpade Mohanty, "'Under Western Eyes' Revisited: Feminist Solidarity
through Anticapitalist Struggles," *Signs* 28, no. 2 (2003): 530.

2

THE EMERGENCE OF
A TWENTY-FIRST CENTURY
APPAREL INDUSTRY

*We have kept the same strategy all along—to put fashion
on an industrial basis.*

—LUCIANO BENETTON[1]

Clothing and Power

For millennia, cloth and clothing have been trafficked over long distances,
linking far-flung regions. They have also been what Eric Wolf has called
"carrier industries" of the Industrial Revolution. The possibility of selling
cotton cloth abroad drove the development of the British textile industry;
at one point cloth alone constituted half of England's exports. In the early
industrial period, British factories competed with those of the Netherlands
and with Indian handicraft industries. Dutch cottons and Indian calicoes,
muslins, and silks were of higher quality than anything England could produce in its own factories. By reducing the costs of production, British weavers undercut their Dutch rivals, but dealing with Indian textile manufacture
required political intervention. British firms pressured the state to pass a
law preventing the British East India Company from importing cloth, and
later to establish stiff tariffs on imports. In this protected position, the

1. Cited in Kenneth Labick, "Benetton Takes on the World," *Fortune,* June 13, 1983,
192.

English mechanized and improved their spinning and weaving over the course of the nineteenth century. Lowering their costs and increasing their volume substantially, they began exporting massive quantities of their cheap new fabrics to India, Asia, and Latin America. By the late nineteenth century these developments had effectively broken the back of the hand-loom industry in India, and the subcontinent became a net importer of textiles.[2] Andean nations were exporting the raw fiber of sheep, llamas, and alpacas to England and reimporting the woven cloth.[3]

Native cloth and clothing thus became invested with meanings forged in the colonial experience. For nationalists like Gandhi, indigenous fabrics and styles, and the cottage industries that produced them, were proud markers of heritage.[4] For colonialist elites, they signified backwardness. These elites viewed the styles of Western industrial nations as conveying a certain kind of modernity, while to nationalist and ethnic movements they appeared degraded and cheap and a threat to rich indigenous handi-craft traditions. This situation became more complex in the late nineteenth century as many countries sought to develop their own industrial base by investing in modern textile mills, which now competed with their own na-tional handicraft production. By the 1930s, nations like India and Mexico had developed thriving textile and apparel industries serving their national markets.

In the United States and Europe, apparel production made the transfor-mation from a household craft to an industry serving a mass market in the late nineteenth century. At the end of the twentieth century it changed again, this time from a patchwork of small firms to a field dominated by a few enormous companies. Late twentieth-century apparel firms developed new practices of branded marketing that revolutionized the industry's com-modity chains, while competitive pressures led them to relocate their pro-duction to distant parts of the world. Wall Street analysts, and the CEOs of large apparel firms, proclaimed that the innovations of the 1990s proved the industry was on a roll. It had shed its reputation as an old-fashioned business and reinvented itself with a formula for success in the new econ-omy. To understand what happened in the 1990s, it helps to go back and

2. Eric Wolf, *Europe and the People without History* (Berkeley: University of California Press, 1982), 278, 268–78.

3. Benjamin Orlove, *Alpacas, Sheep and Men: The Wool Export Economy and Regional Society in Southern Peru* (New York: Academic Press, 1977).

4. Susan S. Bean, "Gandhi and Khadi, the Fabric of Indian Independence," in *Cloth and Human Experience,* ed. Annette B. Weiner and Jane Schneider (Washington, D.C.: Smithsonian Institution Press, 1989).

trace the key changes in technology and work organization that accompanied the move to production for mass markets. We can then turn to the innovations of our own era, in which power became concentrated in the hands of a few key players, most of them in the industrialized centers of the world's economy.

The Rise of Mass Production and Mass Markets in Apparel

Up until the 1850s, even in the industrializing nations of Europe and America, families produced most of their clothing in the home. Women sewed and knit a wide range of items for their families, although by the 1830s they usually used purchased cloth and yarns. Tailors produced made-to-order garments for those wealthy enough to afford them. These artisans and their assistants made virtually all purchased clothing in the United States and Europe in the 1850s. People referred to the few ready-made, or off-the-rack, garments that circulated as "slops" and took them as a marker of poverty.[5]

Tailoring was a trade, and most shops consisted of a skilled worker who, with the help of apprentices and family members, sewed an entire garment from start to finish. Most tailors were men, although seamstresses specialized in women's dresses and underwear. Despite the predominance of men in the trade, garment work has historically been the largest employer of women after domestic service. In shops and through homework for tailors, women performed a wide array of tasks at many skill levels. The industry also provided employment for many of the immigrant women and men who arrived in the United States from the 1840s until 1920.[6]

The structure of the garment industry changed significantly with the invention of the sewing machine in the 1850s. Walter Hunt had begun working on a mechanical sewing device as early as 1834, and Elias Howe patented a lockstitch machine in 1846. But the technology took off with Isaac Singer's addition of a treadle in 1854 and with his ardent promotion of his ma-

---

5. Claudia B. Kidwell and Margaret C. Christman, *Suiting Everyone: The Democratization of Clothing in America* (Washington, D.C.: Smithsonian Institution Press, 1974), 15.

6. Susan A. Glenn, *Daughters of the Shtetl: Life and Labor in the Immigrant Generation* (Ithaca, N.Y.: Cornell University Press, 1990), 98–99; Nancy L. Green, "Women and Immigrants in the Sweatshop: Categories of Labor Segmentation Revisited," *Comparative Studies in Society and History* 38, no. 3 (1996): 411–33; Barbara Wertheimer, *We Were There: The Story of Working Women in America* (New York: Pantheon Books, 1977), 61.

chines.[7] The revolution in production that the sewing machine unleashed was complemented by a contemporaneous revolution in retailing, as department stores and mail-order houses became the purveyors of clothing produced by the new machines. In the 1860s, wholesale establishments like Marshall Field's set up retail lines, and dry goods firms like Macy's expanded into full-fledged department stores. These new retail establishments sold a broad range of consumables to growing urban markets; they included ready-made apparel among the goods they purveyed. In the 1870s Aaron Montgomery Ward reached out to rural consumers through his mail-order firm, followed in the 1880s by Sears, Roebuck and Company.[8] Mail order took off with the improvement of rural roads and the development of rural free delivery after the turn of the century.[9] Twenty-first century branded manufacturers of apparel build on these late nineteenth-century precedents in manufacturing and in mass distribution and sales.

Producing for mass markets revolutionized the apparel industry, as clothing went from being "made for somebody" to "made for anybody." Most important, it led to a shift away from a system in which one or a few individuals made whole garments. Instead, the shops implemented "section work," in which each operator sewed the same piece—a collar or a sleeve— over and over again, and whole garments emerged out of a process much like what later came to be called an assembly line.[10]

By the early days of the twentieth century, very few sewing workers produced whole garments. A first-class white shirt passed through twenty-five to thirty hands before completion, and the manufacture of a coat involved thirty-nine operations performed by thirty-nine individuals.[11] Owners of apparel factories applauded the "unerring accuracy that is gained by . . . years of practice at one thing only. Probably any of the girls . . . could make a complete shirt from separate pieces; but it would be made slowly, awkwardly and probably inaccurately when compared with work, each stage of which is done by experts in that particular portion."[12]

Tailoring involved carefully measuring a client, adapting a pattern, cut-

---

7. Kidwell and Christman, *Suiting Everyone*, 75–77; Nancy L. Green, *Ready-to-Wear and Ready-to-Work: A Century of Industry and Immigrants in Paris and New York* (Durham, N.C.: Duke University Press, 1997), 35–36.

8. Alfred D. Chandler Jr., *The Visible Hand: The Managerial Revolution in American Business* (Cambridge: Harvard University Press, 1977), 218–19, 230.

9. Malcolm Gladwell, "Annals of Retail: Clicks and Mortar," *New Yorker*, December 6, 1999.

10. Kidwell and Christman, *Suiting Everyone*.

11. Ibid., 94–95.

12. *Haberdasher*, 1905, cited in Kidwell and Christman, *Suiting Everyone*, 95.

ting fabric, sewing, pressing, hemming, and trimming, then making various fittings and adjustments to ensure the final outcome. Each step required specific hand operations and a series of calculations to achieve a fit. Tailors drew on their knowledge and experience to select fabrics of appropriate weight and characteristics, the proper thread for each weight and type of fabric, and the correct needle size. Once they began to use sewing machines, tailors needed to know how to set up and maintain their equipment. They had to choose the right plate size, correct feed guards, and appropriate stitch tension.

With the move to mass production of ready-to-wear garments, individual body measurements gave way to a set of standard sizes. Pattern makers translated each design into a guide and graded, or configured, it to produce many sizes. The cutter produced a marker or plan for the layout of the pattern on the fabric. He or she would spread and inspect the fabric and cut it according to pattern. The cutter's assistant would then bundle the cut parts and distribute them to operators for sewing. On receiving a packet of pieces, each operator performed a sewing task: stitching up a sleeve, basting a sleeve or collar to the body of a garment, cutting or stitching buttonholes, attaching a lining, and so on. At several points along the way, it might be necessary to press the garment.

The introduction of scientific management practices to the apparel industry after World War I further "rationalized" this section work.[13] By the 1930s, most factories had organized their sewing lines into what was called a progressive bundle system. When workers completed an operation, they placed the garment in a buffer or bundle. Factory owners laid out their machines to facilitate shuttling these bins of garments between workers. At the end of the line, workers gave the item a final pressing, attached labels, and packed it for shipping. Managers assigned each of these tasks a target time in standard allocated minutes (SAM), and time study engineers calculated SAM for each operation.[14]

These changes reallocated responsibilities among workers and reduced the total number of tasks required of any one operator. Nevertheless, individual tasks still required precision and care as well as a knowledge of machines and of fabrics. Over time, however, there was a tendency for managers to reconstrue skill as speed. As several authors have argued, the ability

13. Glenn, *Daughters of the Shtetl,* 152.

14. Frederick H. Abernathy, John T. Dunlop, Janice H. Hammond, and David Weil, *A Stitch in Time: Lean Retailing and the Transformation of Manufacturing: Lessons from the Apparel and Textile Industries* (New York: Oxford University Press, 1999), 27–28.

to work at high speed became a new "skill," inadvertently created by deskilling.[15] The practice of paying workers by piece rate, and the adoption of standard allocated minutes for each task, fueled this trend. Because of the difficulty of further mechanizing a process involving limp fabric, the progressive bundle system and piecework continued to characterize garment production throughout the twentieth century.

Labor struggles in the apparel industry recognized that section work and the progressive bundle system eroded craft control. In the first years of the twentieth century in Chicago, a group of Swedish seamstresses, who remained committed to sewing whole garments as tailors had done in the past, formed the Custom Clothing Makers' Union. Their goal in this union — the first in U.S. history to be headed by women — was to resist the spread of section work. At the height of its power the CCMU had 3,000 members, and it fought for and won a (shorter) nine-hour day, higher wages, and a ban on child labor in its shops. Its resistance to section work proved futile, however. After it affiliated with the American Federation of Labor, that organization ordered the CCMU to merge with the United Garment Workers. The UGW did not oppose section work, and it forced the CCMU to use the UGW label instead of its own. This undermined the seamstresses' attempt to market "custom-made" clothing as a distinct product and led to the demise of their movement.[16]

The garment workers' unions were sites of ongoing gendered struggles for craft control. In the early twentieth century the Amalgamated Clothing Workers of America, which represented menswear workers, and the International Ladies' Garment Workers' Union both emphasized the interests of male cutters rather than female sewing workers and of those who worked in factories rather than those (mainly women) who worked at home. They did so even though in the 1920s women made up two-thirds of the ILGWU and one-third of the ACWA.[17] Cutters had a long history as a craft guild,[18] and union leaders Sidney Hillman and David Dubinsky (both cutters) felt they could most easily press claims to skill for these workers. They argued that by organizing cutters first, the union could gain leverage to organize and represent the much larger groups of sewing machine operators.[19] In

15. Angela Coyle, "Sex and Skill in the Organization of the Clothing Industry," in *Work, Women and the Labour Market,* ed. Jackie West (London: Routledge, 1982); Glenn, *Daughters of the Shtetl,* 100.

16. Wertheimer, *We Were There,* 320–21.

17. Glenn, *Daughters of the Shtetl,* 171.

18. Cynthia Cockburn, *The Machinery of Dominance: Women, Men and Technical Know-How* (London: Pluto Press, 1985), 47–48.

19. Abernathy et al., *Stitch in Time,* 31.

fact, however, cutters' claims to skill did not "trickle down" to the rest of the workforce. For much of the century, garment workers' unions sought to defend the "craft" nature of their work by these strategies, which Alice Kessler-Harris has called mechanisms of "social closure."[20]

Kessler-Harris has argued that in their efforts to preserve and extend the socioeconomic position of their members, the apparel unions distanced themselves from groups without political power. These included groups who were perceived as easily replaceable within the workforce and whose skill could be understood as innate rather than acquired through training and apprenticeship. After the Amalgamated Clothing Workers of America split from the United Garment Workers in 1914, both that organization and the ILGWU provided a haven for immigrant men who sought to consolidate their claim to practice a skilled trade. Although women made up the majority of the workforce in apparel throughout the twentieth century, they faced a constant struggle to have their voices heard within these unions.[21]

The greatest outpouring of resistance and activism in the garment industry followed the introduction of the "rationalized" production practices of section work and the innovations of scientific management in the first two decades of the twentieth century. The "uprising of 20,000" in 1909–10 in New York City began in the Triangle Shirtwaist shop and ultimately spread to young women making shirtwaists all over the city. After a dispute with their employer, young women at the shop approached the ILGWU to inquire about affiliating. Managers fired the workers who had taken this action. When their coworkers began picketing to show support for the women who were fired, managers called in thugs, who assaulted them, and the police, who arrested them. After five months marred by frequent violence, the uprising reached an anticlimactic conclusion as a number of shops signed individual agreements with the union and ILGWU leaders called off the strike. Two key demands that managers did not meet at the Triangle shop were unlocked doors and functioning fire escapes. This led to the deaths of 146 young women in the Triangle Shirtwaist fire the next year.[22]

In the Great Revolt of 1910, 60,000 ILGWU cloak makers walked out to demand a reduction in the workweek, the elimination of subcontracting,

20. Alice Kessler-Harris, "Problems of Coalition-Building: Women and Trade Unions in the 1920s," in *Women, Work and Protest: A Century of U.S. Women's Labor History*, ed. Ruth Milkman (New York: Routledge, 1985), 120–21.

21. Ibid.; also, Alice Kessler-Harris, "Organizing the Unorganizable: Three Jewish Women and Their Union," in *Class, Sex and the Woman Worker*, ed. Milton Cantor and Bruce Laurie (Westport, Conn.: Greenwood Press, 1977).

22. Wertheimer, *We Were There*, 297–310.

paid holidays, weekly payment in cash, and grievance procedures. The union reached a historic settlement with employers that became known as the Protocol of Peace. The Triangle Shirtwaist fire in March 1911 gave rise to a renewed outpouring of protest and resulted in government investigations and the introduction of a new industrial code in the state of New York.[23]

Because it could draw on low-cost immigrant labor clustered in urban centers, the apparel industry did not move south with textile mills in the 1880s. But with the passage of restrictive immigration laws in the 1920s, this situation began to change. While the urban centers of the Northeast, Cleveland, Chicago, and later Los Angeles have remained important hubs of garment production, with the restriction of new waves of immigration apparel manufacturing firms began to open up sewing shops in small southern towns. By 1950 the South had 154,000 apparel workers, and by 1960 that number had risen to over 308,000.[24] Of all apparel jobs in the nation, 44 percent were in the South in 1974, compared with 17 percent in 1950.[25] By 1982 the South had surpassed the Northeast in its share of employment in undergarments and children's wear, while the Northeast retained a slender lead in women's outerwear.[26] Apparel firms moved south in search of a "favorable business climate," which included low wages, low rates of unionization, right-to-work laws, cheap resources, and community subsidies.[27] The strategy of attracting industry through cheap labor would leave southern communities vulnerable in later periods. In 1998, when Tultex Corporation closed one of its sewing shops in a small southern town, a laid-off worker asked the mayor what could be done. "I told her I was mighty sorry," he reported. "But years [ago] . . . companies came out of the north for cheap labor. Now they're going on south to Honduras and Mexico."[28]

Early twentieth-century department stores and mail-order houses used

23. Ibid., 313.

24. James Hodges, "J. P. Stevens and the Union Struggle for the South," in *Class and Community in Southern Labor History,* ed. Gary M. Fink and Merl E. Reed (Tuscaloosa: University of Alabama Press, 1994), 54.

25. NACLA (North American Congress on Latin America), "Capital's Flights: The Apparel Industry Moves South," *NACLA Report on the Americas* 11 (1977): 10–11.

26. Roger D. Waldinger, *Through the Eye of the Needle: Immigrants and Enterprise in New York's Garment Trades.* (New York: New York University Press, 1986), 71.

27. John Gaventa, "From the Mountains to the Maquiladoras: A Case Study of Capital Flight and Its Impact on Workers," in *Communities in Economic Crisis: Appalachia and the South,* ed. John Gaventa, Barbara Ellen Smith, and Alex Willingham (Philadelphia: Temple University Press, 1990), 85.

28. Dan Kegley, "Tough Luck for Tultex Employees?" *Smyth County News and Messenger,* January 21, 1998.

new techniques of mass distribution and branded marketing to develop the market for the large quantities of clothing that could be produced through scientifically managed section work. Both department stores and mail-order houses made their profits on volume, not markup. As business historian Alfred Chandler has emphasized, mass retailers needed new managerial practices that would allow a high level of stock turn. In this way they could "take lower margins and to sell at lower prices and still make higher profits than small specialized urban retailers."[29] Such competition brought strident protests from smaller local businesses, which could not match prices and so lost sales to these national firms.

Mass retailers established operations that could rapidly administer immense flows of goods. Only in rare cases did they manufacture their own products. Rather, each department had specialized buyers who were responsible for procuring most of what the company sold. Operating departments received incoming goods, stored them, assembled orders, and shipped them. By 1905, firms were using miles of internal conveyor belts and intricate scheduling systems to process as many as 100,000 orders a day.[30]

Mass marketing grew throughout the twentieth century, fostered by improvements in the speed and regularity of transportation and communication. Once a firm had developed an organizational structure that could manage the flow of goods required, it could more efficiently use its capacity by adding more outlets and incorporating new lines. Thus department stores evolved into chain stores, and the number of departments expanded. As the century progressed, firms also spent unprecedented amounts on advertising, often employing independent agencies to develop their campaigns.[31]

In addition to the rise of mass marketers, the late nineteenth century saw the emergence of named brands. Beginning with cigarettes, this trend quickly expanded to grains (Quaker Oats), canned goods (Campbell's soup), soaps (Procter and Gamble), and toothpaste (Colgate). Firms developed logos to advertise their brands in print and jingles for radio commercials. Consumer products companies selling branded goods initially expanded into new geographic regions and markets, but they soon took advantage of economies of scope to move into related product lines. Economies of scope result from using a single operating unit to produce or distribute more than one product.[32] Firms selling branded merchandise used their marketing and dis-

29. Chandler, *Visible Hand,* 229.
30. Ibid., 232.
31. Ibid., chap. 7.
32. Ibid., 17.

tribution networks to manage several lines and transferred resources and knowledge from one production line to another; they sometimes even made joint use of factories.[33]

Brands grew in importance through the twentieth century. They came to signify not just a product, but a way of life, an attitude, or a set of values. Naomi Klein has argued that entire corporations became able to "embody a meaning" for consumers. According to Klein, the defining moment in this trend came in 1988, when Philip Morris purchased Kraft for $12.6 billion, six times what the corporation was worth on paper. The price difference was widely attributed to Kraft's name recognition.[34]

The branding of clothing began early in the twentieth century with Levi's jeans, but it took on new importance beginning in the 1970s. During this decade the ascendancy of brands brought a sea change in apparel manufacture. It was no longer enough for a firm to produce a well-made and fashionable item. Manufacturers had to have a brand, and if they did not, they had to produce for a company that did. By the 1990s, retail establishments were allocating floor space not to categories of clothing but to particular brands. And a new type of apparel concern emerged—one that had no factories or manufacturing capacity of its own but that "caused clothing to be manufactured" by others. These firms made significant investments in the design and marketing functions necessary to build a brand image.

These developments required new kinds of organizational capacity and raised the cost of entry for new firms. They also reshaped the international division of labor in apparel. Textile and clothing industries were once "the most geographically dispersed of all industries," growing up in many parts of the world in a manner largely parallel to what has just been described for the United States.[35] But as we shall see, the emergence of new forms of branded marketing transformed apparel production from a national industry to a transnational enterprise and broadly redistributed elements of the apparel commodity chain across national spaces.

Concentration in the Apparel Industry

As noted in chapter 1, the apparel industry has been known for its historically low levels of concentration and its conditions of near perfect competi-

33. Ibid., 169.

34. Naomi Klein, *No Logo: Taking Aim at the Brand Bullies* (New York: Picador, 1999).

35. Peter Dicken, *Global Shift: Transforming the World Economy*, 3d ed. (New York: Guilford, 1998), 282.

tion. It was traditionally the most labor-intensive and fragmented industry in the United States textile complex—a family industry comprising, as Fariborz Ghadar and his coauthors have noted, "thousands of small companies averaging less than a hundred employees and producing an extremely narrow product line."[36] Ghadar noted that the industry restructured itself in the 1970s, increasing its productivity faster than that of the industrial sector as a whole. During this period, larger firms' share of output increased, but in general changes were very slow. As late as 1991, the industry continued to be made up of many small firms, employing an average of forty-three workers per establishment. In that year, 63 percent of plants employed fewer than twenty workers.[37]

This situation began to change rapidly as the industry moved into the 1990s. One analyst suggested that whereas a company doing $100 million of annual business was large enough to survive in the early 1990s, by 1999 only firms operating at the $2 billion mark were secure and thriving.[38] Others concurred, noting that "a handful of powerful retailers and manufacturers continue to grow, often fueling each others' expansion, while small players find themselves at ever greater risk."[39] A changing competitive situation drove this increase in concentration, while a wave of mergers and acquisitions made it possible.

The changes in the competitive environment were partly a product of the brutal price competition of the 1990s. As table 2.1 shows, the consumer price index for apparel was lower in 2000 than in 1991. At the end of the decade, consumers were paying less for many items of apparel than they were at the beginning. Yet costs for producers rose steadily between 1985 and 2001.[40] Manufacturers complained that retailers were demanding items "floor ready"; that is, garments already prepared with bar codes, price tags, and hangers. They estimated that this raised their operating costs by 7

36. Fariborz Ghadar, William H. Davidson, and Charles S. Feigenoff, *U.S. Industrial Competitiveness: The Case of the Textile and Apparel Industries* (Lexington, Mass.: D. C. Heath, 1987), 3–4.

37. Kitty Dickerson, *Textiles and Apparel in the Global Economy*, 2d ed. (Englewood Cliffs, N.J.: Merrill, 1995), 289.

38. Andree Conrad, "Scaling the Heights in a Discount World," *Apparel Industry Magazine*, June 1999.

39. Sharon Edelson and Anne D'Innocenzio, "Seminar's Focus: Megafirm's Clout," *Women's Wear Daily*, March 26, 1998, 14.

40. Kristi Ellis, "Producer Prices for Apparel Fall below October 2000," *Women's Wear Daily*, November 12, 2001, 19. This article cites Labor Department data indicating that in October 2001 producer prices for apparel fell below the previous year's levels for the first time since January 1985.

Table 2.1. Consumer price index for apparel

Year	All items	Apparel
1980	82.4	93.0
1985	107.6	104.3
1987	113.6	109.6
1988	118.3	114.4
1989	124.0	117.1
1990	130.7	122.8
1991	136.2	127.4
1992	140.3	130.2
1993	144.5	131.9
1994	148.2	131.2
1995	—[a]	129.3
1996	156.9	128.5
1997	160.5	129.4
1998	163.0	129.3
1999	166.6	127.8
2000	172.2	126.2

Source: American Association of Footwear and Apparel Manufacturers, *Trends: A Quarterly Compilation of Statistical Information on the Apparel and Footwear Industries* (Arlington, Va.: AAFA, 2000).

Note: 1982–84 = 100.

[a] Not available.

percent.[41] By the end of the decade, apparel was flooding the market, and in the face of oversupply, retailers often refused to pay for unsold merchandise or asked their suppliers for "markdown money" to subsidize what didn't sell. They instituted "charge backs" on orders that they claimed deviated from packing and shipping specifications in any way. These kinds of pressures on firms created tremendous incentives to lower the costs of labor.[42]

It was growing concentration in their sector that gave retailers the leverage to demand these things from manufacturers. Table 2.2 presents overall measures of concentration for department stores, large discounters, and apparel specialty stores. While the degree to which power is concentrated in the hands of the largest firms appears striking from these data, the more refined measures that industry analysts use present an even more dramatic picture. *Apparel Industry Magazine* reported that in 1990, twenty firms con-

41. Shirley Fung, "Vendors Play the Margin Game," *Women's Wear Daily,* December 13, 2000, 11.

42. Thomas J. Ryan, "Analyst Tells Vendors: Be 'Naughty,'" *Women's Wear Daily,* April 3, 2000, 19; Thomas J. Ryan, "Small Firms Need Size to Survive," *Women's Wear Daily,* November 13, 2000, 22–24; Vicki M. Young, "Making the Most of the Midmarket," *Women's Wear Daily,* May 15, 2000, 29–30.

Table 2.2. Concentration in the retail sector, 1992, 1997

Type of store	Percentage of sales accounted for by firms			
	Four largest	Eight largest	Twenty largest	Fifty largest
Department stores				
1992	55.9	78.3	93.6	99.4
1997	62.1	84.2	95.9	99.8
Discount and mass merchandising				
1992	78.7	87.9	97.9	99.8
1997	87.9	94.9	99.6	100.0
National chains				
1992	100.0	100.0	100.0	100.0
1997	100.0	100.0	100.0	100.0
Clothing stores (all)				
1992	17.9	27.9	41.3	52.4
1997	25.5	34.3	46.6	59.2
Women's clothing stores				
1992	27.6	35.4	48.3	59.8
1997	27.2	36.9	51.9	64.5
Family clothing stores				
1992	35.3	52.3	66.8	76.6
1997	43.3	56.5	70.9	83.8

Source: U.S. Census Bureau, Economic Census, Retail Trade, table 6, "Concentration by Largest Firms, 1992, 1997."

trolled 38 percent of the apparel market. By 1998, those retailers' share had increased to 47 percent. Among department stores in 1999, the six largest companies captured nine out of every ten consumer dollars spent.[43]

Because of their highly concentrated purchasing power, these large retail firms held enormous leverage over clothing manufacturers and could demand not just lower prices but more rapid response to orders and investments in innovations that made supply chain integration possible. These innovations included bar coding, electronic point of sale data collection, real-time Internet-based transaction capabilities, and the software to integrate these data collection functions and transactions. Large retailers were able to hold manufacturers to a price point. "The large merchandising chains can afford to squeeze hard," reported Richard Appelbaum and Gary Gereffi. And as they did so, they "[turned] up the pressure on their contractors to make clothes with more fashion seasons, faster turnaround times, lower profit margins, greater uncertainty about future orders and frequently

43. Edelson and D'Innocenzio, "Seminar's Focus: Megafirm's Clout"; "Apparel's 'Big Six' Retailers Grab a 90% Share," Industry News, Apparel Industry Magazine, June 1999.

worse conditions for workers."[44] While all firms struggled with these pressures, large, well-capitalized firms had a significant advantage.

Large firms reduced their unit costs by renovating and rationalizing the distribution process with new information and telecommunications technologies. Using these technologies, firms developed what has been called an "information-integrated supply channel."[45] The concept of a supply channel is much like that of a commodity chain–it includes all the firms and relationships necessary to get a product to market. In apparel, this starts with yarn spinning, textile production, and manufacture of other necessary materials; moves on to apparel design, cutting, and sewing; and ends up with distribution to a retailer, sale to a customer, and any service that follows the sale.[46] In the 1990s, new forms of electronic data interchange made it possible to link firms within a supply channel through standardized data transmission. Through bar coding, the retailer could track the garment from its preassembly state (as part of a bolt of cloth) to the moment of sale. If workers attached tags to garments and bagged them or placed them on hangers in the factory, they could be shipped directly to the retailer, bypassing distribution centers and the extra handling they entailed. Customer purchasing could then "pull merchandise through the supply channel" in response to demand. As one recent analyst of industrial change has noted, the new information technologies "practically eliminated the physical costs of communications."[47]

It was true that costs were eliminated once the software and equipment were in place. But in the late 1990s, the initial investment for a firm could range from $10 million to $75 million.[48] While this promised savings in the long run, many small firms could not afford such large initial investments. As the industry press noted, "Apparel manufacturers, especially the thousands of modest-sized companies that are not very technologically proficient, have been pulled into EDI compliance because retailers demand it."[49] It is because of the need to make these large initial investments that "the big tend to dance with the big" in the apparel industry and that "concentra-

44. Richard Appelbaum and Gary Gereffi, "Power and Profits in the Apparel Commodity Chain," in *Global Production: The Apparel Industry in the Pacific Rim,* ed. Edna Bonacich, Lucie Cheng, Norma Chinchilla, Nora Hamilton, and Paul Ong (Philadelphia: Temple University Press, 1994), 52, 60.

45. Abernathy et al., *Stitch in Time,* 263–70.

46. Ibid., 2.

47. Peter Drucker, "Will the Corporation Survive?" *Economist,* November 3, 2001, 15.

48. Rocío María Winger, "The E-Zone," *Apparel Industry Magazine,* November 1998; "Ready to Ware: Software and Hardware That Is," *Forbes* April 15, 1999, 30–32.

49. Winger, "E-Zone."

tion among retailers seems likely to lead to concentration among manufacturers."[50]

Firms that adopted these new technologies could engage in "quick response" production. Quick response (QR) is an initiative that gained favor
across many sectors in the United States in the 1980s as companies sought
to emulate the success of just-in-time strategies in Japanese firms. It encompasses a set of practices designed to shorten production cycle time by
electronic data transmission from retailers to various segments of manufacturing.[51] It uses information and telecommunications technologies to link
retailers and manufacturers into a single supply channel that is able to
respond quickly to demand movements.[52] Whereas in the past retailers ordered goods based on past years' sales and demand projections, under QR
they order close to the selling season in small quantities and replenish stock
as needed. Most of the enhanced speed is due not to more rapid manufacturing but to the faster movement of materials.[53]

In addition to allowing companies to use quick response techniques,
the new information and telecommunications technologies helped them to
lower their unit costs in another way. They made it possible to manage a
geographically dispersed production network. While producing offshore
added transport time, Internet-based data management reduced the time
of all of the other business transactions associated with an international
order to practically zero. Companies could track orders in real time and make
adjustments throughout the process. It was this ease of communication that
led the manufacturer quoted in chapter 1 to say that "there's no difference
manufacturing in North Carolina or El Salvador; it's the same everything
except the cost of labor." While the cost of building a garment factory in
Mexico or Central America was only about $5 million in the 1990s, the cost
of establishing state-of-the-art information systems to manage that facility
from afar was much larger and represented a substantial barrier to entry.

Larger firms thus were more able not only to meet retailer demands for
supply chain integration and quick response but also to organize offshore
production. As Chandler has noted, mass distribution has always required

50. Dickerson, *Textiles and Apparel*, 299; Edna Bonacich and Richard Appelbaum, *Behind the Label: Inequality in the Los Angeles Apparel Industry* (Berkeley: University of California Press, 1990), 90.

51. Dickerson, *Textiles and Apparel*, 265.

52. Janice H. Hammond, "Quick Response in Retail/Manufacturing Channels," research
paper, Harvard University Center for Textile and Apparel Research, 1993, 191.

53. Scott Malone, "Cut It Out: Vendors and Merchants Keep Finding New Ways to Slash
Time from the Production Cycle," *Women's Wear Daily*, March 24, 1999, 24.

an organization that is capable of managing the flow of goods and main-taining a high level of stock turn. Accomplishing this across vast distance and national borders is a daunting proposition. In addition to the costs of establishing information systems, small firms had difficulty obtaining access to import quotas, which were traded on a secondary market and were often "reserved" for larger firms. Doreen Massey has argued that global sourc-ing strategies in the industry require a minimum size of operations. Edna Bonacich and Richard Appelbaum have suggested that nine out of ten apparel firms in Los Angeles are too small to afford the costs of shifting production overseas. These authors estimate that companies with annual sales under $40 million will have difficulty managing a globally dispersed network.[54]

Moving production operations offshore or developing subcontracting re-lations with offshore factories was the single most important step that ap-parel firms could take to survive the price competition of the 1990s. Despite innovations in design and distribution, apparel production remains one of the most labor intensive of industries, and labor costs remain the most significant production factor. While these costs represent only about 6 per-cent of the total retail price of a garment, they constitute between 15 and 20 percent of the overall costs of manufacture.[55] In addition, labor costs are the most geographically variable of the industry's production expenses.[56] In 1993, firms producing in Mexico had labor costs (including wages and any benefits, food, or transportation) that were one-quarter those in the United States. In Malaysia those costs were 10 percent of U.S. levels, and in China, 3 percent.[57] In 1999, managers at Tultex Corporation said they could save $10,000 to $15,000 a year for each job they moved to Mexico. By the end of the 1990s, even firms like Levi-Strauss, with a long-standing commitment to U.S. manu-facturing, were closing their domestic factories and sourcing from abroad.

Another important advantage possessed by the large, well-capitalized firms of the 1990s was the ability to invest in the design and marketing ini-tiatives necessary to build a brand. Labels like Nike, the Gap, Liz Claiborne, Tommy Hilfiger, Polo Ralph Lauren, and Calvin Klein came to dominate the scene in apparel marketing. Advertising consultants argue that brands work by creating lifestyle associations with a particular label. This gives the consumer a way to sort through hundreds of thousands of products by

54. Doreen Massey, *Spatial Divisions of Labor: Social Structures and the Geography of Production,* 2d ed. (New York: Routledge, 1995), 158, 164; Bonacich and Appelbaum, *Behind the Label,* 7.

55. Bonacich and Appelbaum, *Behind the Label,* 2.

56. Dicken, *Global Shift,* 295.

57. Dickerson, *Textiles and Apparel,* 201–2.

marking those that suit certain demographic profiles. Stuart and Elizabeth Ewen have suggested, more cynically, that the success of the garment industry has been linked to its extraordinary ability to "produce and distribute standardized goods, laced with the lingo of individual choice and self-expression."[58] They argue that much of the power of the massive late twentieth-century U.S. advertising complex is its ability to train consumers to recognize highly nuanced differences among basically similar goods.

According to this view the same sweatshirt, labeled Tommy Hilfiger, Nike, Guess, or Fubu, will appeal to very different groups. Add a logo for a professional sports team or a university, and its market shifts still further. Use a lighter-weight cotton yarn, add some polyester, and step down quality control, and the same garment can be sold at a major discounter for one-fifth the price of the branded shirt. These items can all be produced in the same factory, using the same machines, with extremely small changes in procedures. This is true for other apparel products as well. An article in Forbes quotes a manufacturer as saying that the "cost to make a pair of jeans runs from $8 for the cheapest to $15 for top of the line. Quality and weight of fabric account for some cost difference. But when all is said and done, jeans are just jeans." Despite this fact, a single issue of Elle magazine in 1995 ran sixty pages of ads for designer jeans, ranging in price from $30 to $150.[59] Adding a brand name can create an illusion of distinctiveness among garments that are numbingly similar.

Brand name proliferation gives the impression that a large number of firms are entering the market, but this is often an illusion as well. As Smith has noted in the case of bakeries, rustic brown bread is produced not only by small shops, but under trendy-sounding names by the same large corporations that make white bread.[60] In 2002, Liz Claiborne marketed clothing under twenty-six brand names. Department stores and mass retailers introduce their own "private label" brands at different price levels with styles targeted to particular demographic groups. All of this is expensive, entailing design costs and massive expenditures in marketing and advertising.[61]

Firms that purvey brands have expanded into what Gereffi and others

58. Stuart Ewen and Elizabeth Ewen, *Channels of Desire: Mass Images and the Shaping of American Culture* (New York: McGraw-Hill, 1982), 226.

59. Joshua Levine, "A Lifestyle in a Label," *Forbes,* November 1, 1996, 155.

60. Chris Smith, "Flexible Specialization, Automation and Mass Production," *Work, Employment and Society* 3, no. 2 (1989): 215.

61. Bonacich and Appelbaum provide the following figures: Nike spent $211 million on advertising in 1997, Levi-Strauss spent $100 million, and firms such as Polo Ralph Lauren, Calvin Klein, Wrangler, and Tommy Hilfiger spent over $30 million each (*Behind the Label,* 215).

have called "high value added" activities within the apparel commodity chain. These firms recognize that profits within the chain derive not so much from scale, volume, and technology as "from unique combinations of high value research, design, sales, marketing and financial services that allow the firms to act as strategic brokers in linking overseas factories with evolving product niches in the main consumer markets."[62] This strategy, while costly to put into practice, is also quite profitable. Eileen Rabach and Eun Mee Kim have argued that product conception and design, along with marketing, are the most lucrative and profitable segments of any commodity chain.

Branded marketers of apparel concentrate on these activities while farming out riskier and lower-return tasks such as manufacturing itself.[63] Firms like Nike, for example, have been able to develop as design, distribution, and marketing enterprises, retaining control over highly profitable nodes in the commodity chain while avoiding the rigidity and pressures of the more competitive nodes. In an article on that company, Miguel Korzeniewicz quotes Neal Luridson, Nike's vice president for Asia Pacific, as saying, "We don't know the first thing about manufacturing. We are marketers and designers."[64] While Nike is a paradigmatic branded marketer, in the sense that it does not own any of the factories where its goods are produced, other firms (like Levi-Strauss) incorporate the branded marketing of apparel into their general business strategy while continuing to produce some merchandise in factories of their own. Still others, like the Gap and the Limited, are similar to branded marketers in subcontracting all of their apparel production but different in that they market it primarily through their own stores.

Unlike garment manufacture, this kind of branded marketing has high barriers to entry. According to Gereffi, "The lavish advertising budgets and promotional campaigns required to create and sustain global brands, and the sophisticated and costly information technologies employed by today's mega-retailers to develop quick response programs . . . illustrate recent techniques that have allowed retailers and marketers to displace traditional manufacturers."[65]

62. Gary Gereffi, "International Trade and Industrial Upgrading in the Apparel Commodity Chain," *Journal of International Economics* 48 (1999): 43.

63. Eileen Rabach and Eun Mee Kim, "Where Is the Chain in Commodity Chains? The Service Sector Nexus," in *Commodity Chains and Global Capitalism*, ed. Gary Gereffi and Miguel Korzeniewicz (Westport, Conn.: Praeger, 1994), 136.

64. Miguel Korzeniewicz, "Commodity Chains and Marketing Strategies: Nike and the Global Athletic Footwear Industry," in Gereffi and Korzeniewicz, *Commodity Chains and Global Capitalism*, 252.

65. Gereffi, "International Trade and Industrial Upgrading," 44.

As *Apparel Industry Magazine* noted, in the 1990s firms needed to create brand recognition, which was expensive. They had to do good market analysis and meet the challenge of filling orders precisely and on time, which required greater capitalization than ever before.[66] In addition, pressures on firms to reduce costs made global sourcing imperative. This required expertise in order to negotiate complex quota systems and import requirements. It also required new electronic data interchange that made far-flung production operations as responsive to market shifts as small shops in the garment districts of New York and Los Angeles.

While the practice of branding provides firms with many advantages, it also contains an important contradiction. When corporations brand a product, they are effectively taking responsibility for it, staking their reputation on the items they sell. In the late 1990s, antisweatshop activists took advantage of the visibility of some key brands, like Nike and the Gap, to link large corporations to low wages and poor working conditions in the factories where their goods were made. When it was possible to discover where a company produced branded items, protesters were able to scrutinize the production process and pressure firms to improve conditions. Brand names are vulnerable to bad press, and socially concerned consumers can use this fact to demand that a firm take responsibility for conditions along its commodity chain.[67]

Gereffi argues that large apparel firms in the 1990s derived profits from three kinds of "rents," or returns from scarce assets. The first of these were relational rents, or profits derived from the firm's ability to establish and manage effective supply chain relationships. The second were trade policy rents accruing to firms that had learned to access quota within a complex set of international trade policies. The third were brand name rents, which are the returns from the "product differentiation techniques" used by firms.[68] Investing in these kinds of relationships, knowledge, and reputation placed firms in a privileged position to manufacture and sell their wares. The best suppliers and support firms, like the most desirable quota, were limited, and the number of successful brands the market would bear was finite. For these reasons, apparel companies that were able to team up with the most desirable supply chain partners, obtain quota allotments for the countries where they wanted to produce, and purchase the advertising expertise to establish themselves as "hot" brands were able to translate those

66. Stuart Hirschfield, "Industry Factors Challenging Apparel Manufacturers and Suppliers," *Apparel Industry Magazine,* August 1998, 3.

67. "The Case for Brands," *Economist,* September 8, 2001, 11.

68. Gereffi, "International Trade and Industrial Upgrading," 43–44.

advantages into tremendous market share, cost advantages, and profits. Large firms were better able to make the initial investments required. Not only did they accrue what Chandler called first mover advantages, but the high costs involved and the limited supply of these "goods" created barriers to entry for less capitalized firms.[69]

Firms that operate in this way possess what Bennett Harrison has called "concentration without centralization." They have pared down their mix of core activities, subcontracting the riskier and less profitable tasks. Harrison argues that despite a disproportionate emphasis on small business entrepreneurship in the popular press, production in many sectors is dominated by firms that are decentralized and flexible, yet large and powerful.[70] In articles written in 1994 and 1999, Gereffi has contributed to this critique by explaining how a trend toward concentration without centralization has extended to consumer goods industries. In these "buyer-driven commodity chains" there are few economies of scale, and the industrial structure is more fragmented and less concentrated than in producer-driven industries like oil, steel, or aluminum.[71] Gereffi's discussion of the rents accrued by large-scale apparel firms is important in showing how the competitive pressures associated with retail consolidation and globalization of production have made "bigger better" even in buyer-driven apparel commodity chains.

Late twentieth-century apparel firms grew in a variety of ways. In the 1980s, the U.S. economy saw a massive 25 percent per annum increase in mergers across a wide range of sectors, and this trend continued through the economic growth of the 1990s.[72] While the apparel industry was slow to join this trend, the 1990s saw the rise of the apparel corporate giant.[73] Firms sought mergers, acquired smaller firms, and forged licensing agreements. In 1999 alone Liz Claiborne acquired, or completed licensing agreements with, six other firms, including such well-known design houses as Kenneth Cole, Donna Karan, and Segrets. In addition to growth through acquisitions and mergers, firms within the apparel industry expanded their clout through "virtual mergers" or new forms of collaboration within a sup-

69. Alfred D. Chandler Jr., *Scale and Scope: The Dynamics of Industrial Capitalism* (Cambridge: Harvard University Press, 1990).

70. Bennett Harrison, *Lean and Mean: Why Large Corporations Will Continue to Dominate the Global Economy* (New York: Guildford, 1994), 247.

71. Chandler, *Scale and Scope*.

72. Ash Amin and Anders Malmberg, "Competing Structural and Institutional Influences on the Geography of Production in Europe," in *Post-Fordism: A Reader*, ed. Ash Amin (Cambridge: Blackwell, 1994), 234; "America Bubbles Over," *Economist*, April 18, 1998.

73. "Fashion's Wheel of Fortune," *Women's Wear Daily*, September 7, 1999.

Table 2.3. Concentration ratios in select branches of apparel industry, 1992, 1997

| Subsector | Number of firms | Percentage of sales accounted for by firms | | | | Herfindahl-Herschmann index[a] |
		Four largest	Eight largest	Twenty largest	Fifty largest	
Men's/boys' shirts						
1992	527	28	42	60	78	315.0
1997	387	42.9	55.4	71.9	85.6	659.3
Women's/girls' dresses						
1992	3,943	11	17	30	45	61.0
1997	747	14.2	23.7	39.4	60.4	111.3
Men's/boys' suits/ coats						
1992	249	39	50	68	88	580.0
1997	193	42	55.5	75.1	92	845.7

Source: U.S. Census Bureau, Census of Manufacturers, Concentration Ratios in Manufacturing, table 3, 1992; table 3, 1997.

Note: Between 1992 and 1997, the U.S. Census Bureau shifted from using the Standard Industrial Code (SIC) for classifying industries to using the North American Industrial Classification System (NAICS). The apparel subsectors presented in the table were chosen because they were standard apparel items and items where it was possible to establish that the SIC code and the NAICS code were directly comparable.

[a] The Herfindahl-Herschmann index is calculated by summing the squares of the individual company percentages for the fifty largest companies.

ply channel.[74] Large retailers and branded manufacturers that controlled the channel could thus enjoy the advantages of coordinated production without the risks of direct ownership. Fiorenza Belussi has referred to this pattern as the emergence of "concentrate regimes," which she believes represent new forms of oligopolistic power concealed within a structure of apparently independent firms.[75]

These kinds of contracting relationships make it difficult to obtain accurate data on concentration in the apparel industry, particularly when the contracts are international in scope. As table 2.3 indicates, census data show a tendency toward greater concentration in key segments of the industry over the period 1992–97. But the data are likely to underestimate concentration for three reasons. First, the factories that the census counts are frequently not producing goods on their own account but are under contract to large branded marketers or retailers. Second, the census does

74. Thomas J. Ryan, "M&A: The Rush to the Altar: Efficient = Big," Women's Wear Daily, November 10, 1999, 18–21.

75. Fiorenza Belussi, "Benetton, Italy: Beyond Fordism and Flexible Specialization; The Evolution of the Network Firm Model," in Computer-Aided Manufacturing and Women's Employment: The Clothing Industry in Four EC Countries, ed. Swasti Mitter (London: Springer-Verlag, 1992), 78.

Table 2.4. Concentration in the apparel industry and selected other industries, 1997

| Industry | Number of firms | Percentage of sales accounted for by firms | | | | Herfindahl-Herschmann index[a] |
		Four largest	Eight largest	Twenty largest	Fifty largest	
Apparel	15,839	17.6	23.2	29.8	38.8	100.6
Textiles	3,863	13.8	21.7	35.9	52.9	94.4
Machinery	27,983	11.5	15.6	23.9	34.3	55.4
Transportation equipment	10,979	49.7	57.8	68.6	77.5	797.6
Computer/electronics	15,492	19.1	28.1	41.1	55.0	136.6

Source: U.S. Census Bureau, Census of Manufacturers, *Concentration Ratios in Manufacturing,* table 2, 1997.

[a] The Herfindahl-Herschmann index is calculated by summing the squares of the individual company percentages for the fifty largest companies.

not count large branded marketers as manufacturing establishments if they only "cause to be manufactured." And third, there are no reliable data on the offshore production of apparel that is marketed by U.S. firms. Still, table 2.3 demonstrates that the percentage of sales accounted for by large firms is increasing across all categories. It also shows a clear decline in the number of apparel firms.

Table 2.4 shows how concentration ratios in apparel compared with those in several other sectors of the economy in 1997. One of the most surprising aspects of the data is that apparel has become more concentrated than the textile industry. As recently as 1992, all branches of the textile industry were more concentrated than any branches of apparel, largely because of the greater investments required in looms and knitting machines. By 1997 this had changed. While apparel is still far less concentrated than industries like transportation equipment, it is no longer the highly fragmented arena of "near-perfect competition" that it has been in the past. The available data indicate that concentration has indeed become a fact of life in the industry and that "a disproportionate amount of the profits needed to reinvest in the industry lies in the hands of only a few companies."[76]

The Growth of Global Sourcing

For U.S. consumers scanning the labels in the clothing section of a local department store in the 1990s, it was increasingly rare to find items that

76. Appelbaum and Gereffi, "Power and Profits in the Apparel Commodity Chain," 47.

were "made in the U.S.A." The U.S. trade deficit in apparel was $52.3 billion in 2000–2001, up from $34.7 billion in 1995.[77] Approximately 90 percent of imports during this period were from developing nations. But for the most part these imports were not the product of developing country firms. Fledgling entrepreneurs in South America and Southeast Asia were not moving into apparel production at the first rung on the ladder of economic development, then upgrading their capacities and learning to export. This may have been the case for Japanese and Taiwanese firms in many sectors during the "East Asian miracle," but it was not the situation for apparel in the 1990s. Rather, U.S. companies scanned the global landscape to find low-wage locations for their garment assembly, and it was these firms that organized the production process and reimported the goods to U.S. markets. Sometimes these firms relocated their factory operations, but more frequently they avoided the headaches and risks of ownership by subcontracting with foreign concerns. As Peter Dicken has noted, "The globalization of these industries has been driven primarily by developed country firms. Indeed, it is paradoxical that a significant proportion of the textiles, and especially the clothing, imports which are the focus of such concern in developed countries, are in fact, organized by the international activities of these countries' very own firms."[78] Thus it is more accurate to think of the changes in the provenance of U.S. apparel in recent years as a result of the growth of global sourcing rather than the growth of imports.

Many observers have pointed to the influence of free trade pacts on apparel firms' sourcing decisions. "Free trade" is a misnomer when applied to the apparel industry, however, since the traffic of shirts and slacks around the world is governed by an extraordinarily complex and arcane web of agreements. Since 1974, trade in garments has been organized by a set of bilaterally negotiated import restrictions under the overarching rubric of the Multi-Fiber Arrangement. This agreement encompasses "no fewer than 1000 different allotments, covering scores of categories from dozens of countries."[79] The quotas established under the MFA play a major role in shaping the investment and sourcing strategies of large apparel firms.[80]

77. Data for 2000–2001 are from "Textile and Apparel Trade Balance Report," U.S. Department of Commerce, Bureau of the Census, International Trade Administration and can be found at http://otexa.ita.doc/gov/tbrimp.htm. Data for 1995 are from Dicken, *Global Shift*, 292.

78. Dicken, *Global Shift*, 303.

79. "The Great Quota Hustle," *Forbes*, March 6, 2000, 120.

80. Paul Charron, chief executive officer of Liz Claiborne, has claimed that during the period of the MFA, 40 percent of his firm's sourcing decisions were based on quota availability (Lisa Rabon, "Season of the Consumer," *Bobbin*, December 2000, 1).

The complexity of apparel quota allotments in the 1990s led to bizarre situations in which cashmere from China was shipped to Madagascar (where quota was abundant) to be knit into sweaters, or Chinese workers were sent to Mauritius (which was quota-rich but lacked experienced labor) to sew clothing for U.S. and European markets. In other cases firms hired workers to cut and partially sew garments in Sri Lanka, sent the clothing to the Maldives for more sewing, and then back to Sri Lanka for finishing, since that country had the appropriate quota resources.[81] Not surprisingly, a lively secondary market in quota itself emerged. And also somewhat predictably, transshipment through countries with unused quota allotments became a problem. In 1995 the World Trade Organization took charge of eliminating quotas on textiles and clothing in three stages over a ten-year period. As the 2005 end date approaches, U.S. apparel importers have expressed concern that Congress will use ad hoc "antidumping" and "countervailing duties" measures to replace the system of quotas. Legislation fostering such measures in Congress in 2001 and 2002 has given such fears credence.[82] At the same time, many industry analysts warn manufacturers that they will face an onslaught of merchandise from cheap-labor countries like China if quotas are truly abolished and "market forces" prevail.[83]

The "free trade" agreements that have had the most dramatic effects on the location and sourcing decisions of U.S. apparel firms are regionally specific and focused on Mexico, the Caribbean basin, and more recently Africa. Item 807 of the U.S. Tariff Code provided the first special arrangements for the import of apparel into U.S. markets, in conjunction with Mexico's "border industrialization" and "maquiladora" programs. Item 807, established in 1963, specified that if articles (of any kind) were assembled abroad of components fabricated in the United States, they could be reimported paying duties only on the "value added" in assembly. Apparel assembled from U.S.-made fabric became eligible for such treatment. Mexico was a prime location for 807 assembly, not only because of its proximity to U.S. markets but because of Mexican government policies of the late 1960s that established special benefits for maquiladoras, or plants that were producing for an export market. These policies eliminated restrictions on foreign ownership for factories along the northern border, allowed duty-free import of materials and machinery, and helped foreign companies gain access to land.

81. "Great Quota Hustle, 120; Kristin Larson, "Sourcing's New Dynamic," *Women's Wear Daily*, May 30, 2001, p. 7.

82. Brenda Jacobs, "Duty Measures Spark Concern," *Bobbin*, February 2001, 64.

83. Kathleen DesMarteau, "TDA Implementation: The Clock Is Ticking," *Bobbin*, November 2000, 6.

In 1972 the Mexican government extended these provisions to all but the most highly industrialized regions of Mexico, making the nation a compelling environment for offshore production for many U.S. firms.

Investors used the "yarn forward" provisions of Item 807 to establish new regimes of garment assembly in some other nations as well. When the Reagan administration implemented the Caribbean Basin Initiative in 1983, it specifically excluded clothing from duty-free treatment. The administration removed this exclusion with CBI II in 1986 and used a "super 807" clause to guarantee that apparel made in the Caribbean basin from U.S. fabrics could enter U.S. markets. The tariff reduction provided by these measures, combined with the proximity of the nations, created incentives for U.S. firms to source apparel in Mexico and the Caribbean basin countries even when the cost of labor was higher than in some other parts of the world.

The passage of the North American Free Trade Agreement in 1994 created further incentives for U.S. firms to produce in Mexico. NAFTA preserved a targeted 807A rule, or "special regime," that gave U.S. companies permission to reimport clothing from Mexican assembly plants, without duties or quotas, if they used fabrics manufactured and cut in the United States. Over time, it also reduced duties for apparel made from fabrics that were not produced in the United States. The agreement gave Mexican factories special exemptions to perform finishing processes such as stonewashing and permanent press treatment without forfeiting duty benefits. These measures, combined with the NAFTA's simplification of import procedures and a massive devaluation of the Mexican peso, generated a rapid response. In 1997, Mexico overtook China as the leading source of U.S. apparel imports.[84]

While many factors besides trade agreements combined to undercut the industry's U.S. manufacturing base, U.S. apparel jobs—which had hovered around one million in the early nineties—had dropped to 520,000 ten years later.[85] By the end of the decade, manufacturers who had not established global sourcing capabilities were increasingly unable to compete. The Trade Development Act passed by Congress in 2000 extended NAFTA-like benefits to seventy countries in sub-Saharan Africa and the Caribbean basin. It ex-

---

84. In 2001, Mexico accounted for $9.6 billion of U.S. textile and apparel imports, or 12.7 percent. China's share was $9.5 billion, or 12.6 percent. Hong Kong, Canada, and South Korea were the next most important provisioners of U.S. apparel. Data are from OTEXA (Office of Textile and Apparel), U.S. Department of Commerce, International Trade Administration, "Textile and Apparel Trade Balance Report, 2000–2001."

85. Joanna Ramey, "More Industry Job Losses in May," *Women's Wear Daily*, June 10, 2002, 3.

empted apparel assembly in those countries from quotas and reduced tariffs to value added if the clothing used U.S.-made fabrics. NAFTA and the Trade Development Act created incentives for not only U.S. firms, but also Asian and European firms, to invest or source production in beneficiary countries in order to gain favored access to the U.S. market.

To call these labyrinthine measures "free trade" is to stretch the meaning of the term beyond recognition, but all fell under the rubric of broader neoliberal policies. The measures combined highly selective import restraints with occasional market opening and divided the interests of a formerly cohesive apparel and textile bloc that had advocated a more overt and across-the-board protectionism. For firms with substantial resources and a global strategy, these measures opened the door to the construction of multinational operations of a size never before seen in the industry. For firms that lacked such resources or vision, the rapid downward pressure on prices caused by new global sourcing patterns led to crisis and bankruptcy.

As William Greider has noted, the "global economy divides every society into new camps of conflicting economic interests,"[86] and global sourcing brought profound contradictions to the U.S. apparel industry. Firms with a global production process advocated free trade policies as a way to enhance their investments, while companies producing in the United States lobbied for protectionist trade legislation to shield their operations from competition with goods produced abroad. The American Apparel Manufacturers Association[87] had historically taken a protectionist stance, but by the late 1980s many of its larger and more powerful members were producing offshore—either in factories they owned or in factories where they subcontracted goods. Because of the strength of these members, by 1989 the organization had shifted to advocacy of trade liberalization. By 1999 its growing record of support for a range of free trade agreements led Senator Ernest Hollings of South Carolina (a staunch advocate of protectionist measures for the textile and apparel factories in his state) to refer to the organization as the "Central American Apparel Manufacturers Association."[88]

Textile manufacturers, represented by the American Textile Manufacturers Institute and backed by powerful politicians such as North Carolina's

86. William Greider, *One World, Ready or Not: The Manic Logic of Global Capitalism* (New York: Simon and Schuster, 1997), 18.

87. The AAMA merged with the Footwear Industries of America to become the American Apparel and Footwear Association in 2000.

88. "Parity Bill Still Afloat," *Apparel Industry Magazine*, November 15, 1999. Paul Charron, CEO of Liz Claiborne Incorporated, became president of the association in 2002.

Jesse Helms, fought hard to protect their industry through the 1990s. They continued to advocate use of Item 807 and related measures to ensure that if apparel manufacture moved offshore, foreign factories would continue to purchase U.S. fabrics. By the time the Trade Development Act was passed in 2000, however, some textile firms had begun to relocate their knitting and weaving operations offshore, and even the formerly protectionist ATMI found itself sharply divided over "yarn forward" rules. More globally organized textile firms began to oppose the rules, while manufacturers who retained U.S. mills continued to advocate them. In that year, ATMI president Roger Milliken—a South Carolina mill owner who advocated protectionism—quit his position in protest over the organization's support of the extension of trade benefits to Africa and the Caribbean basin.[89]

Generating further rifts within the industry were its three growing powerhouses: the new "branded retailers"; traditional retailers who had begun to produce their own private labels; and large manufacturers who subcontracted most of their product. These groups had a strong interest in removing barriers to imports and in lowering the costs of importing. They formed the U.S. Association of Importers of Textiles and Apparel (USA-ITA) to represent their views. This group was joined in most of its positions by the National Retail Federation. As trade bills came before Congress in the 1990s, no single lobby represented the apparel and textile industry. Instead, the industry sported a complex array of competing groups whose interests were shaped by the ways their operations were distributed across the global landscape.

The Dialectic of Fashion and Dualism in the Apparel Industry

Nancy Green has written that since the late nineteenth century, the fashion industry has operated through a dialectic of innovation and standardization. The houses of fashion introduce a new style, and those who wear it are marked as clever and au courant. But then other companies imitate the style, and it becomes commonplace. In the days before mass production, poorer folks imitated the styles set by the wealthy by sewing them at home with less expensive fabrics. But as most clothing production moved into factories, the dialectic between innovation and standardization became the

89. Scott Malone, "Dramatic Departure: U.S. Advocate Milliken Quits ATMI over CBI," *Women's Wear Daily*, October 4, 2000, 1, 14.

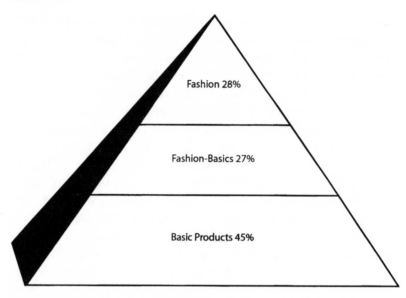

Figure 2.1. The fashion pyramid. From Frederick H. Abernathy, John T. Dunlop, Janice H. Hammond, and David Weil, "Executive Summary of Preliminary Findings, Study of the U.S. Apparel Industry," research paper, Harvard University Center for Textile and Apparel Research, 1995.

motor of an industry. "Torn between art and industry," Green writes, the women's apparel industry markets "individualism to the masses."[90]

The result of this dialectic is what many industry analysts call a "fashion pyramid." At the top of the pyramid are designer and "designer bridge" clothing (see fig. 2.1). Firms producing these items participate in the innovation part of the dialectic. The value of these garments lies largely in the novelty of their design, so their selling life is relatively short. According to research conducted at the Harvard University Center for Textile and Apparel Research, approximately 28 percent (by value) of all apparel sold falls into this category.[91] "Fashion-basic" or "moderate" items make up the next tier of the pyramid. Firms that produce these items participate in the standardization part of the dialectic—they seek to copy the styles introduced by top-tier designers, but in less expensive versions. These items have a longer selling life. Department and specialty stores market them, and they generate approximately 27 percent of apparel sales. At the bottom of the pyramid are basic apparel items–things like T-shirts and underwear that do not experience rapid style change and that can remain on a retailer's shelf without

90. Green, *Ready-to-Wear and Ready-to-Work*, 15.
91. Abernathy et al., *Stitch in Time*, 9.

losing much of their value. Mass merchandisers sell most items of basic apparel, but department stores market a small proportion as well. Basic items account for 45 percent of all apparel sales.

Many apparel industry analysts believe that since the 1960s the dialectic or cycle of fashion has intensified. This has happened partly because of a proliferation of styles and products. Frederick Abernathy and his coauthors use the example of men's suits sold with two pairs of pants. When Bond Stores of New York introduced this new product in the late 1940s, they report, "the line of hopeful buyers at its Times Square store stretched around the block." Today, these authors note, a staple item like a man's dress shirt is produced in "dizzying diversity in fabric, design and style."[92] Consumers have come to expect much greater variety. According to Jonathan Zeitlin and Peter Totterdill, changes in consumers' tastes and demographics, the volatility of demand, and the apparel industry's own efforts at product differentiation have "fragmented the mass market in the advanced countries. . . . The struggle for competitive advantage has come to center increasingly on retailers' and manufacturers' efforts to target specific groups of customers defined in new ways; to seduce customers with attractive, fashionable garments; to respond rapidly to short-term trends in the sales of individual product lines."[93]

In 1988 apparel manufacturers introduced 2,368 new stock-keeping unit (SKU) numbers, which corresponds to the number of unique new products; in 1992 that figure had increased to 3,688.[94]

Not only are there more kinds of apparel on the market than ever before, but the fashion cycle has speeded up. Whereas in the past stores changed their stock twice a year, the number of fashion "seasons" has now expanded to six to eight, and many fashion-oriented retailers change their lines monthly.[95] *Forbes* reported that the average fashion trend in 1999 lasted six to twelve weeks. The magazine points out that whereas car designs change every few years, clothing designs change every few weeks. "And garments don't just come in several models, but in two genders and a myriad of shapes, sizes, colors and styles, which complicates the supply chain process beyond what most product makers face even in their worst night-

---

92. Ibid., 1, 7.

93. Jonathan Zeitlin and Peter Totterdill, "Markets, Technology and Local Intervention: The Case of Clothing," in *Reversing Industrial Decline? Industrial Structure and Policy in Britain and Her Competitors,* ed. Paul Hirst and Jonathan Zeitlin (New York: St. Martin's Press, 1989), 162.

94. Abernathy et al., *Stitch in Time,* 46.

95. Gereffi, "International Trade and Industrial Upgrading," 6; Bonacich and Appelbaum, *Behind the Label,* 29.

high end stuff we
are imitating's
made way it was in past!

mares."[96] So not only do manufacturers introduce many more products than in the past, but cycles of innovation and standardization are now faster.

Many industry analysts have suggested that the dialectic between innovation and standardization is important in structuring the way apparel is produced—that the cycle of introducing new products and disseminating them to a broader market is linked to dualism in the production process. In this view, high-end fashion goods require one kind of production process and standardized goods for mass markets another. More pointedly, analysts contend that whereas companies can produce basic apparel in factories located wherever labor is cheapest, using the progressive bundle system, the same is not true of fashion goods. According to this argument, fashion merchandise requires the skill and creativity of the small shop and the close community of designers, fabric concerns, and sewing operations that only the garment districts of industrialized cities can provide.

For these reasons, proponents of this view argue that manufacturers will continue to produce high-end fashion clothing in small, flexibly organized shops.[97] "The large apparel company," Roger Waldinger writes, "while well-suited for making staple goods, is too cumbersome an entity to . . . respond to sudden and unanticipated fluctuations. . . . Because apparel is a product very much subject to the vagaries of fashion change and the volatility of consumer spending, there is a role for . . . the small facilities that are best suited to producing small quantities of short-lived fashions."[98]

Allen Scott further develops this view. He argues that manufacturers cannot produce high-quality fashion merchandise through subcontracting and section work. They are more likely to construct fashion garments, he argues, on "making through" principles, giving a single operator or team responsibility for putting the whole garment together.[99] Production of these items retains, in other words, many of the elements of tailoring.

Based on this reasoning, some authors have suggested that high-end apparel is ideally suited for production under industrial paradigms of flexible specialization. Flexible specialization paradigms emphasize the re-integration of manual and mental work in ways that give firms the flexibility to alter production in response to changes in demand. They involve

---

96. "Ready to Ware: Software and Hardware That Is," *Forbes,* April 15, 1999, 31.

97. Allen J. Scott, *Metropolis: From the Division of Labor to Urban Form* (Berkeley: University of California Press, 1988); Waldinger, *Through the Eye of the Needle;* Zeitlin and Totterdill, "Markets, Technology and Local Intervention."

98. Waldinger, *Through the Eye of the Needle,* 189.

99. Scott, *Metropolis,* 102.

"the manufacture of specialized goods by means of general purpose resources."[100] Advocates of this approach argue that its success requires workers to develop and use a wide array of skills and to play a role in design and in the decision making surrounding production.

In *The Second Industrial Divide,* Michael Piore and Charles Sabel point to the women's garment industry as a classic example of the craft models of production that they see as precursors to flexible specialization. They argue that frequent changes in fashion have long required apparel firms to constantly reorganize the ways they use materials and the skills of workers.[101] Green has built on this argument by suggesting that "the garment industry was an example of flexible specialization before the term was coined."[102] For many authors, however, the speedup of fashion cycles and proliferation of products in the 1980s and 1990s made new versions of flexible specialization techniques even more important to the fashion segment of the industry.

Zeitlin and Totterdill have argued that the fragmentation of the consumer market and proliferation of styles has led to a decline in scale economies for apparel firms. The challenge of designing and manufacturing the widest range of styles at the lowest cost can be accomplished in part, they have suggested, through the introduction of new technologies such as computer assisted design (CAD), computer controlled cutting, and new information systems for inventory control. But sewing operations are more intractable, since no one has yet developed a technology that can replace the worker who handles limp fabric. "As production runs become shorter and style changes more frequent in the industry as a whole," they write, "even the larger firms have been forced to require their machinists to become proficient at a wider range of sewing operations to avoid costly bottlenecks and line imbalances. Broader initial training and continuous retraining, and higher basic wages for more versatile operatives . . . are being used by larger companies in their efforts to shorten the learning curve and reduce the cost penalty associated with frequent style changes."[103]

Many analysts see the flexibility of work processes as crucial to achieving "quick response," which is crucial in the case of fashion merchandise. But for firms producing at the high end of the fashion pyramid, the quality of

100. Charles Sabel, "Flexible Specialization and the Re-emergence of Regional Economies," in *Post-Fordism: A Reader,* ed. Ash Amin (Cambridge: Blackwell, 1994), 139.

101. Michael J. Piore and Charles F. Sabel, *The Second Industrial Divide: Possibilities for Prosperity* (New York: Basic Books, 1984), 118.

102. Green, *Ready-to-Wear and Ready-to-Work,* 5.

103. Zeitlin and Totterdill, "Markets, Technology and Local Intervention," 170, 176.

their garments is also an important concern. As with responding to product proliferation and implementing quick response, these analysts feel, traditionally organized mass production firms would have a problem maintaining quality standards. According to this view, high-quality production requires a tailorlike, flexible process. While plants producing large runs of low-quality goods may be able to "farm out" assembly to disparate locations, manufacturers producing small batches of high-quality garments tend to perform skilled, attentive work within their own shops, where they can provide constant and careful supervision. Such work is most easily managed, in this view, within the garment districts of cities like New York and Los Angeles.[104]

Arguments about the dualism of apparel production have had a geographical dimension. Scott suggests that high-end fashion production requires the "agglomeration" of complementary producers in a particular place. "Different productive activities interpenetrate with one another," he says, "in a tangled network of linkages. . . . They cluster compactly in geographic space, and in this way they form a specialized garment district in the core of the city."[105] Zeitlin and Totterdill have taken this geographical argument one step further by suggesting that manufacturers are less likely to move the production of fashion goods for niche markets outside the industrialized countries, "since lead times are too long, minimum production runs too large, and quality control too difficult."[106] This view has been echoed by other scholars studying the apparel industry. Bonacich and Appelbaum, for example, write that "the consensus seems to be that the production of basics, for which there are big runs of the same line and styles do not constantly change, [is] likely to leave Los Angeles. The smaller companies, and those that specialize in fashion, for which runs are short, and styles are constantly changing, will remain."[107]

Analysts from the industrialized nations are fond of this line of argument because it suggests that there will be a continued role for some segments of the apparel industry in their parts of the world. In an era when so many manufacturers were moving production to developing countries to reduce their labor costs, the "dualist" perspective suggested that the industrial nations could hope to retain factories making short runs of high-end fashion goods.

104. Scott, *Metropolis*, 102–4.
105. Ibid., 74.
106. Zeitlin and Totterdill, "Markets, Technology and Local Intervention," 167.
107. Bonacich and Appelbaum, *Behind the Label*, 71.

In summary then, dualist accounts of the apparel industry have argued that high-end fashion production faces three intractable problems that cannot be solved using mass production methods: the need to shift production runs rapidly to meet the needs of a changing market (the product proliferation problem); the need to reduce turnaround times to a minimum (the quick response problem); and the need to produce goods that meet stringent standards (the quality problem). Until the end of the 1980s, these accounts held out hope that the high end of the apparel industry could provide good jobs, using and recognizing the skills of its workers and organizing its work in ways that drew on and rewarded their creativity. This view circulated not only among academic observers and industry analysts but in the larger culture as well. A Virginia news publication, reporting on job loss in the southside communities where apparel companies like Tultex had operated, expressed a somewhat chauvinistic version of the argument: "Manufacturers believe U.S. companies always will have a future producing specialty items, with the nearby U.S. market counting on higher-end products that demand the expertise of skilled American workers."[108]

The idea that only U.S. workers have the expertise necessary for high-end production contains within it a profound contradiction. While the production of fashion merchandise may require somewhat flexible work processes, it has another characteristic as well. To paraphrase Scott, it requires "attention" and "careful work." The production of fashion apparel is unavoidably labor intensive. Gereffi has suggested, in contrast to the preceding accounts, that the incentive to reduce the cost of labor may be highest for firms producing these goods.[109] He argues that companies selling near the top of the market face the imperative to turn out short runs of new products in a timely way combined with the need to produce intricately worked, high-quality garments. The labor intensity of the process creates strong incentives to find ways to operate flexibly–but in low-wage settings.

It has become apparent across many industries, in any event, that "the confident presumption that certain high-caliber work can be done only by certain people (mainly, it is assumed, by well-educated white people in a few chosen countries) is mistaken" and that people "who exist in surroundings of primitive scarcity are making complex things of world-class quality,

108. Page Boinest Melton, "How Global Trade and NAFTA Hit a Vital Virginia Business," *Virginia Business,* August 2000.

109. Gary Gereffi, "The Organization of Buyer-Driven Global Commodity Chains: How U.S. Retailers Shape Overseas Production Networks," in *Commodity Chains and Global Capitalism,* ed. Gary Gereffi and Miguel Korzeniewicz (Westport, Conn.: Praeger, 1994), 96, 102.

mastering modern technologies that used to be confined to a select few."[110] In the apparel industry this trend is clear, since by the end of the 1990s, firms were subcontracting all but the highest tier of tailored clothing, including exclusive-label men's suits, in Mexico and China. Manufacturers may have (shamelessly) lamented that workers in these sites, including managers, were hindered because "they have never purchased high quality garments" and did not know how they should look or feel. But they also noted that "low labor cost sites can afford to put in a great deal of handwork." U.S. imports of tailored garments shot up 50 percent between 1994 and 1999, with much of this growth from countries with low labor costs.[111]

Addressing the question of how firms achieve high-quality production in low labor cost environments raises important issues of skill, labor control, and shop floor politics. Apparel firms relocating their production operations are not simply seeking the lowest hourly wage but are combining the sweating of labor with complex new systems of quality—and thus labor—control. These new "hyper-Taylorist" methods of work organization allow apparel firms to simultaneously solve the three problems outlined above. Like a skilled juggler, they manage to pay low wages while producing top-quality goods, and to do so on a just-in-time basis. For apparel workers these new work regimes also require a juggling act. They must try to maximize their production under a piecework system while inspectors monitor the quality of their production using systems of "statistical process control."[112]

The quest to achieve flexible high-end production in low labor cost settings raises questions for firms about how they will invest in, and relate to, the places where they produce garments. "Cheap labor" strategies and fly-by-night operations are not consistent with the need for skilled and experienced workers and top-of-the-line work processes. At the same time, making significant investments in a place and developing a low-turnover workforce implies operating costs that reduce the average rate of profit. Extricating themselves from long-term commitments to workers and communities motivated many firms to relocate their operations in the first place. Managers of apparel firms in the 1990s sought ways to balance these concerns.

Whether they were producing for the high or low end of the market, firms confronted "localization" questions—how much to invest in their new

110. Greider, *One World, Ready or Not,* 20.

111. Jules Abend, "The Out-Sourcing Revolution," *Bobbin,* May 2001, 40.

112. Jane L. Collins, "Flexible Specialization and the Garment Industry," *Competition and Change* 5 (2001): 165–200.

locations, how to structure their relationship with workers, and how to organize work. Offshore production introduced the factor of geographic distance, but it often entailed new forms of economic organization as well. Subcontracting introduced new layers of social relations between workers and owners and altered the legal relationship between employees and firm. The nature of the employment contract and the social responsibilities of employer to worker could be quite different in Mexico, China, or Indonesia than in the United States.

Market forces alone do not produce the cheap labor that employers seek. It is a product of the social relations that structure workers' opportunities and freedoms. In the apparel industry, where such a large percentage of the workforce is female, gender plays a crucial role in shaping these opportunities and freedoms. As Lourdes Arizpe and Josefina Aranda have noted, the supposed "comparative advantage" of low-wage regions often relies on "women's disadvantages."[113] Or as Cynthia Enloe has written, the low cost of women's labor is referred to in public policy "as if cheapness were somehow inherent in women's work. In reality, women's work is only as unrewarded or as low-paid as it made to be."[114]

Relocations across space are also social relocations. Moving or subcontracting abroad makes it possible for industrialized country firms to restructure labor relations in ways that could not have happened in the former context of work, law, and social regulation. In the following chapters we will examine some of the ways that firms establish their production regimes and develop relationships with workers and local communities. We will look at how they balance the benefits of deterritorialized production regimes that develop few connections to regions and workers against the need to localize their operations in ways that enhance productivity and the quality of work. To address these issues, we will look first at the story of how one firm sought to extricate itself from its decades-long production history in a community in the southern United States and to reestablish its operations in a very different setting in Mexico.

113. Lourdes Arizpe and Josefina Aranda, "The 'Comparative Advantages' of Women's Disadvantages: Women Workers in the Strawberry Export Agribusiness in Mexico," *Signs* 7, no. 2 (1981): 453–73.

114. Cynthia Enloe, *Bananas, Beaches and Bases* (Berkeley: University of California Press, 1989), 160; my italics.

3

TULTEX: MASS-PRODUCING KNITWEAR IN SOUTHERN VIRGINIA

The new despotism is the "rational" tyranny of capital mobility over the collective *worker.*

—MICHAEL BURAWOY, *THE POLITICS OF PRODUCTION*[1]

Garment shops began to produce ready-made apparel in the second half of the nineteenth century, and the industry prospered with the rise of the department store and mail-order marketing. Fueled by the labor of successive waves of immigrants, small apparel factories thrived in northern cities until the restriction of immigration in the 1920s. The history of Tultex Corporation is bound up with these shifts. The founder of the company traveled north in the early years of the century to learn knitting mill technology from an upstate New York firm, then transplanted it, in the 1920s, to a southern setting where labor was "abundant and cheap." Over the next sixty years, a complex and contradictory form of paternalism grew up between the firm and its workers, which the coming of a union in 1994 overturned only with difficulty. The case of Tultex illustrates how a U.S.-based firm produced for mass markets. At the same time, it provides an example of a localization strategy that involves densely embedded

1. Michael Burawoy, *The Politics of Production* (London: Verso, 1985), 150.

and multistranded relations between a company and the site of its production.

The Sweatshirt Capital of the World

Entering the town of Martinsville, Virginia, from the east on Route 58, the highway passes through miles of tobacco fields, broken only by occasional patches of pine forest, seasonal vegetable stands, and the town of Danville, where textile mills—some functioning, some empty—dominate the skyline. Alternatively, coming into town from the north on Route 220, the road descends from the hardscrabble farmlands of the Appalachians into the gentler foothills, or Piedmont, where the town lies (fig. 3.1). The Piedmont of Virginia and the Carolinas lies between the broad plains of the tidewater region to the east and the mountains to the west and is the site of the fall line for the region's rivers. For nineteenth-century entrepreneurs, it was thus a prime location for water-powered industries. While its rural character and the continuing presence of farms may suggest to a casual observer that the economy has an agricultural base, from the early decades of the twentieth century more of its inhabitants have made their living working in factories than on farms. Tobacco processing, furniture manufacture, apparel and textiles, small machinery, glassworks, and leather were the lifeblood of the region.

When I drove into Martinsville in the summer of 1999, signs posted at the city limits proclaimed it "the sweatshirt capital of the world." The company primarily responsible for this distinction operated in an imposing multistory red brick building on Franklin Street (fig. 3.2). This was the headquarters of Tultex Corporation, at that time the largest producer of sweatshirts in the world, and one of the top thirty apparel firms in the United States. The factory site was a renovated and expanded hundred-year-old cotton mill that contained over a million square feet of operating space. That summer the firm employed nearly 5,100 people in its Martinsville plant and several other small yarn-spinning and sewing facilities in southern Virginia, North Carolina, Montego Bay, Jamaica, and Tamaulipas, Mexico. It was the focal point and economic anchor of this small southern town. About two miles south of town along Route 87, a visitor could find the gray Quonset hut that served as headquarters for the company's union, UNITE Local 1994.

The town of Martinsville was home to only about 16,000 people in the 1990s, but with surrounding Henry County added in, the total population

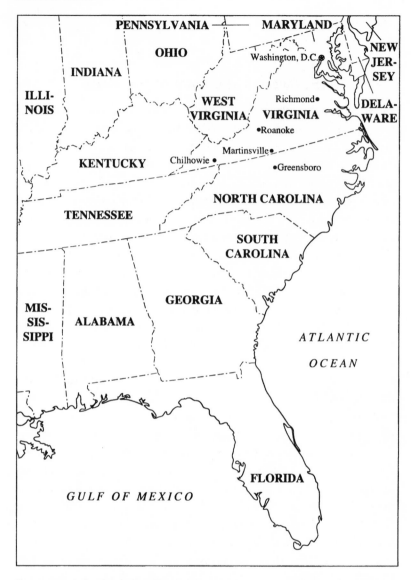

Figure 3.1. Map showing Martinsville, Virginia.

came closer to 80,000. Approximately three-quarters of the residents were white and the rest were African American, with only a sprinkling (less than 1 percent) of other ethnic groups.[2] In the eighteenth and nineteenth centuries, tobacco plantations formed the backbone of the region's economy, and

2. United States Census Bureau, *Provisional Estimates of Population for Virginia Counties and Cities* (Washington, D.C.: Government Printing Office, 1998).

A

B

Figure 3.2. Tultex in 2002, after plant closing.

the legacies of slavery were addressed only slowly in the twentieth. In 1890 almost half the population of the city and county was black, but many of the area's African American residents migrated to cities of the North and Midwest during the 1930s and 1940s.[3]

The region's light industrial base made it more prosperous than many southern counties. In the 1990s about three-quarters of adults had graduated from high school or some institution of higher learning, and the average household income was $30,000. In June 1999 the unemployment rate for Henry County was just over 5 percent. Of the top ten employers in the county, four made textiles or apparel, four made furniture, one produced plastic film, and another prefabricated housing.[4]

The firm that came to be known as Tultex Corporation was founded in 1937 in the wake of a wave of unrest in the textile industry. This unrest culminated in the General Textile Strike of 1934, when more than 400,000 workers across the country walked off their jobs in the largest single labor conflict in American history. In the late 1930s mill owners faced New Deal labor legislation with trepidation, and highway and transportation improvements were resulting in the dismantling of the "mill village." What led William Pannill to start a textile venture under such uncertain conditions was the allure of new knitting machines.

In 1903 Pannill was working for Mayo Cotton Mills in Mayodan, North Carolina, when his employer sent him north to learn about the technologies for knitted textiles. He took a job as a janitor in a knitting mill in Utica, New York, where he secretly observed the plant's operations and took notes. When he returned to North Carolina with his notes and diagrams, he helped Mayo Cotton Mills start a new knitting division. While some southern textile concerns had already moved into knitted hosiery production, this was the first southern factory to produce knitted garments such as underwear.[5]

Pannill moved to Winston-Salem, North Carolina, in 1916 to work for P. H. Hanes Knitting, but in 1925 he established a mill of his own — Pannill Knitting — in Martinsville, Virginia. Over the next twelve years, he started two other mills in the town. He later sold one, Bassett-Walker, to the giant

3. Eric Rise, *The Martinsville Seven: Race, Rape and Capital Punishment* (Charlottesville: University Press of Virginia, 1995), esp. 26; Henry Wieneck, *The Hairstons: An American Family in Black and White* (New York: St. Martin's Press, 1999).

4. Patrick Henry Development Council, *Community Profile* (Martinsville, Va., 2000).

5. Dorothy Cleal and Hiram H. Herbert, *Foresight, Founders and Fortitude: The Growth of Industry in Martinsville and Henry County, Virginia* (Bassett, Va.: Bassett Printing, 1970).

textile firm VF Corporation and Pannill Knitting itself to the corporate conglomerate Sara Lee. Pannill started the third firm, Sale Knitting, in 1937.
He turned this firm over to his son-in-law, Ernest A. "Mike" Sale. Sale
Knitting, which specialized in fleece-lined sweatshirts, is the company that
went on to become Tultex Corporation. Pannill's key strategy in establishing
his mills was to take advantage of the South's lower costs in order to undercut northern firms on price.[6]

Knitting mills, then and now, combine features of the textile and apparel
industries. They make cloth from yarn, using knitting machines rather than
looms. Like textile mills, they dye or bleach the cloth. But unlike most
mills, they also cut the cloth, make the trimmings, and sew the pieces into
a finished garment. The new knitting mills were the most desirable sources
of employment for textile workers in the 1930s. Historians of the period
have written that knitting work was "better paying, physically easier and
cleaner" than cotton mill jobs. The machinery was not as dangerous, and
the air in the factories was not laden with dust. When people left the mill
they did not walk down the street covered with the lint that branded others
as mill workers. Knitting mill jobs were more complex and carried more
prestige than other factory work.[7]

Pannill did not build his knitting mills in an isolated hamlet that included housing for workers. Mill owners believed that the close ties of
workers in mill towns had contributed to the union activity that led up
to the General Textile Strike. In addition, the growing availability of automobiles and the expansion and improvement of highways made it possible, for the first time, to draw workers from a broad hinterland. In light
of these trends, Pannill built his mills in the growing town of Martinsville, Virginia, where he employed the wives and daughters of local furniture workers and as well as rural women and men who had access to
automobiles.[8]

Sale Knitting remained a family enterprise for nearly fifty years. When
Mike Sale retired in 1953, he turned the company over to his brother-in-
law, William Franck, who was also married to one of Pannill's daughters. In
time William Franck turned the firm over to his son John. Under family
ownership, the company went from a mill with 50 employees to a complex
of knitting mills, spinning mills, and sewing shops employing over 6,000

6. Ibid., 161.
7. Jacqueline Dowd Hall, James Leloudis, Robert Korstad, Mary Murphy, Lu Ann Jones,
and Christopher Daly, *Like a Family: The Making of a Southern Cotton Mill World* (New York:
Norton, 1987), 255–56.
8. Cleal and Herbert, *Foresight, Founders and Fortitude.*

workers. Even when the firm moved to public ownership in the 1980s, and to a unionized workforce in the 1990s, the legacy of family management continued to shape its practices.

Historical Antecedents in Textile Production

Knitting mills used different machinery than other textile operations, but there were similarities in the work and a shared tradition of labor practices. While a few textile mills had existed in the South since before the Civil War, most were established in the region between 1880 and 1920, when they became a primary force in the reconstruction of the southern economy. Southern businessmen with roots in tobacco or other forms of agriculture in the antebellum period started these mills. They depended heavily on northern capital, however, often receiving credit from commission houses in return for cloth or stock subscriptions. In the 1880s an average of six new mills were built every year, and mill construction became synonymous with town building and community prosperity.[9] In 1899 the Northeast had 68 percent of the nation's spindles. By 1940 its share had dropped to 14 percent as a result of the growth of southern operations.[10] The South outpaced the North in looms as well. Between 1923 and 1933, 40 percent of New England's textile factories closed, and the South's share of textile jobs rose to 68 percent. Northern firms were undercut by southern wages, which amounted to only 60 percent of those of northern workers. As Jacqueline Hall and her coauthors note, by the 1930s the center of American textile manufacturing had moved definitively southward.[11]

Southern mill owners who entered the business in the 1880s were able to take advantage of new developments such as the ring spinning frame and the Northrop loom. These new technologies simplified operations in ways that made it possible for owners to wrest craft control from hand weavers and mule spinners. They permitted mills to return to their earlier practice of employing women and children and to recruit new workers without experience in the industry. From the beginning, southern firms adopted a Rhode Island, or family labor, system as opposed to a Lowell, or boardinghouse, system based on the employment of young single women.[12]

9. Hall et al., *Like a Family*, 24–26, 30; Cathy McHugh, *Mill Family: The Labor System in the Southern Textile Industry* (New York: Oxford University Press, 1988), 6–7.

10. Herbert J. Lahne, *The Cotton Mill Workers* (New York: Farrar and Rinehart, 1944), 91.

11. Hall et al., *Like a Family*, 81, 197.

12. Linda Frankel, "Southern Textile Women: Generations of Survival and Struggle," in *My Troubles Are Going to Have Trouble with Me: Everyday Trials and Triumphs of Women*

Mill owners purchased the labor of families as a package, "paying adult workers less than a living wage and offering employment to children." Most specified a minimum of three workers per family as a condition for employment.[13]

Mill owners recruited their first generation of workers from the small farms of the Appalachian hills west of the Piedmont. These were white families, many of them headed by widows with dependent children. Others were households of farm laborers; some were headed by "failed" farmers who had lost their land through crop liens or inability to pay taxes.[14] As late as 1923, most mill workers were first generation off the farm. Mill owners portrayed themselves as protectors of the widowed women who came to them for work and as providing an "honorable alternative" for impoverished white men who could not make a living at farming.[15] The villages built around mills rented housing to workers, often with a rule of one room per family member employed. Many families took in boarders to help meet this requirement and pay the rent. Mill towns often had a store that maintained wage accounts and subtracted credit purchases before distributing wages. Most also had a church, a post office, and sometimes a local law enforcement branch. At the beginning of the twentieth century, 92 percent of southern textile workers lived in mill villages; as late as 1938 two-thirds of families still did.[16]

Women were the mainstay of southern textile industry, outnumbering men two to one in North Carolina's forty-nine textile mills in 1880, with children working in numbers equal to men. Women earned only about 60 percent of men's wages, however. Cathy McHugh notes that while managers did not consider children to be particularly good workers, they employed them because they believed it was good to begin their training early. Managers claimed that mothers begged to bring their children to the mills rather than leaving them alone at home or roaming the streets. But the presence of children in the workforce depressed wage levels; McHugh calculated that

Workers, ed. Karen Brodkin Sacks and Dorothy Remy (New Brunswick, N.J., Rutgers University Press, 1984).

13. Hall et al., *Like a Family,* 52.

14. Ibid., 32.

15. J. Rhyne Jennings, *Some Cotton Mill Workers and Their Villages* (Chapel Hill: University of North Carolina Press, 1923), 124; Gary Freeze, "Poor Girls Who Might Otherwise Be Wretched: The Origins of Paternalism in North Carolina's Mills, 1836–1880," in *Hanging by a Thread: Social Change in Southern Textiles,* ed. Jeffrey Leiter, Michael D. Schulman, and Rhonda Zingraff (Ithaca, N.Y.: ILR Press, 1991).

16. McHugh, *Mill Family,* 20; Hall et al., *Like a Family,* 114; Lahne, *Cotton Mill Workers,* 36.

for each $1 increment in child workers' earnings, the wages of male heads of households were reduced by 70¢.[17]

The paternalist social relations of mill villages have been a subject of extended debate among historians of the South. Paternalism has been described as a system that united white workers and their employers in a conservative and racialized consensus.[18] Mill owners argued that their relationship with workers was like that of a father dealing with his children. The factory and the community that surrounded it were portrayed as a "family" with shared interests. The owner, however, was always the one who determined what those interests were. Paternalism operated by providing nonwage goods and services, maintaining an ideology of beneficence, and cultivating deferential relations between workers and bosses. Some have argued that through such means it transformed power relationships into moral obligations—a system of mutual responsibilities, duties, and ultimately even rights.[19]

Historians of the southern United States have disagreed about whether paternalism ultimately provided any benefits to workers. Hall and her co-authors have described the literature as divided into boosterism and muckraking in this regard.[20] "Benign" accounts of paternalism emphasized the tutelary role that factory owners adopted, the welfare services they provided, and the fact that the factory was a refuge for families whose small farms had failed and who had few other employment alternatives. Muckraking accounts argued that textile mill workers were "white slaves" who had no liberties and a frightfully low standard of living. They argued that the southern mill village was a total institution that left workers without autonomy.[21]

17. Gary Freeze, "Poor Girls," 25, provides the data on composition of the workforce; wage differentials are from McHugh, *Mill Family,* 45, and Hall et al., *Like a Family,* 67; McHugh reports the arguments for child labor (52), and calculates the impact of child labor on wages (39).

18. Harry Boyte, "The Textile Industry: Keel of Southern Industrialization," *Radical America* 6, no. 2 (1972): 4–49.

19. Linda Frankel, "Jesus Leads Us, Cooper Needs Us, the Union Feeds Us: The 1958 Harriet-Henderson Textile Strike," in *Hanging by a Thread: Social Change in Southern Textiles,* ed. Jeffrey Leiter, Michael D. Schulman, and Rhonda Zingraff (Ithaca, N.Y.: Cornell University Press, 1991), 106; Dolores Janiewski, "Southern Honor, Southern Dishonor: Managerial Ideology and the Construction of Gender, Race and Class Relations in Southern Industry," in *Work Engendered,* ed. Ava Baron (Ithaca, N.Y.: Cornell University Press, 1991).

20. Hall et al., *Like a Family,* xvi.

21. Holland Thompson, *From the Cotton Field to the Cotton Mill: A Study of the Industrial Transition in North Carolina* (New York: Macmillan, 1906), and Broadus Mitchell, *The Rise of the Cotton Mills in the South* (Baltimore: Johns Hopkins University Press, 1921), present paternalism as relatively benign. Frank Tannenbaum, *Darker Phases of the South* (New York:

These differences stem from the divergent political perspectives of those who wrote about the institution, but also in part from the fact that paternalism was many things in many places and times, continually being reworked to adapt to new conditions. Robert Blauner saw a decline in paternalist practices with the end of the mill village and the tendency to locate new mills in small towns and cities.[22] As Dolores Janiewski has observed, however, this represented a change in practices and not a simple decline. In her words, there was a constant unraveling and reworking of the fabric of control in the transition from Old South to New South and from New South to Sunbelt.[23] In an attempt to capture this variability, Bryant Simon has argued that paternalism was a managerial style. It was based on material power, but it blended symbols, gestures, and welfare programs into a style of control that featured personal involvement and accessibility. His account of paternalism characterizes it as based on a shifting balance of consent and force. Consent could be bought with "a public face of good will and largesse," but the threat of force always lurked in the background. The elements of this complex system could be combined and recombined in different settings and places; in some, relations between firms and managers could be characterized as consent, while in others force might predominate.[24]

Racial hierarchies were an integral part of paternalism.[25] One had to be white to be a member of the "mill family," and mill jobs offered racial exclusivity as part of the "wages of whiteness."[26] As one late nineteenth-century proponent of segregation expressed the situation, being part of an all-white workforce "excites a sentiment of sympathy and equality . . . with classes above them, and in this way becomes a wholesome social leaven."[27] In

---

G. P. Putnam, 1924); Wilbur J. Cash, *Mind of the South* (New York: Alfred A. Knopf, 1941); Herbert J. Lahne, *The Cotton Mill Workers* (New York: Farrar and Rinehart, 1944); and Dwight Billings, *Planters and the Making of a "New South": Class, Politics and Development in North Carolina, 1865–1900* (Chapel Hill: University of North Carolina Press, 1979), present a more negative, "muckraking" view.

22. Robert Blauner, *Alienation and Freedom: The Factory Worker and His Industry* (Chicago: University of Chicago Press, 1964).

23. Janiewski, "Southern Honor, Southern Dishonor," 90.

24. Bryant Simon, "'Choosing between the Ham and the Union': Paternalism in the Cone Mills of Greensboro, 1925–30," in *Hanging by a Thread: Social Change in Southern Textiles,* ed. Jeffrey Leiter, Michael D. Schulman, and Rhonda Zingraff (Ithaca, N.Y.: Cornell University Press, 1991), 82.

25. Boyte, "Textile Industry"; Eugene Genovese, *Roll, Jordan, Roll: The World the Slaves Made* (New York: Random House, 1976); Janiewski, "Southern Honor, Southern Dishonor."

26. David Roediger, *The Wages of Whiteness: Race and the Making of the American Working Class* (New York: Verso, 1991).

27. John W. DuBose, cited in Boyte, "Textile Industry," 20.

Janiewski's words, "A brotherhood of white men bound together planter, industrialist, landlord, mill worker, and tenant farmer in defense of an ideal that denied their conflicts of interest and disguised the real differences in power."[28]

It is not completely true, as Jeffrey Leiter and his coauthors assert, that "the traditional web of cross-class ties in the paternalistic community did not envelop blacks because they were excluded from mill employment."[29] Although not permitted to work alongside whites on looms or spindles, black workers were present in the warehouses of the mills and as sweepers, groundskeepers, loaders, cooks, and janitors. But as Adler has explained, these workers were not included among those taken "under the company's paternalistic wing."[30] In Virginia the racial segregation of mills was enforced informally, but in South Carolina it was law until 1964. The majority of mill workers who were female were not included in this "brotherhood of white men" in a straightforward way. In fact it is more accurate to portray their fathers, brothers, and sons as members of this pact. In the gendered rhetoric of racial segregation, mills promised male kin that they would provide a "safe" and "respectable" work environment for white women workers.[31] "Protecting" white women from contact with black workers was considered an integral part of this safety and respectability.

Hall and her coauthors have made a convincing case that workers never took the rhetoric of family very seriously, at least in the sense of believing they were bound to the mill owner through reciprocal ties. They point to high rates of absenteeism and turnover as evidence of workers' autonomy.[32] Initially this may have been related to the persistence of connections to the land, as workers continued to cultivate gardens and to hunt. It remained important, however, as a way of dealing with frustration, unfair treatment, and abusive overseers. A U.S. Senate document from 1907 reported that "the cotton mill hands in the South are an extremely independent set of people who do not hesitate, upon a slight provocation, or from a pure whim, to leave one mill and go to another."[33] In 1907 the annual turnover rate in southern mills was 176 percent, with 20–40 percent of workers in a "floating population" that moved freely between plants. One manager claimed that

---

28. Janiewski, "Southern Honor, Southern Dishonor," 91.

29. Jeffrey Leiter, Michael D. Schulman, and Rhonda Zingraff, eds., *Hanging by a Thread: Social Change in Southern Textiles* (Ithaca, N.Y.: Cornell University Press, 1991).

30. William M. Adler, "A New Day in Dixie," *Southern Exposure* 12, no. 1 (1994): 20.

31. Freeze, "Poor Girls."

32. Hall et al., *Like a Family*, 106–9.

33. McHugh, *Mill Family*, 22.

in order to have a full complement of labor in the mill each morning they needed to carry a "surplus" of 20–25 percent spare help. Another complained that he was being taken advantage of by people who wanted to work only enough to live.[34]

The mobility and absenteeism of workers in the early twentieth century were possible because there were more jobs than workers and mills were always shorthanded. Wages were rising, and competition led mills led to "pirate" their neighbors' workers by offering them inducements to change jobs. Labor scarcity increased during World War I, when mills sought hands to fulfill military contracts. Owners complained that wage increases only caused most mill hands to work shorter hours, as they adjusted their workweek to meet their immediate needs.[35]

This situation changed drastically with the end of the war, however. Demand for textiles dropped precipitously, and by 1920 the South found itself in a textile depression.[36] Mills attempted to cut wages and rescind the concessions they had offered during the wartime boom. They also responded to these problems by attempting to rationalize work itself by adopting "scientific" methods derived from the principles of Frederick Taylor. Some of the innovations included running the mills twenty-four hours a day, using two or three shifts in order to spread overhead across a greater volume of goods, and introducing new spooling and warping equipment. The most significant change, however, was the adoption of a "multiple loom" system. Operators previously had responsibility for all of the work associated with a few looms, including cleaning, repair and doffing of cloth.[37] Under the new system, the mill gave lower-paid workers responsibility for maintenance tasks and assigned weavers more looms. Workers deeply resented this innovation, which was known as the "stretch-out." It set them "tending machines 'by the acre,' filled every pore in the working day and robbed them of control over the pace and method of production."[38] One worker complained that "hundreds of folks go to jail every year for doing things not half so bad or harmful to their fellow man as the stretch-out."[39] Mill owners enforced the new arrangements by paying piece rate and with hard-driving supervision. Not only was this "rationalization" of work incompati-

34. Hall et al., *Like a Family,* 107; McHugh, *Mill Family,* 25; Robert Sidney Smith, *Mill on the Dan: A History of the Dan River Mills, 1882–1950* (Durham, N.C.: Duke University Press, 1960), 105.

35. Hall et al., *Like a Family,* 110, 184.

36. Ibid., 190.

37. Ibid., 199–208.

38. Ibid., p. 211.

39. Simon, "'Choosing between the Ham and the Union,'" 90.

ble with child labor, but managers often forced sick and elderly workers into retirement by giving them more looms.[40]

Workers responded to the wage cuts and the stretch-out by joining unions and by walkouts and strikes. Forty-three locals of the United Textile Workers of America were chartered in North Carolina alone in the summer of 1919. Between 1919 and 1921, workers in Columbus and the Horse Creek Valley of South Carolina, and in Charlotte, Belmont, Concord, and Kannapolis, North Carolina, walked off their jobs.[41] As the full weight of the textile depression began to be felt, firms placed additional burdens on their employees, fueling their discontent. In one worker's words, "They cut off help and loaded the next man [sic] up with his job. And it began to be where you was running three jobs for the price of one. And the more that happened, the more they was invitin' the unions to the South."[42]

Conditions continued to deteriorate through the 1920s, and the burden fell particularly heavily on women. As "rationalized" plants turned away from child labor, women became responsible for a greater share of family income.[43] The gender composition of the strikes and walkouts reflected the strain women felt. Sixty percent of participants in the Henderson, North Carolina, strike of 1927 were women; in the Elizabethton, Tennessee, strike of 1929, three-quarters were female.[44] Linda Frankel has argued that women were particularly sensitive to alterations in the intensity and hours of work because of their home responsibilities. Family and community members also supported their activism. In her words, "When management actions violated communal norms and family welfare, the close kinship, work and neighborhood ties provided a source of oppositional unity."[45]

Increasingly violent strikes and confrontations spread through the South in 1929 and the early 1930s. Workers invoked Protestant values to criticize their bosses, calling them money lovers and accusing them of abandoning Christian values.[46] Mill workers argued that the new work rules associated

40. Hall et al., *Like a Family*, 297.

41. Ibid., 187–90.

42. George Stoney, Judith Helfand, and Susanne Rostock, *Uprising of '34* (film), Point of View, Public Broadcasting Services, 1995.

43. Hall et al., *Like a Family*, 310.

44. Frankel, "Southern Textile Women"; Mary Frederickson, "I Know Which Side I'm On: Southern Women in the Labor Movement in the 20th Century," in *Women, Work and Protest: A Century of U.S. Women's Labor History*, ed. Ruth Milkman (Boston: Routledge, 1985).

45. Frankel, "Southern Textile Women," 40.

46. Frankel, "Jesus Leads Us, Cooper Needs Us, the Union Feeds Us," 15.

with the stretch-out robbed them of an "American way of life" by withholding a living wage. In this way, Simon argues, they "placed the mill masters in opposition to the values of both Christ and the founding fathers."[47] Workers took encouragement from the Roosevelt administration's adoption of a Cotton Textile Code that promised textile workers a minimum wage, a reduction of working hours, and the right to organize and bargain collectively. As one worker said, "The best thing that ever happened to working people was when President Roosevelt got in. . . . He raised the legal age for work and got those young'uns out of the mills. . . . He cut our hours down from twelve hours a day to eight hours a day."[48] They believed John L. Lewis's claim that "the President wants you to join a union." But Roosevelt's policies did little to alter the intensification of work through "scientific management."

Resistance to the stretch-out, and to such harsh laborsaving measures in the midst of the Great Depression, culminated in the General Textile Strike of 1934. Actions began in July 1934, even before the United Textile Workers of America called workers out on strike. By September "flying squadrons" of cars and trucks were making their way from town to town closing mills; by midmonth 400,000 workers were out on strike. The president called out the National Guard, and martial law was declared in some areas. Police shot and killed seven workers in Honea Path, South Carolina. Mill owners evicted and blacklisted strikers. When, after three weeks, Roosevelt asked the UTWA to call off the strike, its leaders complied. There was no clear resolution of workers' grievances, however, and although Roosevelt asked employers to take back striking workers, few did so. Most workers who had participated in the strike or had union ties lost their jobs. The "settlement" agreed to by the UTWA involved little more than the initiation of a government study board.[49] When makers of a documentary film tried to interview strike participants in the 1990s, they ran into a determined silence about the period. "The few townspeople we were able to find who had been members of the local were bitter about a labor uprising that had cost them their jobs, got their families evicted, and ostracized them from their communities. Many had told no one—not even their children—of their part in the uprising."[50] As one of the individuals filmed said, "[We]

47. Simon, "'Choosing between the Ham and the Union,'" 97.

48. Victoria Byerly, *Hard Times Cotton Mill Girls: Personal Histories of Womanhood and Poverty in the South* (Ithaca, N.Y.: ILR Press, 1986), 165.

49. Lahne, *Cotton Mill Workers,* 230–31.

50. Judith Helfand, "Sewing History," *Southern Exposure* 22, no. 1 (1994): 43.

never mention it. After that happened down here, union wasn't never mentioned again. 'Cause they know they killed them. They were afraid. And they still are afraid."[51]

The textile industry continued to play a central role in the southern economy after World War II, wielding almost as much influence as it had from 1880 to 1945. But the labor unrest of earlier decades subsided. The CIO's "Operation Dixie," launched in 1946, signed up only 10,000 members over a seven-year period. Right-to-work laws were passed in several southern states in the late 1940s. Strikes in Danville, Virginia, and Henderson, North Carolina, in the 1950s were violently suppressed. When workers at the Deering Miliken plant in Darlington, South Carolina, voted to unionize in 1952, the company closed the plant without repercussions.[52]

Meanwhile, the 1950s and early 1960s saw the rise of the civil rights movement. Mill towns, as bastions of paternalist social relations, remained a world largely apart from these developments. A black woman who worked in the warehouse at Cannon's Kannapolis, North Carolina, mill noted, "There were no demonstrations at Kannapolis. The first sit-ins were over there at Woolworth's in Greensboro, a boy out here was one of them. But his daddy is still working in the mill so we don't tell that. We whispered such as that."[53]

Although black workers were employed in nonproduction jobs before 1964, mills had separate toilets and drinking fountains and maintained separate eating spaces for black and white workers.[54]

Only after the passage of the Civil Rights Act in 1964 did textile mills begin to integrate their production lines. But once integration began, it proceeded rapidly. In 1965 nearly all the workers at the J. P. Stevens plant in Roanoke Rapids, North Carolina, were white. By 1973, 40 percent of the workforce was black.[55] At Oneita Knitting Mills in Andrews, South Carolina, 75 percent of the workforce was African American by 1971, and 85 percent of black workers were women.[56] At the Cannon plant in Kannapolis, management proceeded cautiously, hiring two black women for each of three shifts and putting them to work in a separate warehouse with one white woman

51. George Stoney et al., *Uprising of '34.*

52. James Hodges, "J. P. Stevens and the Union Struggle for the South," in *Class and Community in Southern Labor History,* ed. Gary M. Fink and Merl E. Reed (Tuscaloosa: University of Alabama Press, 1994); Frankel, "Jesus Leads Us, Cooper Needs Us, the Union Feeds Us."

53. Byerly, *Hard Times Cotton Mill Girls,* 155.

54. Wieneck, *Hairstons,* 51.

55. Adler, "New Day in Dixie," 20.

56. Frederickson, "I Know Which Side I'm On," 174.

and one white man. After eighteen months without incident, they hired black women in large numbers.[57] Managers attempted to extend their social networks to black workers through a recommendation system. As one black employee at J. P. Stevens put it, "In those days, a black person had to know somebody who knew a white somebody to get on" at the mill.[58]

Recruiting through networks was not sufficient to ensure a compliant and antiunion workforce, however. As blacks gained rights in many spheres of civic life, unions provided a means to protect and pursue those rights in the workplace. Mary Frederickson has noted that

> as the number of black women in southern mills began to increase in the late 1960s and early 1970s, the number of successful union elections also multiplied. Black women took the lead in contacting unions, getting cards signed, fighting management's legal obstacles, and participating in contract negotiations. A majority of black women workers within a plant could usually convince younger white women to join them in supporting the union; with this interracial coalition, an election could be won.[59]

An organizer for the Textile Workers Union of America reported that when he entered a plant in the 1960s, he counted the number of African American workers and knew that he could count on at least that many votes.[60] While unions did not always retain the confidence of their black (or white) members over time, in the 1960s they offered rules that would equitably govern work assignments, overtime shifts, and rotations—practices that had formerly been governed by white social networks from which blacks were excluded.

A Vertically Integrated Production Process

The Tultex plant in Martinsville, located in its renovated and expanded hundred-year-old cotton mill, hovered over the small and deteriorating downtown area. Inside, it contained space larger than "twenty-two football fields," divided into warehouse, manufacturing, and office areas. Townspeople described it as a "city within a city" because it combined so many processes and distinct work areas under one roof. Over the years, Tultex had vertically integrated its operations to encompass all stages of

57. Byerly, *Hard Times Cotton Mill Girls,* 152–53.
58. Adler, "New Day in Dixie," 17.
59. Frederickson, "I Know Which Side I'm On," 174.
60. Carolyn Ashbaugh and Dan McCurry, "On the Line," *Southern Exposure* 4, nos. 1–2 (1976): 34.

fleece production, reaching out to a handful of regional satellite factories for operations it could not perform in Martinsville.

The company spun its yarn, for example, in three plants in Mayodan, Longhurst, and Roxboro, North Carolina. It performed most of the cutting, knitting, dyeing, and finishing in Martinsville, although a small factory in Asheville, North Carolina, did some dyeing and finishing work. It established sewing shops in Martinsville, Bastian, South Boston, Roanoke, and Chilhowie, Virginia, and in Mayodan and Marion, North Carolina. Only in the 1980s did the firm set up sewing operations in Montego Bay, Jamaica, and Tamaulipas, Mexico. In the 1990s it began subcontracting some sewing to factories that it did not own. The company's warehousing and distribution facilities were also in Martinsville. In 1991 it invested $80 million in a new twelve-acre, state-of-the-art distribution center on the outskirts of the city, only to find it ill suited to new practices of rapid replenishment.[61]

The company worked mostly with cotton yarns, adopting polyester blends in the 1970s but never working exclusively with synthetic fibers. Each of the North Carolina plants produced a specific kind of yarn: backing thread, top fleece, or jersey. Nearly all the cotton used was grown in the United States. The yarn plants performed opening (which spreads out, cleans, and blends cotton fibers), carding (which filters out short fibers, makes remaining fibers parallel, and twists them to make sliver), drawing (which draws multiple slivers into a single strand and twists it), and open-ended spinning (which feeds the sliver into a rotor, spins and twists it, and winds the yarn onto a cone). The yarn plants were capable of producing 1.5 million pounds of yarn per week and meeting 85 percent of the firm's needs at peak production. They employed 285 workers in making yarn.[62]

Trucks carried yarn from the North Carolina plants to the five large knitting rooms at Martinsville. Tultex's machines produced tubular fabrics, eliminating the need for side seams in its sweatshirts and T-shirts. To produce fleece, workers arranged cones of yarn for the face, backing, and tie on creels around the bottom of the large machines. The machines drew in yarn and extruded it as fully formed tubes of various sizes. To produce jersey, which the plant began making in the 1980s, workers needed to use only a single type of yarn.[63] Equal numbers of women and men worked in the knitting rooms. Management paid these workers a base rate with piece rate incentives.

61. Tultex Corporation document, *Facilities* (1999).
62. Tultex Corporation documents, *Operations* (1998); *The Manufacturing Process* (1999).
63. Tultex, *Operations; Manufacturing Process.*

The job of knitter required ten weeks of training and involved loading and unloading bobbins, checking for faulty needles, and examining the emerging cloth for defects.[64] In the early days, workers tended two or three of these machines. By the 1990s, that number had increased to eleven or twelve. One woman, who had been at Tultex for twenty years, recounted: "We have to walk farther now to keep check on all the machines. The walking makes it hard. And we have to carry much more yarn than we used to. Each cone is ten pounds, and we carry three at a time. A human being's not meant to carry like that all day long."

This worker talked about a twenty-seven-year-old man in the knitting department who had bought some special gloves designed for arthritis sufferers that he thought might ease the pain he was experiencing from work. She said, "If a young boy has pain doing the job, you can imagine what its like for me." A coworker added that new machines adopted in the late 1980s were "raised up" and a "catwalk" was added. This forced people to work with their arms stretched above their heads. Both women noted that managers required them to use a small blower to blow lint out of the machines and onto the floor and that there was lint in the air all the time. The *Qualifications Book* that contained job descriptions for positions at Tultex acknowledged that "noise, wet, and air particles" were characteristics of the job.[65] When operating at peak production, Tultex ran five hundred knitting machines and produced 1.8 million pounds of knit fabric per week.[66]

After knitting, workers turned the tubular cloth inside out using a vacuum technique (for later "fleecing") and moved it to the "dye house." They had moved the fabric on carts until the 1990s, when the company adopted a system of chutes for dropping it to lower floors. Despite its name, the dye house was not a separate building but a unit in the basement of the plant. The workers in dyeing were nearly all men, which people argued was necessary owing to the heat and smell and the need to handle heavy wet cloth. The *Qualifications Book* listed the ability to lift up to one hundred pounds and to work in "a hot/humid/odorous environment" as prerequisites for the job. The position of dye-jet operator involved twelve weeks of training. In the past it was among the highest-paid jobs in the plant, receiving an hourly wage rather than piece rate.[67] By the 1990s, however, piece rates had risen faster than hourly wages, and the pay of dye-house workers

64. Tultex internal document, *Qualifications Book* (1999).
65. Ibid.
66. Tultex, *Operations*.
67. Tultex, *Qualifications Book*.

lagged behind—a source of consternation for those who remained on the job.

In the past, workers dyed cloth in huge vats or tubs in a fairly inexact process. In the early 1980s managers introduced a computerized jet-dyeing system. Under this system, workers dyed cloth in closed tanks that could accommodate 1,000 to 6,000 pounds of cloth. They set cotton fabrics at 185 degrees and polyesters at temperatures of up to 265 degrees, generating tremendous heat in the surrounding area. Dyeing a single load of fleece took from six to twelve hours. Operators set the color by computer, managing and monitoring the controls and occasionally climbing up on the dye vats to untangle the fabric.[68] One worker noted that the vat itself was hot, and that "you have to poke your head down into cavities where the heat is so intense it burns your skin." Cloth that was not dyed was bleached, and after dyeing or bleaching, workers treated it with fabric softeners and dried it.

Managers described the dye house of the 1990s as a technological marvel, where they were able to produce sweatshirts in hundreds of colors, including five distinct shades of navy blue, and where they could test the "trueness" of colors using a spectrophotometer. Operators consistently described the area as "hot and stinky." They complained bitterly about the heat, which was relieved only slightly by an antiquated air conditioner. They were also concerned that several of the chemicals they worked with were not labeled, and when they tried to look them up in the specifications log to see what they contained, they found their ingredients were classified as a "trade secret."

After dyeing and drying it, workers took the fabric, which was still inside out, to a napping or finishing area. They placed it on a large rotating dowel that used sharp bristles to break the threads of the backing and create the soft "fleece" found on the inside of a sweat shirt. Both men and women worked in the napping area. After napping, operators turned the tubular cloth right side out again using a vacuum, or air turnpole. Then they calendered or compacted the fabric by squeezing or steaming and sized it so it would hang well and retain its shape. They ran the fleece through a series of tests for strength, durability, and "pilling," then moved it on to the cutting room.[69] The firm paid finishing workers, like knitters, a base rate plus piece rate incentive. A worker who had been with Tultex for eighteen years said that when he started, he could finish 8,000 pounds a day and was up to 13,000 pounds now. He claimed that his son-in-law could

68. Tultex, *Operations*.
69. Tultex, *Operations; Manufacturing Process*.

finish 15,000 to 16,000 pounds a day but that he himself was "too old to work that hard."

The next step was cutting. Cutting marked the transition from textile fabrication to apparel assembly. In the 1990s it was a highly mechanized operation that used the latest European machines with automated die plates and a vertical knife that could slice through many layers of fabric.[70] Cutting room operators, who were mainly women, received twelve weeks of training. They laid out the fabric in stacks using a machine. They needed to have good math skills to set the machine properly and to ensure that sleeves, collars, bodies, and trim were produced in the right proportions.[71] Once workers had cut the fabric, they compressed it, then baled or bundled it for transport to the sewing room, to one of the outlying sewing shops, or increasingly over time, to Jamaica or Mexico.

Sewing operators stitched collars and cuffs, banded bottoms, and attached sleeves to bodies. T-shirts and sweatshirts are simple items that do not require a great deal of complicated handling and finishing. Managers expected operators to pay close attention to detail, however, performing visual checks for shading and defects on the fabric while sewing. They subjected their work to rigorous quality control.[72] The *Qualifications Book* listed the requirements for sewing operators as follows: "Good hand and finger dexterity. Lift up to 30 pounds. Ability to follow written and oral instructions. Basic math. Standing/sitting."[73] People who worked in other areas of the plant thought that sitting for long hours, as seamstresses did, was a mixed blessing. Although their legs were tired at the end of a shift, they liked the freedom to move about that sewing operators did not have. One seamstress summed up the work: "Sewing piece rate is hard work. It's monotonous. And you really do get carpal tunnel from it. Sitting all day you do get back problems. I tried to learn every job in the room to ease this 'doing the same thing over and over' and so I would be qualified for other jobs."

Nearly all the workers in the sewing shops were women. Sewing machine operators did not work the twelve-hour shifts (three days one week, four the next) that were typical of the rest of the plant in the 1980s and 1990s. Rather, they worked four nine-hour days plus a half day on Fridays. The wage for sewing workers was a base rate plus piece rate, but the base rate

70. Ibid.
71. Tultex, *Qualifications Book.*
72. Tultex, *Operations; Manufacturing Process.*
73. Tultex, *Qualifications Book.*

was several dollars less per hour than for other workers in the plant. Historically, managers had set wage increases for sewing workers separately from those for other workers. Workers said it was pay cuts in the sewing shops that led to union drives in 1979 and 1981 and to the successful drive for the Amalgamated Clothing and Textile Workers Union (ACTWU) in 1994. As one sewing worker noted: "The cuts were what did it. They made people mad. Once or twice maybe people would take a cut to help keep the plant running. But we didn't see an end to it."

The final steps in the production of a sweatshirt took place in the company's distribution center, located in an industrial park on the outskirts of town. Its operations were known to operators as "pick and pack." The employees in this division were mostly women, who worked eight-hour days for base pay plus piece rate. In the "pick" section of the operation, workers pulled items from stock to match orders. In "pack" they attached tags to the garments, put them in plastic bags or on hangers, added stickers, and packed them in boxes. Male workers then moved these boxes to the nine-story warehouse, where they remained until they could be loaded on trucks. Each order slip specified the number of minutes the operator should take to fill it. By the 1990s, managers used bar coding to track and time most orders.

The Economic History of the Firm

Tultex emerged from the wartime production of the 1940s with a strong position in the national fleecewear market. The three firms that William Pannill had started in Martinsville filled 80 percent of what was then still a small market for fleece garments. They were collectively responsible for pushing Martinsville ahead of Utica, New York, as the sweatshirt capital of the world. Most people considered jobs in the industry to be "good" work—with wages at the top of the local market and the prestige of a semiskilled "craft." Although Tultex did not operate in an isolated mill village, its internal relations in that period were distinctly paternalist. Managers bought their workers' consent with public generosity, backed by an implicit threat of force.

Throughout its history, the owners and managers of Tultex had played powerful and visible roles in the political and civic life of Martinsville and Henry County. The Pannill family, though not originally from Martinsville, was a member of the regional elite, who could trace their ancestry back to supporters of Charles I. They had owned properties along the Virginia–North

Carolina border since the middle of the seventeenth century.[74] William Pan-nill was born just after Reconstruction and was one of the first generation of planters to grow up knowing he would have to seek his fortune in indus-try. In many ways the collaborative relationships among the three knitting mills he established were similar to the links that planters established be-tween family properties in an earlier era.

Local businessmen, through the Kiwanis Club, had persuaded Pannill to establish his mills in Martinsville, and he and his sons-in-law depended on their close ties to local bankers and businesses throughout their careers. Mike Sale had been vice president of a bank in Covington, Virginia, before he married Pannill's daughter. William Franck, who took over the firm when Sale retired in 1953, was a particularly active member of the Martinsville community. He was an elder in the First Presbyterian Church and served several terms as president of the Chamber of Commerce. He served on the school board and led a bond issue drive to fund the local hospital. He also helped start a country club, housed in one of the region's old plantation homes.[75] This kind of civic mindedness persisted past the period of family ownership and well into the union era. CEO Charles Davies and other manag-ers in the 1990s continued to be active on the local school board, in the Chamber of Commerce, in local churches, and in a variety of charitable orga-nizations.

Such demonstrations of civic leadership and largesse showed that Tultex owners and managers were concerned about the community. They undoubt-edly contributed to local economic development and to the welfare of many community members. At the same time, they extended the firm's influence and control into these other arenas of life. That workers saw their bosses playing important roles in churches, political forums, and schools was not always a source of reassurance, to them, since problems at work could rever-berate in these other arenas. As one said, "People here are scared of the rich people who run the town. They're scared to speak up."[76]

An important dimension of a paternalist managerial style was what some have called "management by personal appearance." Bill Franck was well known for the time he spent on the factory floor and for his ability to call "hundreds of workers by first names."[77] Under his management, the com-

74. Judith Hill, *A History of Henry County, Virginia* (Baltimore: Regional Publishing, 1983), 237–44.
75. Cleal and Herbert, *Foresight, Founders and Fortitude,* 177.
76. Frank Swoboda, "Labor's Day in Martinsville," *Washington Post,* September 5, 1994, F1.
77. Cleal and Herbert, *Foresight, Founders and Fortitude,* 177.

pany gave substantial Christmas bonuses and honored exemplary workers with "employee of the month" awards. In periods of downturn, Franck would walk out on the shop floor and ask for extra hours or for belt tightening. "I built this company with you," workers remembered his saying. Most spoke positively of these aspects of his managerial style. In contrast, they described the company's professional CEO in the 1990s as having "his nose in the air" for not speaking to workers when he walked through the plant.

A third way paternalism operated was through the close ties between workers and their immediate supervisors. As in the mill town period, it was normal for more than one member of a family to work in the Tultex plant: husbands and wives, parents and children, cousins and other extended family members. Some of these individuals would eventually be promoted to supervisory positions. This infused "simple control" (the right of the overseer to direct and discipline the worker) with a highly personal flavor. As Richard Edwards has shown, in close-knit communities the supervisor's authority leverages status and relationships outside the workplace.[78] Thus, if employees caused problems, their family members could find their jobs threatened; kin could be held responsible for the behavior of their relations. But at the same time, abusive supervisors had to face those they worked with outside the factory, and workers could take them to task for actions they perceived as unfair. The fabric of relationships inside the walls of Tultex also imported distinctions of class from the community outside. When managers promoted more "respectable" members of the community to supervisory roles, this reverberated with, and seemed justified by, their position in a hierarchy of class.

The firm's hierarchies, and its paternalism, had a racial dimension. The former tobacco-growing region of Virginia's southside had a reputation for "racism, nativism and parochialism." Although Martinsville's race relations were deemed relatively harmonious by local standards, local whites continued to have deep-seated expectations of racial deference up until the 1970s.[79] At midcentury Martinsville's neighborhoods were strictly segregated, and black communities lacked basic amenities.[80] Attention was drawn to the racial politics of the community by a 1949 court case in which seven black men were executed for the rape of a white woman. The issuing of

78. Richard Edwards, *Contested Terrain* (New York: Basic Books, 1979), 34–36.

79. Rise, *Martinsville Seven*, 25–27.

80. Andrew Buni, *The Negro in Virginia Politics, 1902–1965* (Charlottesville: University Press of Virginia, 1967), 72.

the death penalties revealed the persistence of white southern practices of retribution for contact between black men and white women; it was also telling that the defense relied in part on an argument that the victim had not properly conformed to the ideals of southern womanhood, since she had walked alone in a black community.[81]

Like other southern mills, Tultex reflected these norms. It practiced racial segregation until the mid-1960s, limiting black workers to positions on the loading docks or in janitorial services. But when managers began to employ black workers on production lines beginning in 1964, new forms of discrimination emerged. White managers administered job rules and work assignments through their social networks, leaving black workers with the least desirable jobs and last in line for overtime. These networks excluded black workers, who neither received their benefits nor experienced their subtle forms of discipline. The hiring of black workers introduced new sets of social ties, new forms of hierarchy, and ultimately new sources of resistance within the plant.

Change was brewing outside the plant as well. By the late 1960s the company's steady growth had attracted the attention of potential investors. The beginning of a fitness boom was expanding the market for jogging wear, and sweatshirts became "acceptable . . . on the college campus, the beach, the bowling alley, the ski slope and even at the Key Biscayne White House."[82] Since the 1940s, Sale Knitting had relied on the Henry J. Tully Company of New York City as a selling agent. In 1971 it merged with the firm, changing its name to the Tully Corporation of Virginia and then, in 1976, to Tultex Corporation.

Workers first began discussing a union at Tultex in the 1970s. They said the issue first arose when Robert Freeman, a representative for the Textile Workers Union of America, began writing leaflets that he circulated to workers at the plant. People remember them as long, single-spaced missives on legal-size paper, detailing problems in the plant and telling how the union could address them. Black women in the sewing shop were among the first workers to get involved. They obtained enough signatures to move to a union vote in 1979 and again in 1981. In both cases the drive was defeated.

Union issues were put on hold for most of the 1980s, as the firm entered what managers and workers alike described as its heyday. Sales of fleece in the United States grew from $300 million a year in 1975 to $2 billion in

81. Rise, *Martinsville Seven*, 50.
82. Cleal and Herbert, *Foresight, Founders and Fortitude*, 174.

1982.[83] As one manager explained the changing fortunes of the company, "Up to that point in time—the early 1980s—there were four companies in the fleece business and sweatshirts and three of them were here [Martinsville]. . . . Then fleece came out of the locker room . . . and became acceptable casual wear. Of course, the whole world was going more casual. Women, particularly, found it was a very versatile garment. . . . Tops and bottoms, color-coordinated, dressed up with scarves or other sorts of accessories. . . . It became acceptable street wear." While this man's fashion sense may have been slightly off-key, his reading of the market was echoed by other managers: "It was an under-produced market. Supply could not get even close to demand. We could sell every piece we could make. We could go through and pick out the best customers that were most credit-worthy." Apparel industry analysts echoed managers' stories: "Though many thought the fitness fad wouldn't last, a more affluent, leisure-oriented society adopted sweatpants and sweatshirts as a uniform. After their stock of sweatpants and sweatshirts sold out in 1986, companies such as Tultex and Russell Corporation expanded production to meet the increased demand. Earnings of those companies rose dramatically."[84]

In this climate, Tultex thrived beyond what its owners had ever envisioned. To meet the growing demand, it began purchasing small factories in outlying communities. In 1981 the firm instituted "continuous process" scheduling to keep the plant running twenty-four hours a day. It placed workers on twelve-hour shifts, three days one week and four the next. During the week that they worked forty-eight hours, they earned overtime pay. They rotated between day and night shifts in a complex pattern that kept the plant running continuously throughout the year (except for seven holidays). This innovation in scheduling allowed the company to increase production without expanding its facilities, making more intensive use of the existing infrastructure. Managers argued that the move to twelve-hour shifts also permitted more efficient use of the dye house, since fabric could not be allowed to sit in the vats overnight. The new system avoided the need to spend time each evening to cool down, clean out, and shut off the dyeing vats and to heat them up again the next morning.

Despite the long shifts and complicated scheduling, workers liked the new arrangements, partly because of the overtime pay and partly because

---

83. Jeff Sturgeon, "Martinsville, Virginia Apparel Company Dissolving amid Financial, Policy Woes," *Roanoke Times*, March 6, 2000.

84. Kitty Dickerson, *Textiles and Apparel in the Global Economy*, 2d ed. (Englewood Cliffs, N.J.: Merrill, 1995), 249.

of the long blocks of time they got off. Many workers argued that the shifts were "ideal" for families, since if husband and wife worked different shifts on the same days, or the same shift on different days, the children never had to be in day care. One woman who worked twelve-hour night shifts explained that she could leave work in time to take her son to school. She slept each day from 8:00 a.m. to 1:00 p.m., then picked him up. If he had an activity at school, she skipped a few hours of sleep to attend. "He never hardly knows I work," she said. While Bassett-Walker was the first plant in the region to use the twelve-hour system, Tultex was the second. By the 1990s, twelve-hour shifts had become the standard for a range of industries in the Virginia–North Carolina region.

The firm's economic success in the 1980s drew the attention of Wall Street. The company made the transition from private to public ownership in the middle of that decade and was listed on the New York Stock Exchange. The Pannill family heirs continued to play a major role in the firm, however. William Franck remained chairman of the board, and his son John became CEO, a position he retained until 1994. O. Randolph "Randy" Rollins, a well-known lawyer and John Franck's brother-in-law, served as the firm's general counsel and chief financial officer for many years.

The boom in consumer demand for active wear that fueled the firm's growth did not subside, but by the late 1980s the market had changed significantly. Many new companies began producing fleece and quickly increased their capacity. Within a few years, a situation of undercapacity became a glut. In one manager's words, "The late '80s was the last heyday of the fleece business. . . . When everybody got in the act . . . all of a sudden supply drew even and then started to overshadow demand, and you needed a rationalization of the market. . . . And that makes business tough."

Tultex took a variety of actions to cope with these new competitive conditions. In the late 1980s it diversified into jersey (T-shirt) production. It sold T-shirts and sweatshirts to wholesalers, who would screen print the garments with designs and logos. It sold higher-end items to professional and collegiate sports teams and to branded marketers like Nike. At the lower end of the market it produced private-label active wear for Wal-Mart, Kmart, Target, and Ames. Recognizing that it suffered from not having a "brand" to purvey, the firm developed the Discus Athletic line, which it marketed through athletic specialty stores.

By the 1990s the firm was beginning to feel strain on many fronts. The first was simply the saturation of the market, with many firms entering the business and competing for consumer dollars. This included low-end producers like Hanes and Fruit of the Loom, firms with midrange products like Russell and Champion, and high-end branded marketers like Nike and Adidas, who diversified from footwear into apparel and sourced the bulk of their product overseas.

The second strain was pressure from retailers. Beginning in the 1970s, mass merchandisers such as Wal-Mart and JC Penney began to innovate in electronic data management, using new techniques of bar coding and point of sale computer terminals. This allowed them to develop supply chain efficiencies that other firms lacked.[85] At the same time, they had resources to source goods from other countries, which greatly reduced their costs. These two factors allowed them to offer consumers a greater variety of goods in a more timely fashion and at lower cost than their competitors. It forced less agile retailers, particularly those whose procurement strategies favored U.S. operations, out of business.

Concentration gave retailers new power to dictate the prices they would pay for goods as well as to demand compliance with increasingly complex packing and tracking procedures. One manager at Tultex explained, "The number of retailers that are out there has gone down. So many of them have been gobbled up by larger retailers. There's also been a lot of them going bankrupt. Quite a few have filed Chapter 11. . . . So we've got to have a stronger alliance with Wal-Mart, Kmart, Target, Sears, and Ames. . . . Without a doubt our leverage has decreased because of the situation. It has definitely weakened the strength of all the manufacturers. The retailers, they have the upper hand, they can decide . . . where they're going to shop. . . . They'll typically say, 'Here's a product and we think we want to retail this at X.' The retailer pretty much dictates the price."

The third difficulty the firm faced was competing with manufacturers who were already moving their production offshore and thus were rapidly reducing costs. Tultex had little in the way of international expertise. It had a "hands-on" philosophy that emphasized control over each step in its vertically integrated production process. And it felt a commitment to the local community. As one manager reported in 1999, "We were forced to move south in terms of our assembly operations, our labor-intensive operations. It's not fun shutting down a plant. . . . It's painful. It's distressing. Nobody likes doing it. But you have to make decisions in the best interest of the majority of workers. And many companies were in the Caribbean and Mexico before we were." The firm thus moved slowly and awkwardly toward

---

85. Frederick H. Abernathy, John T. Dunlop, Janice H. Hammond, and David Weil, *A Stitch in Time: Lean Retailing and the Transformation of Manufacturing; Lessons from the Apparel and Textile Industries* (New York: Oxford University Press, 1999), 49–51.

establishing offshore production sites. It began by purchasing and running its own facilities, and only when that proved too costly did it turn to the by then "industry standard" practice of subcontracting.

Finally, in an era when "branding" had become the key strategy for market expansion among consumer products firms, Tultex moved slowly into this arena. Until it employed its first professional CEO in 1995, it had spent almost nothing on advertising. In the first year after Charles "Chuck" Davies began his tenure, the firm spent $25 million on promotions. Whether he spent those funds wisely (on a "celebrity" endorsement from Troy Aikman, sponsorship of a race car in the Busch Grand National series, and prime-time advertising on ESPN and TNT) was a separate question; nevertheless, the firm was ill prepared to face what one local news columnist called "the whoop-de-doos of retailing."[86] In a world where people increasingly chose goods according to a tiny alligator or a swoosh, Tultex sweatshirts were predominantly boring, unlabeled commodity items.

All these problems weighed heavily on the company. In 1989 it experienced the worst financial year since its founding and began cutbacks. It cut the wage rates of sewing workers most heavily, which led workers to renew their mobilization for a union drive. As in 1979 and 1981, workers gained enough signatures to move to a vote, but as in those years the union was defeated, though this time by a mere 250 votes.[87]

Encouraged by the close election, Tultex workers tried again in 1990. This attempt proved especially contentious. Managers organized resistance to the drive through an organization called Tultex Employees against the Union. They recognized the strength of support for the union among black employees. To address that support, they held a rally at the Martinsville high school with free hot dogs and sodas. They invited a guest speaker, Golden Frinks, who claimed to have been a civil rights leader and to have worked with Martin Luther King Jr. and the Southern Christian Leadership Conference. Frinks is reported to have said that half of Tultex's employees were black and that the firm put good money in their pockets. He urged workers to oppose the union because "with the economy flirting around at this time and black workers holding marginal jobs," a union victory might cause the firm to cut employees.[88] Given the difficulty black workers had

86. Jeff Sturgeon, "The Tultex Tale," *Roanoke Times,* February 4, 1996.

87. George Kegley and Patricia Lopez Baden, "Union Defeated Again at Tultex," *Roanoke Times,* September 21, 1990.

88. George Kegley, "Tultex Blacks Told to Vote against Union," *Roanoke Times,* September 11, 1990.

experienced in working through seniority systems controlled by white networks, this not so veiled threat had a bite. If layoffs occurred, it was credible
that African American workers would be the first to go. The threat to black
jobs was hardly assuaged when the Southern Christian Leadership Conference immediately disavowed any knowledge of Frinks and his claim to represent it, adding that "any attempt to suppress workers' rights to form a union
in any manner is not condoned by this organization nor any of its leadership
or members."[89]

In addition to appealing to race, Tultex was reported to have told workers
(erroneously) that legislation repealing Virginia's "right to work" laws was
pending and that all workers would be forced to pay union dues whether
they were members or not. Employees at the firm's Bastian, Roanoke, and
Chilhowie plants petitioned to be allowed a vote in the election, but their
petition was denied. In all, the firm's financial records indicate that it spent
over $3 million in legal and consulting fees to fight the union in 1990.[90]
The vote was 1,179 for the union, 1,484 against, with 119 challenges.

The firm's financial situation improved slightly in 1991–92, allowing it
to invest in a new distribution center and to add several auxiliary plants.
But by 1994 it was experiencing another serious slump. It had lost a $25
million contract with Sears in 1993.[91] One local news reporter captured the
magnitude of the decline by noting that whereas in 1984 the company's
profits could have run the entire city of Martinsville for a year, in 1994
they could not have supported the police department.[92] In response to this
downturn in its fortunes, the company instituted a more drastic series of
cuts. These included wage cuts (from an average of $9 an hour to an average
of $7), the end of contributions to the employee savings plan, and cur-
tailment of other benefits. The firm suspended length-of-service parties and
awards and Christmas bonuses. Local news sources calculated that the average worker was losing $5,658 in annual take-home pay, in addition to bene-
fit cuts. Workers were angry that top executives took no pay cuts and received additional stock options at the same time that they slashed wages
and benefits for other employees.[93]

These cuts created a new wave of interest in the union, even among

89. George Kegley, "Anti-union Speaker Disclaimed," *Roanoke Times,* September 13,
1990.
90. Sandra Brown Kelly, "In This Mill Town, Its as Much about Respect as Pay," *Roanoke
Times,* July 17, 1994.
91. George Kegley, "Tultex Outgrows Fleecewear," *Roanoke Times,* March 26, 1993.
92. Sturgeon, "Tultex Tale."
93. Kelly, "In This Mill Town, Its as Much about Respect as Pay."

those who had opposed it in the past.[94] When workers approached Bruce Raynor of the ACTWU in 1994, he was reluctant to support another drive, given the history of unsuccessful campaigns. He told workers they had one week to assemble the required number of signed authorization cards. When the workers obtained 1,300 signatures within the week, the ACTWU sent forty staff members to Martinsville for the two months leading up to the vote. The final tally, in August 1994, was 1,321 in favor of the union, 710 against. It was the largest victory for the ACTWU since its successful drive at the J. P. Stevens plant in Roanoke Rapids in 1974, and the second largest victory in its history.

The union victory represented a break with the firm's paternalist tradition. Some workers noted its passing with sadness and saw unionization as the culmination of changes already initiated when the firm became a public company. One woman commented, "When I first came to work here it was still a small company and people knew everybody. It was a small, family company and then it got bigger and workers were not important."[95] Other workers echoed this view: "When I first started it was a relatively good place to work. Over the last five years I've seen a change. It's expansion, corporate greed. They've forgotten about those people who are making the products." Another said, "They pushed out older supervisors and brought in younger ones. It just wiped out that family feeling." The union representative at the plant simply noted, "I think the perception was that [John Franck] played the family card one time too many." For some employees, however, the break with paternalism was long overdue. In one man's words, "This is a historic change for workers here. The town's been controlled by the same families for a long time. This has always been an antiworker town. I graduated from high school here in 1966, and not much has changed. But it's a new day in Martinsville."[96]

Within a month of the union vote, John Franck stepped down as CEO of the company. The local press reported that he didn't think the union "was good for the company" and "was wounded by personal attacks by the union during the organizing campaign."[97] While Franck continued to chair the board, Charles Davies was promoted from vice president of operations to CEO. Seventy percent of Tultex workers joined the union, and in March 1995 they approved their first contract 1,237 to 0. It provided for raises of 5

94. Swoboda, "Labor's Day in Martinsville"; Southern Exposure, "News Roundup: Workers Win Biggest Victory since Stevens," 22, no. 3 (1994).

95. Swoboda, "Labor's Day in Martinsville."

96. Southern Exposure, "News Roundup."

97. Sturgeon, "New Leader Has Earned His Stripes," *Roanoke Times,* February 4, 1996.

percent the first year and 4 percent in each of the next two years. It promised Christmas bonuses, improved health insurance and retirement benefits,
and overtime pay after eight hours in a day rather than forty hours in a
week. Perhaps the greatest change, however, was the issuing of clear-cut
rules for work assignments, overtime, absences, job bidding, and short time.
The contract established grievance and arbitration procedures and contained a no-strike/no-lockout clause. It established a labor management
cooperation committee to discuss productivity and efficiency issues, cost
reduction, and work redesign.[98]

The year 1995 was a turning point for the firm, in which the rhetoric of
paternalism gave way to the rhetoric of contract and the firm renovated
its business practices to compete in what it was rapidly recognizing was a
new competitive environment. Both William Franck and John Tully (of the
Henry J. Tully Company) retired from the board of directors in May. The
company spent its first advertising dollars and refinanced its debt. By the
end of 1996 it boasted record gains in both operating margins and reve-
nues.[99] The firm slowly began to shift emphasis from manufacturing to marketing, acquiring several smaller companies that produced clothing and
hats bearing professional and collegiate sports logos. By the end of 1998,
branded products made up 25 percent of its sales.[100] In December 1997 Tultex was honored by *Apparel Industry Magazine* with one of its prestigious
"All-Stars" awards. In an article describing the firm's accomplishments, the
magazine emphasized its new diversification and attempts at brand building, collaborative relationships with retailers, and adoption of state-of-the-
art information management software. The firm's annual sales topped $636
million in 1996, up from $350 million in 1991.[101]

During this period the ACTWU (which in 1995 underwent a national
merger with the ILGWU to become UNITE—Union of Needletrades, Industrial
and Textile Employees) began to establish an operating presence at Tultex.
Membership rates held steady at 70 percent, and nearly every department
had a shop steward in place on every shift. The union conducted educational
meetings for workers about rules and rights and about what constituted
a grievance. It provided training for shop stewards and published a small

98. ACTWU, Agreement between Amalgamated Clothing and Textile Workers Union
(ACTWU) and Tultex Corporation, Martinsville, Virginia, April 3, 1995.

99. Tultex Corporation document, Press Release: Tultex Corporation Announces Record
Fourth Quarter and Annual, February 6, 1997.

100. Sturgeon, "Martinsville Virginia Apparel Company Dissolving."

101. Fairchilds, *Textile and Apparel Financial Directory* (New York: Fairchild's Books and
Visuals, 1991, 1999).

newsletter called *Chit Chat!* that provided information on national and international as well as local events. It organized lobbying of local political representatives on such issues such as trade law and the Occupational Safety and Health Administration (OSHA), encouraged workers to keep up attendance when there was a critical order from a major customer, and addressed the ever-present question of trash in the cloth bins. Most grievances filed during this period were for unfair pay rates (35 percent); the rest were for unfair disciplinary actions (23 percent), company violations of work rules (20 percent), provision of improper equipment or health and safety violations (12 percent), unfair termination of an employee (7 percent), and failure to allow the union to conduct its business (3 percent).[102]

By the end of 1996, economic problems began to reappear. Trends toward quick response in the apparel industry had made the company's new warehouse something of a white elephant. The firm began to search for new distribution options, eventually building a 300,000-square-foot facility in Brownsville, Texas.[103] Managers became convinced that the firm needed to have its sewing done in Mexico if it was to be competitive on price. The first efforts at Mexican production were rocky. Retailers refused several shipments owing to quality problems.[104] Nevertheless Tultex began closing its U.S. sewing shops, starting with Marion, North Carolina. By 1998 the firm was sewing 80 percent of its apparel offshore. It reduced the number of sewing workers in Martinsville by 150 and closed sewing shops in Dobson, North Carolina, and Chilhowie, Virginia, laying off 329 workers. It calculated that it could save $10,000 to $15,000 a year for each job moved to Mexico.[105] Despite these cost-cutting measures, it continued to be buffeted by the market. In early 1998 it posted the first yearly loss ($8.5 million) in its sixty-one-year history. As reasons for the loss, the firm cited poor holiday sales, production problems in overseas sewing operations, and the fact that it couldn't "get last year's prices" for its apparel.[106]

The closing of the firm's sewing plant in Chilhowie, Virginia, was particularly poignant. Nestled in the mountains of southwestern Virginia, the

102. Union of Needletrades, Industrial and Textile Employees (UNITE), Local 1994, *Union News* 1, nos. 1–4 (1996); *Union Chit Chat!* 1, nos. 1–3 (1998–99).

103. Sturgeon, "Martinsville Virginia Apparel Company Dissolving."

104. Jeff Sturgeon, "Third Quarter Profits at Tultex Hurt by Problems with Contract Work," *Roanoke Times*, October 24, 1997.

105. Eric Heisler, "Textile Turmoil: Sweeping Changes in the Apparel and Textile Industries Leave Workers and Community Leaders Struggling to Cope with an Uncertain Future," *Greensboro News and Record*, May 23, 1999, A1.

106. Jeff Sturgeon, "Tultex Reports First Yearly Loss," *Roanoke Times*, February 18, 1998.

tiny town had little else going in the way of industry, since several of its gypsum mines had recently closed. Many of the women who worked at the factory were the only providers for their families. The local press described the workplace as one "where mothers sew alongside their daughters, and where lifelong friends have worked together since they finished school."[107] When the shop closed, the women were shocked not only by the loss of their jobs, but by the terms of the severance. Production workers were excluded from the severance benefit and faced a 35 percent penalty for withdrawing their pension funds. In addition, several of the women who sewed for Tultex in Chilhowie had continuing health problems as a result of a 1994 incident in which a malfunctioning forklift spewed carbon monoxide into their work area. Sixty workers had lost consciousness, and some continued to have headaches.[108] One woman said, "We've been very faithful workers. Even after the carbon monoxide we came right on back to work."[109]

Closing two sewing plants and moving the jobs to Mexico was not sufficient to solve the company's problems, however. The price of Tultex's stock fell from $8 a share in the spring of 1998 to 56¢ a share in early 1999.[110] The $36.5 million loss posted in 1998 was seven times that of the previous year. The firm began to sell off the sportswear companies it had acquired only a few years before. In May 1999 it appointed as its new president James Chriss, an executive who had formerly worked with Levi-Strauss, hoping that his extensive marketing experience would help turn things around.[111]

The Stretch-Out in the Era of Globalization

My first visit to Tultex, in early summer of 1999, occurred just after a very difficult shareholders' meeting in which CEO Charles Davies presented his plan for a return to profitability. This plan emphasized conservative measures such as continued debt refinancing, new efforts to collect receivables, and moving more sewing offshore.[112] John Franck, who continued as chair-

107. Lee Ann Prescott, "Tultex Is Leaving Chilhowie," *Smyth County News and Messenger,* January 10, 1998.

108. Dan Kegley, "Tough Luck for Tultex Employees?" *Smyth County News and Messenger,* January 21, 1998.

109. Prescott, "Tultex Is Leaving Chilhowie."

110. Jeff Sturgeon, "Tultex Posts Dramatic $36.5 Million Loss," *Roanoke Times,* February 26, 1999.

111. Tultex Corporation document, Press Release: Tultex Elects New President with Extensive Marketing Experience, May 25, 1999.

112. Tultex, Notes, Shareholders' Meeting, May 27, 1999.

man of the board, announced his "terrible disappointment" with the stock price. He emphasized that while the situation in the industry was "extraordinarily difficult," industry conditions alone did not cause the slump in which the firm found itself. Davies resigned, and John Franck's brother-in-law O. Randolph Rollins took his place as CEO in August 1999.

For workers at Tultex, this was a confusing and distressing time. The initial period after the union vote had been one of high spirits and great energy. Higher wages and new work rules appeared to go hand in hand with the company's improved performance from 1995 to 1997. As it happened, however, this recovery was short-lived, and the era of the union at Tultex coincided with a tightening of competitive pressures in the industry.

It was an unfortunate coincidence that 1994, the year of the union victory, was also the year that the North American Free Trade Agreement (NAFTA) went into effect. With tariffs and quotas relaxed for production in Mexico, many companies began to relocate, or to source their apparel there. This exacerbated the price competition already driven by the shrinking number of large retailers. Knitwear firms such as Starter, Pluma, and Oneita began going out of business.

As Tultex managers felt the pinch of these conditions, they sought ways to cut costs within the framework of the contract they had negotiated with the union. They had little leeway to change wage rates, so they began reorganizing working arrangements in an attempt to enhance efficiency. As in the 1920s and 1930s, the goal was not to increase output but "to cut off help and load up the next worker with the job."

At the peak of its success, Tultex had over 8,000 employees, of whom 4,200 worked in Martinsville and Henry County. After layoffs in the spring of 1999, it employed 5,100, with about 2,600 in Martinsville. Although the firm was operating at a loss, its sales volume was not declining. Thus the firm was asking far fewer workers to produce the same number of garments. Management promoted this arrangement to workers under the guise of multiskilling and cross-training. This new approach placed workers in different jobs on different days or at various times of the day, or forced them to perform a combination of tasks simultaneously. This slowed them down to the point where they could not make their accustomed piece rate, at the same time that it increased stress on the job. Twelve-hour shifts only exacerbated the exhaustion workers experienced.

This situation, which Tultex workers referred to as the problem of "combination jobs," led many employees to file grievances. Examples logged in the union newsletter read: "A first shift employee filed a grievance because he was denied the proper pay for doing a higher paying job." Or "[Three]

repair area girls . . . had additional duties added to their jobs with no increase in pay. They filed a grievance . . . asking for their job to be reevalu-
ated."[113]

A much more involved dispute developed when the company tried to
shift all employees in the cloth room from single to combination jobs. The
firm argued that most of the workers did not have a full day's work on
single jobs. In a rowdy meeting of the General Shop Committee, employees
denied this claim. They argued that the union contract did not allow for
combination jobs and that the company was just looking for a way around
this. "We said 'no way,'" the newsletter reported. "We do not have combination jobs in our contract, and we were not helping them break the contract
by having workers earn incentive [piece rate] on two jobs rather than one.
. . . . Then the company decided since we wouldn't go for the combination
jobs, they would force it on us by changing everyone's pay to hourly, and
off incentive, to be effective in two weeks. We said 'no' again. These jobs
were incentive and will stay incentive. Furthermore, there was no hourly
rate for these jobs, all rates were base rates."[114]

Working combination jobs was a hardship for two reasons. One was the
stress associated with operating additional machines of different types. This
required workers to perform a larger number of complicated tasks, to incur
additional time in setting up and shutting down equipment, and often to
move between different rooms or floors of the plant. This stress was more
intense for workers who were on piece rate or incentive pay. Moving from
one job to another significantly slowed them down, not only because of
startup and shutdown, but because of the difficulty of developing dexterity
and speed in several distinct operations and because changing jobs broke
the steady rhythm of work. Workers relied on incentive pay to make their
average hourly wage of $8.66 an hour; this was why management thought
a threat to remove them from piece rate altogether might be effective.
Armed with the contract, workers won this skirmish in a larger war whose
outline neither they nor their managers could fully perceive.

A particularly dramatic flare-up of issues around combination jobs took
place at a general membership meeting of the union in August 1999. As
the meeting was called to order, about thirty-five people were inside, while
five young African American men who worked in the plant's knitting room
remained outside in the parking lot. They entered the meeting late, after
the prayer and general announcement. The atmosphere in the room was

113. UNITE Local 1994, *Union News* 1, nos. 1–4 (1996).
114. UNITE Local 1994, *Chit Chat!* 1, nos. 1–3 (1998–99).

tense, with a number of women speaking out about the union's failure to resolve grievances. The mill chair—a young black man dressed impeccably in Tommy Hilfiger shorts, shirt, and hat—said that he knew this was causing problems, but that once the grievances moved beyond second step, the mill chairs were no longer involved and the union didn't know how to force the company to act. A broad-shouldered, T-shirt-clad white man from knitting suggested that if there weren't a no-strike clause in the contract they "would get an answer quick." The mill chair explained that the company could ask for an extension in the third step, "and then it just lingers unless someone wants to send papers up to the Equal Employment Opportunity Commission." A heavyset black woman replied, "Isn't this why we pay union dues?" She argued strongly that resolving grievances was the job of the union and that if it couldn't figure out how to do it, then what was the point? "I'm not saying it's you," she added. The mill chair said he had been to Eden, North Carolina, to see the regional UNITE representative and had talked to a lot of other people, but he didn't know how to make the union resolve the grievances.

After this discussion, one of the knitting workers who had been in the parking lot began to speak. He pointed to the young men who had come in with him and said that they were alienated from the union and didn't normally attend meetings, but that they were there to testify to the truth of what he was saying. "I used to do one job," he said. "Now I have to do four." "Grieve it," the mill chair suggested. "I grieved it and they added a job," he replied.

Someone asked if this wasn't the same issue that had been disputed in the cloth room. Another woman agreed that it was and reminded everyone that this practice had been grieved earlier and that the labor-management committee had agreed it was not allowed. The knitter continued, "What they're doing to me is—for almost two years they've had me working between floors. I go in on the weekend, and I'm doing an entirely different job." A white woman from the back row interjected, "That's right. That's what they're doing to him."

"It's this knit-to-lot system," the young man added, referring to the frequent yarn changes required to respond to small-batch orders. "They told us doing more jobs was a way to make more money. But we're working harder and losing money on a daily basis. You bring in the industrial engineer. He throws a bunch of numbers at you that's above your head. He tells you you're making money. But you look in your wallet and see you're not."

The union president, a white man who appeared to be about fifty years old, broke in to say, "This is the first time I've heard about them putting extra work on knitting. When can we talk?" The knitter, now visibly agitated, said *"Now,* man. That's what I'm here for." He went on, "I filed a grievance yesterday and they sent me home." Someone asked who took over his machines. *"No one,* man," he replied. "They stopped the line. It's like they took that harassment brochure and read how to do it. There's not a grievance been won in fleece knitting in the last two years. They treat us like slaves. Like slaves. . . . I mean it. They say 'your union is crap.' Your union [is] so weak it can't do nothing. I've been fighting this for over a year. My machines are running 11:56 of the [twelve-hour] shift. We went to Washington to protest sweatshops. But third-floor knitting is a sweatshop now."

When the union president interrupted again to suggest a meeting, the four young men who had come in with the knitter walked out. Shortly afterward, he left to talk with them. Four or five other workers shared stories of speedup and harassment and of unresolved grievances. Several women from knitting drifted outside to join the conversation in the parking lot. About two hours after it started, the meeting was adjourned.

For workers in the 1920s, the response to the stretch-out had been to go out on strike. Workers at Tultex not only had a no-strike clause in their contract but were painfully aware that companies were moving jobs out of the country at a rapid pace. Employment in the U.S. apparel sector had dropped from a peak of 1.4 million in 1973 to 670,000 in August 1999. Jobs in the textile industry had declined from 1.2 million in the late 1940s to 557,000 that same month.[115] While workers were angry about the intensification of their work, their response was tempered by the threat of corporate relocation or new sourcing strategies.

Hegemonic despotism—the threat of job loss as a means of control—worked to undermine the contract between union and firm almost as soon as it was established. The union found its bargaining position weakened by the expansion of the boundaries of the labor market in which its members participated. That market grew to include thousands of nonunionized workers in Mexico and other parts of the world. While some workers were willing to take their grievances to the mat, union representatives were not as aggressive. The politically constructed economic realities of free trade, and the firm's dire financial situation, tempered their actions.

---

115. *Women's Wear Daily,* "August Apparel Job Loss Is Worst in Six Months," September 7, 1999, 27; United States Department of Labor, Bureau of Labor Statistics, *Employment Hours and Earnings, U.S. 1990–94,* vol. 1, Bulletin 2445 (Washington, D.C.: Government Printing Office, 1994), 583.

Just after the union meeting in which the heated discussion of the stretch-out in knitting occurred, both CEO Charles Davies and new president James Chriss resigned. O. Randall Rollins was appointed both president and CEO of the company. Shares of Tultex common stock traded at 43.75¢ on the New York Stock Exchange. In September the firm closed its next-to-last U.S. sewing plant in Bastian, Virginia. A company press release said that jobs would be relocated to "non-U.S." locations. "We regret the closing of Bastian and the loss of jobs. However, Tultex's costs must come down if we are to be competitive and to return to profitability."[116] That same month, the firm placed its new distribution center on the market. "Today over 85 percent of our apparel is sewn outside the U.S.," the press release said. "Time and money can be saved by shipping more directly."[117] In October the firm announced $9 million in additional cost reductions and the closing of its dyeing and finishing plant in Asheville, North Carolina. In November it announced it would close its Roanoke, Virginia, sewing plant.

The End of the Line in Virginia

The handwriting was on the wall. With hindsight, it seems clear that the company was heading into financial difficulties from which it would not recover. But when Tultex employees were called into meetings on the afternoon of December 3, 1999, and told that their jobs were being eliminated, most were deeply shocked. The prepared statement that came down from O. Randolph Rollins read: "Tultex is not alone in having to transform itself rapidly. Practically every company in the textile and apparel industry is suffering today and is deciding that the only way to survive in the face of foreign competition is to outsource manufacturing needs. Simply put, America's textile and apparel industry has too much high-cost, domestic manufacturing capacity."[118]

Rollins noted that in 1996 a basic white T-shirt sold at wholesale for $2.50. In 1999 the same shirt sold for $1.35 to $1.50.[119] Interviewed at a Martinsville nursing home, William Franck touched on similar themes. He

---

116. Tultex Corporation document, Press Release: Tultex Announces Plant Closing in Bastian, Virginia, September 28, 1999.

117. Tultex Corporation document, Press Release: Tultex Plans to Sell or Seeks Alternative Uses of Its Consumer Service Center, September 9, 1999.

118. Tultex Corporation document, Press Release: Tultex Files Chapter 11, December 3, 1999.

119. Ginny Wray, "Rollins to Reshape Tultex into Different Company," *Martinsville Bulletin,* December 7, 1999.

discussed the movement of textile industry from England to northeastern U.S. cities and from the Northeast to the South. "From there it went out of the country," he said. "It will probably end up in India or some place like that where labor costs are real bad." The company tried to be a good citizen, he said.[120]

At that point Tultex was still claiming it hoped to reorganize under Chapter 11 and to reemerge as a marketer of apparel sourced outside the United States. But a market analyst from a major investment firm raised questions about this approach when interviewed for a local newspaper. "Why would Nike buy from Tultex instead of directly from a plant in Honduras or Mexico?" he asked. "They'll have to develop a brand name or brand following to start marketing on their own."[121]

Workers' initial reaction to the plant closure was "numbness."[122] "I feel like somebody jerked the rug out from under me and hit me over the head with it," one seamstress said. She added, "One of my workers said she cried for an hour. . . . When they told us, our jaws just dropped. It was like someone smashed you real hard."[123] Workers who were not on their shifts during the afternoon of December 3 learned about their termination on the six o'clock news. "People are hurting," said a local Baptist minister. "For some people, it's going to be a bare minimum Christmas."[124]

It was perhaps ironic that a number of union members from Martinsville had traveled to Seattle only days before the plant closing to protest the 1999 meeting of the World Trade Organization in that city. "This week, UNITE members in Martinsville joined with the tens of thousands of workers who were protesting against unfair trade rules in the streets of Seattle, to say that the world trading system is broken and doesn't work for working families," a local organizer said. "Now the grim reality of the global economy has come home to Martinsville, Mayodan and South Boston."[125]

Reflecting on the plant closure, the Henry County administrator recalled receiving a call from O. Randolph Rollins. "Randy told me Tultex was not going to give these employees 60 days notice or offer any severance pack-

120. "Franck: Tultex Hurt by NAFTA, Quickly Changing Industry," *Martinsville Bulletin,* December 6, 1999.

121. Ginny Wray, "Tultex Stock on Hold," *Martinsville Bulletin,* December 6, 1999.

122. "Ex-Worker Now Works at Job Hunt," *Martinsville Bulletin,* December 5, 1999.

123. Eric Heisler and Michelle Cater, "Tultex Issues Layoffs," Depot.com, December 4, 1999.

124. Kiran Krishnamurty, "As Holidays Near, Tultex Layoffs Hit Hard for Southside Workers," *Charlottesville Daily Progress,* December 7, 1999.

125. "Union Vows to Explore Aid for Ousted Workers," *Martinsville Bulletin,* December 3, 1999.

ages," he said. "They were literally turned into the streets with no benefits."[126] In the days immediately following the bankruptcy, local officials
struggled to establish a variety of aid plans for workers, to apply for NAFTA
retraining benefits, and salvage a county budget that would lose about 6
percent of its tax base.[127] They put together a package of incentives for
new industry that included free land for any company that would make a
substantial capital investment. News services across the country picked up
the story of the "Free Land for Jobs" program, and it was covered by Dan
Rather on the Saturday evening news. By February 2000, the unemployment
rate in Martinsville had reached 20 percent.[128]

Both public and private organizations in the area moved quickly to assist
workers, who were facing winter heating bills and the Christmas holidays
without their jobs. The state employment commission held job fairs. The
Salvation Army received $100,000 in donations to help displaced workers
with heating, electrical, and medical bills and to meet mortgages or rent
on an emergency basis.[129] The county established an information hotline
for workers needing assistance. Local churches also helped jobless families
pay bills and collected Christmas gifts for them.

By mid-January the shock had worn off and workers were able to take
stock of how little the company had left them: no Christmas bonuses, no
payment for accrued leave, no severance pay. Some workers found that their
medical insurance claims filed for services received when the firm was still
in operation were not being paid, and people became anxious about the
status of their pensions.[130] In mid-January 2000 about eight hundred former
workers showed up at a creditors' meeting held at the Martinsville High
School. Local papers described the crowd as "rowdy" and the event as a
"near free-for-all."[131] The hearing, which was mediated by a federal trustee,
provided an opportunity for workers to question Rollins about events of
the past six weeks. When they asked why they had received no notification
of the impending shutdown, Rollins replied that early notice "would have
had a jeopardizing effect on running the business." He responded to questions about why the firm wasn't paying for accrued vacation or Christmas

126. Bernard Baker, "Clower: Lessons of Tultex Must Never Be Forgotten," *Martinsville Bulletin,* December 3, 1999.

127. Krishnamurty, "As Holidays Near, Tultex Layoffs Hit Hard."

128. Justin Blum, "Laid Off and Left Behind," *Washington Post,* February 28, 2000, B1.

129. "SafetyNet Gives Help to Newly Jobless," *Martinsville Bulletin,* December 19, 1999.

130. Ginny Wray, "Ousted Workers Sound Off," *Martinsville Bulletin,* January 12, 2000.

131. Jon Cawley, "Tultex Head Fields Questions from Rowdy Crowd," *Roanoke Times,* January 12, 2000, A1.

bonuses by saying that this "had led to many sleepless nights." This did not jibe well, however, with his admission that the company's top five officers would receive a total of $1.076 million in compensation. At this point the crowd erupted into whoops, jeers, and catcalls. When Rollins was unable to respond to workers' questions about health insurance and pensions, the trustee of the federal bankruptcy court ordered him to furnish written answers. Many who attended the meeting felt that Rollins did not provide the kind of straight answers they had hoped for. "I think he squirmed a lot," one woman said. "He's trying to go around a lot of things."[132]

UNITE brought in a lawyer to help workers file claims for back pay as creditors,[133] and local politicians sponsored a bill in the Virginia state legislature that would have provided emergency assistance to laid-off workers. A legislative committee rejected the proposed Textile Workers Relief Act of 2000 (SB 763) in February 2000. By that time the company had given up plans to reorganize and had begun liquidating its assets.[134]

Tultex employees were outraged by the sums being paid to corporate executives when they could not even get back pay. In subsequent public meetings they forced the firm to admit that former CEO Charles Davies had been on the payroll through the end of December (despite his resignation in August) and to detail top executives' salaries and bonuses. Reminiscent of incidents in the 1920s, when workers faced with the stretch-out obtained and published their employers' tax returns,[135] workers dusted off the rhetoric of mutual obligation to argue that managers were taking more than their fair share. While they were successful in getting the firm to reduce payments to top officers, its assets fell far short of paying its debts.[136] Its pension account was underfunded by $9.4 million, so that workers received only partial payment from their pension funds, and red tape delayed even those payments for well over a year.[137]

Tultex executives and local politicians identified foreign competition as the cause of the firm's demise. In his remarks to employees before their dismissal on December 3, 1999, Rollins mentioned such competition as the

132. Ibid.
133. "Workers to File Claims," *Martinsville Bulletin,* January 12, 2000.
134. Ginny Wray, "Textile Aid Bill Is Rejected," *Martinsville Bulletin,* February 11, 2000; John Hale, "Tultex Gives Up," *Martinsville Bulletin,* February 10, 2000.
135. Simon, "'Choosing between the Ham and the Union,'" 91; "Executive Pay Questioned," *Martinsville Bulletin,* January 12, 2000.
136. "Judge Cuts CEO's Request for Severance," *Martinsville Bulletin,* February 10, 2000; "Tultex Says Assets Won't Pay Creditors," *Martinsville Bulletin,* March 29, 2000.
137. "Tultex Checks Slowed," *Martinsville Bulletin,* August 10, 2000; John Hale, "Tultex Pensioners Stunned by Payout," *Martinsville Bulletin,* April 1, 2001.

culprit. The state representative from the district that encompassed Martinsville and Henry County told a local paper, "We need to be more tough [in] negotiating instead of going along with what those other countries want all the time."[138] While this interpretation was correct in understanding that the jobs lost were being moved overseas, it missed the fact that U.S. corporations employed the vast majority of workers in export apparel factories in other parts of the world. Tultex lost out in competition not with Mexican or Chinese firms, but with U.S.-based companies that produced or subcontracted in those countries. In the view of some of its managers, and of many industry analysts, it simply had not moved fast enough to do so itself.

138. Eric Friedhoff, "Clower Says Tultex Move Will be Widely Felt Here," *Martinsville Bulletin,* December 3, 1999.

4

LIZ CLAIBORNE INCORPORATED: DEVELOPING A GLOBAL PRODUCTION NETWORK

Rather than dwindling away, concentrated economic power is changing its shape.

—BENNETT HARRISON, *LEAN AND MEAN*[1]

The Invention of "Fashion Imports"

Liz Claiborne is one of the few apparel firms that has produced its merchandise in offshore factories since the 1970s. The firm is a branded marketer of high-end fashion apparel, although in recent years it has expanded into "fashion moderates," or moderately priced fashion merchandise. The company does not own any of the factories where its goods are produced; it operates through an extensive network of subcontracted firms. Because of this global division of labor, managers and production workers do not live and work in the same communities. The firm's managers occupy a complex of buildings just outside New York City, while its subcontracted production line employees work in thirty-two countries around the world.

Tultex's corporate headquarters had felt comfortable and familiar to me. Their executives embraced a casual down-home style, their offices were in

---

1. Bennett Harrison, *Lean and Mean: Why Large Corporations Will Continue to Dominate the Global Economy* (New York: Guildford, 1994), 8.

a small building attached to the factory itself, and their rhythms seemed connected to it. Yarn, cloth, and sample garments were strewn around. The factory itself evoked memories of the machine shop where my father spent his working life. In contrast, I entered the New Jersey headquarters of Liz Claiborne with some trepidation. Worried about the impression I would make on fashion industry executives, I had bought a Liz Claiborne wool jacket at a thrift store for $10 and wore it on interviews as a talisman. Despite CEO Paul Charron's encouragement of casual dress, the vice presidents I spoke to were, as I feared, impeccable in their understated business attire. I joked with friends that after years of research in the Andes and Brazil, One Claiborne Avenue in North Bergen was by far my most exotic field site.

Liz Claiborne's headquarters is located in two large buildings that look out on a recently restored estuary of the Secaucus River in North Bergen, New Jersey. The lobby of the firm's headquarters is all glass and chrome, but it is decorated with memorabilia from the garment industry's earlier days: photographs of tailors' workshops along with old sewing machines, account books, and adding machines. In the year 2000 the company had 8,300 employees, about a quarter of whom worked in the North Bergen headquarters. That same year, Liz Claiborne did over $3.1 billion in business, up more than 10 percent from 1999. It was the fifth largest apparel firm in the country and was number 509 on the Fortune 1000 list. In addition, *Fortune* magazine consistently listed it among the top five or ten "most admired" apparel companies in the United States. The firm's stock rating made it a Wall Street favorite, something of a rarity in the beleaguered apparel industry of the late 1990s.

Industry analysts attribute much of Liz Claiborne's success to its global sourcing of the apparel it sells. The firm owns no manufacturing facilities and is best characterized as a branded marketer of apparel. Such firms "design and market, but do not make the products that they sell. [They] rely on complex networks of contractors that perform almost all their specialized tasks."[2] In 1999 Liz Claiborne produced over 120 million units of clothing in 256 supplier factories around the world. In the late 1990s, producing or subcontracting outside the country was not unusual. But Liz Claiborne had begun doing so in the 1970s, when this was still an anomaly for purveyors

---

2. Richard Appelbaum and Gary Gereffi, "Power and Profits in the Apparel Commodity Chain," in *Global Production: The Apparel Industry in the Pacific Rim,* ed. Edna Bonacich, Lucie Cheng, Norma Chinchilla, Nora Hamilton, and Paul Ong (Philadelphia: Temple University Press, 1994), 44.

of high-end fashion goods.[3] The firm was an innovator in building a global infrastructure for its garment imports. During an interview in the spring of 2000, the vice president of manufacturing and sourcing at Liz Claiborne boasted that the company had "invented the concept of imported fashion merchandise." Few in the industry would contest the accuracy of that claim.

Liz Claiborne, the designer, started the firm in 1976 after quitting her job with a reputable New York clothing manufacturer to strike out on her own. Claiborne was born in Belgium and lived there until her family fled the Nazis in 1939. She returned to Europe after World War II to study art but came back to New York in the early 1950s to take a job in the fashion industry.[4] In his spacious executive office overlooking the Secaucus River, Robert Zane, the firm's senior vice president for manufacturing and sourcing, told a well-rehearsed story of the firm's origins. The account, as it has been handed down in the company, is that Claiborne wanted to design a new line of clothing for working women. She wanted to produce an alternative to the dark tailored suits that were at that time virtually the only option for women who worked in offices, replacing them with more casual, but still tailored, styles and a broader range of color. According to Zane,

> Liz was a designer, and she had this concept that the clothing American women wore had to evolve as they were entering the workplace. And so she wanted to move away from the traditional blouse or dress or whatever, and she convinced the managers at [her former employer] that this was the right thing to do and they said, "Well go ahead—that sounds like a fine idea." And she said, "and by the way, I would like to have my name on the line," and they said "No. . . ." I guess they didn't say it as politely as that.

So Claiborne set out to establish her own firm, together with her husband Arthur Ortenberg, Jerome Chazen, who was a marketing specialist, and Leonard Boxer, who had experience in garment production. And as women entered the workforce in unprecedented numbers in the 1970s through 1990s, the company's target market turned out to be the leading demographic segment in the industry.

For the first two years the firm produced its garments mostly in Pennsyl-

---

3. Jerome Chazen, "Notes from the Apparel Industry: Two Decades at Liz Claiborne," *Columbia Journal of World Business* 31, no. 2 (1996): 40.

4. Encarta (Microsoft), "Liz Claiborne," *Distinguished Women of Past and Present,* 1995. Distinguishedwomen.com/biographies/claibor.html.

vania, sourcing some items from North Carolina and Alabama. According to managers, it was Jerome Chazen who first suggested manufacturing overseas. His colleagues in the industry were touting the advantages of Taiwan as a production site, and he broached the idea with the other owners. "Are you crazy?" Claiborne is said to have responded; "Managing production in Pennsylvania is difficult enough." No one in the group had experience doing business outside the country. Nevertheless, they authorized Chazen to travel to Taiwan to investigate.

Claiborne later explained that she had changed her mind about importing because of the quality and detail of the work she could obtain from foreign factories. During the firm's first two years, she had trouble finding domestic suppliers who could provide the quality of fabrics and tailoring she wanted. She was shocked to find that she could get "good quality . . . tiny stitches . . . beautiful buttonholes" from factories in the Far East. "I had never seen fine little buttonholes like that," she reported. "I could make any shirt pocket I wanted to. I could put double needle stitching all over the place. I could make two pockets instead of one pocket."[5] The company could obtain this detailed work in the Far East for much less than the cost of production in the United States. "We tested some products with the first company we used in Taiwan," Chazen said, "and we found that we could deliver better products and better fabric at a better price than the competition."[6]

Because all this was happening in the late 1970s, Liz Claiborne garnered what economists call "first mover" advantages from its sourcing strategies. First movers are able to increase their market share by leveraging new types of functional or strategic effectiveness. Through innovating in technology or organizational strategy, they achieve efficiencies that allow them to reduce their costs and to offer a more desirable product or a lower price on the market. As other firms attempt to learn and adapt these techniques, they enter a playing field that is largely shaped by those firms that innovated early on. And they must compete for market share with companies that already have an established presence.[7] Liz Claiborne was committed to production outside the United States almost from the very beginning of its operations. It had invested very little in manufacturing infrastructure and did not have to divest itself of factories and workers in order to move off-

5. James Lardner, "Annals of Business: The Sweater Trade II," *New Yorker,* January 18, 1988, 62.

6. Chazen, "Notes from the Apparel Industry," 41.

7. Alfred D. Chandler Jr., *Scale and Scope: The Dynamics of Industrial Capitalism* (Cambridge: Harvard University Press, 1990), 34–35.

shore. Perhaps more important, however, the firm gained experience and connections, laid a groundwork of contractual arrangements, and learned the apparel quota system that governed international trade long before many of its competitors. As Chazen expressed it, "We sailed in uncharted waters, made our share of mistakes, and attained an enormous competitive advantage."[8]

According to Robert Zane, the firm quickly realized "that Taiwan was not really the center of the [apparel] universe—it was Hong Kong." He continued, "Liz and Art would go to Hong Kong every two to three months, and they would hold court in their suite at the Peninsula Hotel, and they wouldn't leave until the job was done, which meant that the next season's work was designed and production was arranged." According to this manager's account, once factory owners understood the sheer quantities of clothing that would be involved in producing for Liz Claiborne, they "clamored to get on the bandwagon. . . . When Liz ordered one hundred of something, a reorder of one thousand would follow, and ten thousand would follow from that."

The firm developed close relationships with apparel suppliers in Hong Kong, particularly with the firm Fang Brothers. S. C. Fang had run spinning and weaving factories in Shanghai until the 1940s, when "the prospect of revolution, and then the revolution itself, drove two million people from China to Hong Kong."[9] Fang started new factories in Hong Kong and brought his sons into the business. When the Hong Kong apparel industry took off in the 1960s, the Fang Brothers were in the vanguard and ultimately expanded their operations into Thailand, the Philippines, Malaysia, Ireland, and Panama.[10] They participated in a system that Gary Gereffi has referred to as "triangle manufacturing."[11] In this system, U.S. or other overseas buyers place orders with apparel firms in relatively industrialized Asian sites such as Taiwan or Hong Kong, who then shift some or all of the order to affiliated factories in lower-wage countries. According to Zane, when primary sources like the Fang Brothers ran out of production capacity in their Hong Kong factories, "we encouraged [them] to move on, to build more factories themselves. We went from Hong Kong to the Philippines, and from

8. Chazen, "Notes from the Apparel Industry," 43.

9. James Lardner, "Annals of Business: The Sweater Trade I," *New Yorker,* January 11, 1988, 45.

10. Lardner, "Sweater Trade I," 40.

11. Gary Gereffi, "The Organization of Buyer-Driven Global Commodity Chains: How U.S. Retailers Shape Overseas Production Networks," in *Commodity Chains and Global Capitalism,* ed. Gary Gereffi and Miguel Korzeniewicz (Westport, Conn.: Praeger, 1994), 113–15.

Hong Kong to southern China. We were at the forefront of sourcing, all the while maintaining control over the production process and over quality."

Control over the production process was a hallmark of Liz Claiborne's managerial style. According to its managers:

> We treated the factory in Taiwan no differently than we had treated the factory in Pennsylvania. All we did was exchange the labor that was available in, say, Pennsylvania or South Carolina for the labor that was available in Taiwan or Hong Kong. Otherwise, we sent the piece goods, we sent the patterns, we made the markers, we did all the same things. We took what we had here in the States, and we replicated it overseas. And as a result, we were able to bring in a product that was rather well made. They were good factories and they had highly skilled workers, and so we brought in a well-made product that competed very, very well with anything that was available. And Liz understood that labor was *so* much less expensive over there, and she could put all sorts of details into the design that would be impossible to deal with here in a cost-effective way.

This strategy worked well for the firm, which went public in 1981, and led to steady growth throughout most of the 1980s.

The development of a global sourcing strategy also had a political dimension. As described in chapter 2, the primary trade association for apparel manufacturers—the American Apparel Manufacturers Association (AAMA)—had for most of its history advocated policies that would protect firms whose production operations were in the United States. Up through the 1980s, there were no industry coalitions representing the interests of firms whose production was predominantly outside the country. Liz Claiborne played a major role in establishing the United States Association of Importers of Textile and Apparel (USA-ITA) in 1988, as an organization that would lobby for freer trade and fewer customs restrictions. The firm's corporate managers have held key positions in the organization throughout its history. In 2000, for example, Liz Claiborne's vice president of customs and international trade operations chaired the organization. In addition, the firm exercised influence within the AAMA, moving that organization away from its former protectionist position.

According to managers, however, Claiborne's hands-on approach to its contracting led the firm to create its own competition. The overseas factories that worked for Liz Claiborne learned to produce fashion merchandise of a quality and style that appealed to U.S. consumers. "They took the lessons learned from us," Zane said, "and set up a line next to ours that was doing the whole product for whoever wanted it. . . . Retailers were now able to buy directly from the factories, which was something that they were totally unable to do before." Former CEO Chazen tells a similar story. "The competition . . . that followed us started from a different plateau. They demanded and received more from their manufacturers. . . . [They] 'leapfrogged' us."[12] The development of manufacturing capacity among producers outside the United States began to undermine the competitive position of the firm as it moved into the 1990s, eroding the "first mover" advantages it had previously enjoyed.

As Liz Claiborne Incorporated moved into the 1990s, many branded apparel marketers crowded the field, and this took a toll on the company's market share. Competitive conditions became difficult as more and more companies established successful global sourcing patterns. Other factors affected the firm's success as well. Claiborne herself was playing less of a role in design, and the coherence of the brand suffered from the lack of a lead designer with a strong vision. The company had only begun to spend large amounts of money on advertising in the late 1980s and had not perfected its methods. In the words of Paul Charron, who became CEO during that period, "Sales were down, market share was down, profits were down, morale was down, and the Board and the shareholders were most unhappy."[13]

Beginning in 1994, the company sought to change its key strategies. Its new CEO saw the firm's brand name as its strongest asset. He sought to revitalize the brand through consumer research and innovative advertising. He also moved to diversify the "portfolio" of brands associated with the Liz Claiborne name—expanding from seven brands in the late 1980s to twenty-seven in 2002. The company began to market some of its brands through new channels, including such "down-market" retailers as Wal-Mart and JC Penney. In addition, the firm spent $150 million to revamp its information systems, to the point where all its transactions and supply channel functions were online and in real time. It adopted computer-assisted design of fashions. And it backed away from a short-lived initiative toward retailing its own clothing begun in the late 1980s.[14]

Quota and Global Sourcing

One of the keys to the firm's success had always been its global production network. From the outset, Liz Claiborne had possessed strong competitive advantages in its ability to capture what Gereffi has called "trade policy

12. Chazen, "Notes from the Apparel Industry," 43.
13. Lisa Lockwood, "Charron's Catharsis," *Women's Wear Daily*, June 13, 2001, 14.
14. Ibid.

rents."[15] That is, it had developed the ability to control and draw advantage from quota, a resource made scarce by—or more accurately, created by— trade law. The firm's methods of procuring fashion garments from abroad evolved alongside the provisions of the Multi-Fiber Arrangement. From the beginning, the availability of quota under this unusual trade policy instrument shaped its sourcing strategies.

Since 1974, the Multi-Fiber Arrangement has provided the framework for trade in textiles and apparel. The textile and clothing industries were unique in being governed by such special regulations, which grew out of the attempts of the industrialized nations to protect their domestic industries from imports from Japan and Hong Kong beginning in 1957. In that year the United States and Japan signed a short-term agreement limiting exports from Japan to the United States. Thirty-three nations signed a multilateral short-term arrangement in 1961, which they elaborated into a long-term arrangement in 1962 and renewed in 1967 and 1970.[16] These agreements were meant to limit imports into the developed countries for a period during which those nations would presumably restructure their own domestic textile and apparel industries, and then to gradually increase the level of permissible imports over time.

The Multi-Fiber Arrangement was a more comprehensive version of previous agreements. Under its provisions, "individual quotas were negotiated which set precise limits on the quantity of textiles and apparel which could be exported from one country to another. For every single product a quota was specified."[17] The signatory nations extended the original agreement of 1974 in 1977, 1982, 1986, and 1991. In 1994, as part of the Uruguay Round of negotiations, the General Agreement on Tariffs and Trade incorporated rules for trade in textiles and apparel, and ultimately the World Trade Organization took responsibility for administering them. Signatory nations set a plan for the gradual phase-out of quotas during the Uruguay Round, scheduling full liberalization for 2005.

In ways that were sometimes bizarre, apparel production followed the availability of quota around the world. Besides creating incentives for pro-

15. Gary Gereffi, "International Trade and Industrial Upgrading in the Apparel Commodity Chain," *Journal of International Economics* 48 (1999): 43.

16. Edna Bonacich and David V. Waller, "Mapping a Global Industry: Apparel Production in the Pacific Rim Triangle," in *Global Production: The Apparel Industry in the Pacific Rim,* ed. Edna Bonacich, Lucie Cheng, Norma Chinchilla, Nora Hamilton, and Paul Ong (Philadelphia: Temple University Press, 1994), 26.

17. Peter Dicken, *Global Shift: Transforming the World Economy,* 3d ed. (New York: Guilford, 1998), 301.

duction in regions that would not otherwise make sense, quota availability shaped trends in the industry in other unexpected ways. One was the pressure it created to ship high-value items. Because the quotas measured imports by quantity rather than value, manufacturers sought to maximize earnings by producing the highest-value garments possible in a given category.[18] The second type of unanticipated incentive was the pressure to adopt fabrics not covered by the arrangement. This was the origin of ramie, a crinkled cloth made of hemp that was developed specifically to allow firms to sidestep quota limits.[19] Hemp fabric was of course quite old, but it was called ramie for export purposes. Third, quota led manufacturers to alter products slightly so they would fall into a category for which more quota existed. Jackets were shipped without sleeves so they could pass as vests, for example, or skirts and tops were shipped separately and later reattached to form dresses.[20] Fourth, a less creative and less legal measure, but one that was even more significant, was to tranship apparel through countries with available quota. Finally, the highly complex quota restrictions that applied to most of the world made production in Mexico and the Caribbean under the special exemptions of Item 807 customs rules particularly attractive, as did the quota-free environment of NAFTA, Caribbean basin parity legislation, and the Africa Growth and Opportunity Act for their respective regions.

The United States and European nations designed the quota system to protect their domestic textile and apparel industries from emerging competitors in parts of the world where labor was much less costly. Neoliberal economists have long argued that textile and apparel industries are ideally suited to nations in the early stages of developing a national industrial base. They require little in the way of capital and take advantage of abundant labor. For this reason, the industrialized nations argued that poor regions had an unfair trade advantage and that the Multi-Fiber Arrangement was needed to give them time to adjust to competition from the emerging proletarians of developing nations.

In fact, however, the Multi-Fiber Arrangement neither preserved U.S. jobs nor promoted the orderly growth of nationally owned textile sectors in the developing world. Small firms in developing nations were not in a

18. Bonacich and Waller, "Mapping a Global Industry," 28; Kitty Dickerson, *Textiles and Apparel in the Global Economy,* 2d ed. (Englewood Cliffs, N.J.: Merrill, 1995), 432.

19. Bonacich and Waller, "Mapping a Global Industry," 27; Lardner, "Sweater Trade I," 62–64.

20. Bonacich and Waller, "Mapping a Global Industry," 27.

good position to compete for allocations of quota. Political elites often g
erned its distribution and favored those in their networks. As a secondar
market for quota emerged, the cost could be high. Small operations were
also more vulnerable to the effects of losing access to quota. A simple rule
change could make it impossible for a firm to export. For small, nationally
based firms, a season without quota was a season without income. Factory
owners had to shut production down and send workers home.

Those enterprises that thrived under the quota system were transnational firms with multiple production sites. If there was no quota available to produce coats in Hong Kong, a multinational firm could shift the
order to Singapore or Malaysia. While the subcontractor in Hong Kong might
suffer, the large apparel concern would not lose money. Multiple production
sites thus insured against the risks associated with quota availability. This
situation created significant barriers to entry for firms that could not afford
to operate in several countries.

Because countries received quota for specific garments made of specific
fabric types, an apparel firm attempting to put together a full clothing line
might need to operate in a dozen or more countries. This too created difficulties for smaller companies, which might find the number of designs they
could offer limited by the countries where they could operate. Their fashion
ideas and perceptions of consumer demand meant nothing if they could
not also access the quota to produce those items.

In the 1980s journalist James Lardner interviewed Arthur Ortenberg, one
of the founders of Liz Claiborne, about the quota system. Ortenberg told him
that the complexities of the quota system "tended to winnow out potential
competitors and thus made the rewards of success all the greater."[21] Lardner
asked him if it was accurate to say that the system worked much like a
cartel in which those who had strong, ongoing relationships with factories
that held scarce quota controlled the market. Ortenberg replied, "Almost
. . . but you need to remember that we're dealing with nervous suppliers
all over the world. And we do have competitors. . . . But, by and large, the
quota system has worked to our advantage."[22] In his impassioned article,
Lardner argued that Liz Claiborne owed much of its success to having established stable relationships with firms that had large quota holdings. He
noted that Americans paid more for their clothes than they would in a
quota-free world, and that a lot of that money went to importers and overseas manufacturers who had mastered the system. The quotas, he asserted,

21. Lardner, "Sweater Trade II," 63.
22. Ibid., 64.

"amounted to a government program, that among other things had helped Art Ortenberg and Liz Claiborne to buy themselves a private jet."[23] Other large importers have expressed sentiments that support Lardner's view of quota as giving rise to cartel-like dynamics within the industry. The owner of a major children's apparel firm interviewed by *Forbes* magazine twelve years later noted, "I'm in fifteen countries . . . mainly because of quotas. . . . The more complex it is, the better for me."[24]

In 1988 Jeffrey Fang, the Hong Kong–based agent for Liz Claiborne, articulated the benefits that the quota system provided to large firms and the way it required global reach. "If Fang Brothers did not have overseas factories [outside of Hong Kong]," he explained, "it would be unable to fill these orders, and that was indeed the situation with a lot of the smaller companies in Hong Kong: because of the quota system, they could no longer compete. This is the consequence—you kill the small guy."[25] Twelve years later another member of the Fang family told *Forbes* magazine that the quota system "is like smoking opium. When you have protection, nobody wants the protectionist umbrella to be taken away. I'm surprised the U.S. consumer, who is really being hurt, is not asking the government why."[26] The irony of the situation is that the beneficiaries of the protectionism of the Multi-Fiber Arrangement were not U.S. textile and apparel workers, as consumers and the U.S. Congress had been told. They were large branded marketers who had the resources to organize a highly coordinated global factory system and to secure access to quota wherever it existed: from Mongolia to the Maldives, Madagascar to Guyana.

Tapping a Global Labor Force

Operating in thirty-two countries gave Liz Claiborne great flexibility in making its sourcing decisions. According to managers, during each of the firm's six fashion seasons, its fifteen divisions went through the following process: The manager in charge of the division solicited designs from the company's New York studio. Once the sketches came back from the designers, the manager turned them over to pattern makers who interpreted them, constructed a pattern, and conducted fittings to properly size the garment. Once the manager and the division's staff finalized the line and adopted a set of

23. Ibid., 63.
24. "The Great Quota Hustle," *Forbes,* March 6, 2000, 122.
25. Lardner, "Sweater Trade I," 69.
26. "Great Quota Hustle," 122.

styles, they decided which of the firm's 256 supplier factories would produce them.

To a large extent, they based this decision on quota availability. It was certainly not possible to send an order for say, jackets, to Taiwan if the firm did not have a relationship with a factory there that had unused quota for jackets. Liz Claiborne's president, Paul Charron, estimated that 40 percent of the firm's sourcing decisions were based on quota considerations alone.[27] But particular factories also had particular capabilities, which were related to their machinery, the proximity of raw materials, the expertise of their managers, and the skills of their workers. Robert Zane, the company's vice president for manufacturing and sourcing, offered the following explanation of how they might work through this variety of factors:

> Anything made of silk is made in China. . . . Otherwise, structured merchandise . . . we probably get the best ladies'-type suits out of Taiwan and places in China, but where we have to reach a price point and where those price points are combined with American fabric, we tend to do that in El Salvador. We tend to do our ongoing programs in cotton-type pants in the Dominican Republic, and our other-than-basic knits in Saipan. So we have developed our pockets—I don't suppose they are pockets of countries as much as they're pockets of manufacturers.

The firm was also concerned with how quickly a supplier could fill orders. Managers noted that ten or twelve years ago a textile supplier could take ninety days to produce a particular color and weave of fabric for a line. In the 2000 season they could count on the mill to weave the fabric and the apparel factory to make it into a shirt in sixty days. In the 1990s many industry analysts had suggested that adopting "quick response" practices would lead to a "regionalization" of production in order to reduce lead times. That is, firms serving the U.S. market were expected to source more of their garments in Mexico, the Caribbean, and Latin America; those serving Europe would source from Eastern Europe and North Africa; and those serving Japan would source from Southeast Asia. Despite these predictions, in 2000 Liz Claiborne continued to order two-thirds of its garments from Asia. This suggests that the firm cared less about transport time than about the factory's ability to turn an order around quickly.

Liz Claiborne negotiated its orders with suppliers based on landed duty costs, which meant that the supplier was responsible for developing a com-

27. Lisa Rabon, "Season of the Consumer," *Bobbin*, December 2000, 1.

petitive bid that incorporated factors such as handling costs, taxes, tariffs, and transport. For this reason, managers at the firm's headquarters were concerned with labor and transport costs not per se, but only as they contributed to the overall cost of an item. Yet they were still aware of the crucial role that wages played in shaping contractors' ability to meet their price points. As Zane noted, "What we looked for from the factories was to supply skilled labor and for lower cost, that's all. Nothing more and nothing less."

The firm ordered its most labor-intensive items from regions with the lowest hourly wages in the world. Managers sometimes had complex explanations for doing this. One division manager provided the following account:

> Well, right now you know that there's a lot of embellishment going on in fashion, all types of hand embroidery, and there's really only two places in the world that can do it right now for us. There's other places, but we have huge volumes, so we can't just go any place for any product. . . . Generally the best people are India and second would be China. Of course you can make some in Mongolia, you can make some down in Peru, but I would say the lion's share . . . is China. Where they have the manual labor and many times they have that skill.

He noted that it was very common in China, for example, for an urban factory to send an agent into rural Chinese communities with graphs and yarn for sweaters. There women gathered to work in what the firm called "cottage industries." Factory agents would return to pick up the knitted panels to be washed, finished, and assembled.

While this manager suggested that the company sought out workers in these regions because they had certain skills—such as embroidery or hand knitting—ultimately the key issue proved to be labor "availability," which translated very directly into labor cost. He went on to say:

> It's very hard to find enough labor, you know. One "hand knit" may take one person a day. It may take them two days for a hand knit. . . . You always have to keep ahead of your competition, so although you're not necessarily looking for new places. . . . One compelling reason certainly is a drastic price reduction where you're able to get an edge on your competitor and either market that product for considerably less and hopefully drive sales or to get a better margin to support the markdown.

To illustrate the effect of even minimal cost savings—including wage savings—on the firm's bottom line, he noted, "In my division I do 70 million units. For every penny I save per unit, it's about a quarter of a million dollars." He added, "But we won't go into a new factory for just a nickel or a dime. They have to fit within our criteria."

The significance of wage costs to the firm's sourcing decisions was perhaps best revealed by Zane's comments on the quota system. In speculating on the impact of quota removal in 2005, he predicted that

> all commodity apparel—where turn time is not a factor—will be made in China, India, or Bangladesh—places where labor is projected to be cheap and abundant into the future. Other places like Egypt and Sri Lanka will have to change their product capabilities to become more fashion oriented. It's funny, the wages in Sri Lanka are between $90 and $120 a month, and that's not a lot of money. But they are at a competitive disadvantage because wages in China are closer to $60.

While he suggested that the cheapest apparel might go to China, it is worth noting that the company already looked to China to produce its fashion sweaters and that it sourced its "best" ladies' suits there.

Developing Relationships with Supplier Factories

Liz Claiborne drew competitive advantage from the density, complexity, and strength of its relationships with supplier firms. These ties provided what Gereffi has called "relational rents": advantages accruing to firms that can construct strategic alliances with enterprises that perform significant work along the supply chain.[28] The construction of these alliances provided many benefits to the firm.

One of the most important benefits was the reallocation of risk within the supply chain as the firm was able to shift the costs of holding inventory to the manufacturer. As Frederick Abernathy and his coauthors have noted, before the 1990s, when retailers or branded marketers ordered a product, they did so with adequate lead times for each party to produce what they ordered. They gave the apparel manufacturer time to acquire the necessary materials and to make the products before the delivery date. Similarly, the apparel producer gave the textile mill enough time to acquire the yarn and make fabric. Firms did not have to order raw materials or manufacture products on speculation.[29] By the 1990s, however, apparel firms no longer held inventories of finished garments. Rather, they ex-

---

28. Gereffi, "International Trade and Industrial Upgrading," 43.

29. Frederick H. Abernathy, John T. Dunlop, Janice H. Hammond, and David Weil, *A Stitch in Time: Lean Retailing and the Transformation of Manufacturing; Lessons from the Apparel and Textile Industries* (New York: Oxford University Press, 1999), 186.

pected textile manufacturers to hold inventories of cloth and other inputs; textile firms, in turn, expected their suppliers to hold stocks of yarns and dyes. This moved risk down the supply chain and created significant financial pressure on small to midsized producers in both the textile and apparel sectors.

Having reduced their exposure to risk in this way, managers at Liz Claiborne sought to ensure that they always had several sourcing options for every kind of garment. They developed alternatives that would serve as backup should one factory be unable to take an order, or to price it in a way that they found acceptable, and that would allow the company to strategically locate orders based on quota availability and the specific strengths and weaknesses of providers. The firm did not want any factories to become completely dependent on its business, however. According to Zane, the company had decided that it should never account for 100 percent of any factory's production. "Our goal," he said, "is to be somewhere between 30 and 40 percent. So we're always important but never dominating." Another manager added, "We really don't want to be more than two-thirds of volume of any one factory. It's too much pressure on them and on our organization to be the sole supplier of product for a factory. It would be no different than owning our own factories, and that's something we can't live with." At the same time, the company's sales volume provided a powerful lever for obtaining compliance and loyalty. As one executive said, "What vendor is going to risk a relationship that brings them $40 million a year?"

Developing stable and reliable relationships with overseas factories represented an investment in administrative coordination that routinized transactions between units, thus lowering costs. These stable relationships were important in helping the firm resolve the three dilemmas for high-end producers that were described in chapter 2. For firms operating with a geographically dispersed production base, solving the market fragmentation problem, the quick response problem, and the quality problem all required a strong supplier network. Combined with electronic data interchange capabilities, having strong relationships with suppliers permitted the implementation of quick response. It allowed the firm to maximize both its productive capacity and its responsiveness to changing product lines. In combination with programs of supplier certification and statistical process control, it made new forms of quality control possible.

As Liz Claiborne developed more confidence in its supplier factories, it sought to give them more responsibility. It discontinued certain support functions and began to require "full package production."[30] Full package production entailed making the offshore factory responsible for producing a finished garment that would meet specifications. It required them to obtain inputs, handle quota negotiations, and arrange for production in an appropriate site. The company had long worked this way with Hong Kong firms like Fang Brothers. As one manager noted, "We have a lot of requirements, and a lot of times factories aren't ready for it. They have to be well-capitalized. They have to be able to purchase the fabric and trim. . . . We require that they do their own grading and marking." He added, "We want to design and market product. That's what we really want to do. We don't really want to be the manufacturers. We don't want to have warehouses. What we want to be able to do is say, 'Here is our product, here is our label,' and then have these other guys make it and ship it to our customers. It's still going to take some time to get to this point, though." Zane echoed this view. "We like the one vendor concept. . . . At the end of the day, we would like to specify the product, . . . write a check for the product, and rely more on the supplier to do everything in between."[31] Whereas in 1995 suppliers produced a little over half of Liz Claiborne's apparel on a package basis, by 1999 that figure had risen to 93 percent.

Although Liz Claiborne sought full package production as a long-term goal, it still retained a good deal of control over many aspects of production. Managers described the process: Once the head of a division chose a style and decided on a sourcing location, he or she sent the pattern, along with fabric and specifications, to an overseas office in a country that had quota for the item. Individuals from that office visited a factory and requested that they make up a sample of the garment. They talked with the local factory managers about the requirements and about the size and scheduling of the order. The factory then made and sent a "counter sample" to headquarters, where staff discussed and evaluated it. Division leaders sent back suggestions on how to adjust and improve the dress or shirt. If they found the sample acceptable, they authorized a preproduction run; the company's field office examined these items. This degree of hands-on management was unusual in the industry, and Claiborne managers claimed it was part of their formula for success.

30. Gary Gereffi, "Global Shifts, Regional Response: Can North America Meet the Full-Package Challenge?" *Bobbin,* November, 1997, 16–31.

31. Scott Malone, "Mills Move to Sewing Machines," *Women's Wear Daily,* April 6, 1999, 12.

By 1994, Liz Claiborne's global sourcing network had grown to immense proportions. The company had developed relationships with 512 factories in more than forty-four countries. In the words of Robert Zane, "Every time we heard of another opportunity—a quotaless environment over there, a quarter to be saved over here, we would run there. And that's a management problem because we were very, very decentralized."

As part of an effort to consolidate and improve relationships with supplier factories, the firm began to reduce the number of subcontractors it was working with. Zane continued,

> I remember distinctly how we separated one type of factory from another. Some of the factories had become so accustomed to dealing with us that they would show up at our offices in Hong Kong or Taiwan and say, "Well, good morning. It's January First and I'm here for my spring orders please." . . . Other factories would come in and say, "Let's talk strategy. We feel that quota on this will get tight in the next few years and therefore we feel that we should make a move by creating this kind of factory in Malaysia, or this type of situation in Taipei. How do you feel about that?" Well, those are the partners we like. . . . So it became a mentality of "Don't ask what Liz Claiborne can do for you. What is it that you can do for Liz Claiborne?" In conjunction with that, we had to get off this quality thing where— we had some bad quality, and when I complained to the factory, they said, "Why are you coming to us? You're in charge of quality." We had to change the idea that they weren't responsible. So we launched several initiatives at the same time.

In the mid-1990s the firm began to consolidate its factory base. By 1999 Liz Claiborne had reduced the number of factories it worked with to 256 in thirty-two countries, while producing twice as many units of clothing as it had in 1994.

As part of its consolidation program, the company began a "supplier certification" initiative. It established a set of guidelines and requirements for apparel factories as well as for suppliers of fabric and trim. The firm required its subcontractors to use information systems that were compatible with its own, to institute specific quality control procedures, to buy fabric and other components from designated sources, and to follow a "code of conduct" in labor relations. The company's director of supplier certification argued that the emphasis was on establishing good systems and procedures rather than on product. "We look at everything from beginning to end," she said. "Raw materials inspection, housekeeping, safety, preventive maintenance, calibration of the machinery, the training programs for everybody involved, as well as their quality practices and procedures and documentation." Managers saw supplier certification as an important tool for achieving factory compliance with the techniques that would enable quick response and rapid adoption of new designs. They felt that it reduced costs by allowing transactions to be routinized. But perhaps most important, it allowed the company to work closely with suppliers to establish procedures for quality assurance.

Solving the Quality Problem

Industry analysts regard Liz Claiborne as setting an industry standard for quality control procedures in its offshore factories.[32] In 2000, managers had developed what they referred to as a "quality pyramid," which combined a range of types of quality control (table 4.1). Proactive forms involved factory certification, statistical process control, and preproduction meetings between company representatives and factory managers to discuss a production run. Active measures entailed production of a counter sample, which was sent back to headquarters for approval and could then be displayed in the plant as a "sealed sample" of an accurate product. Also, before a full order was undertaken, the factory would produce a short preproduction "pilot" run to ensure that machines were set correctly and operators understood the job. Reactive measures were in-line inspections. Passive measures included final audits at the factories, at the firm's quality assurance centers in the country of production, and at U.S. distribution facilities.

By far the most ambitious of the firm's quality control procedures was statistical process control (SPC), which the company instituted in supplier factories in the 1990s. According to managers, Claiborne borrowed this procedure from more highly automated industries such as heavy equipment and appliance manufacture and applied its principles to apparel assembly. The company worked with industrial engineers to adapt it to garment factory work. The approach required inspectors to measure and record aspects of quality for a statistical sampling of garments that passed through each work station on the garment assembly line. At a given time, inspectors would examine all garments under construction. They would determine whether each operation was performed within upper and lower control limits. Measurements were charted, typically using a line graph that showed ideal measures and allowable variance. Variances that exceeded limits signaled an "unstable situation" and required that the inspector consult with

32. Kathleen DesMarteau, "Liz Launches Global Quality Coup," *Bobbin,* July 1999, 34–38; Lisa Rabon, "Navigating New Terrain," *Bobbin,* August 1999, 34–37.

Table 4.1. "Quality pyramid" at Liz Claiborne Incorporated

Type of quality control	Procedures involved
Proactive (procedures designed to assess and monitor quality continuously)	Factory certification
	Statistical process control
	Preproduction meetings
Active (procedures used to set the standards before production)	Counter sample procedure
	Sealed sample procedure
	Preproduction pilot
Reactive (production has started, so identified faults require in-line correction)	In-line inspections
Passive (identified faults can only be rejected or repaired)	Final audit at factory
	Final audit at quality assurance center
	Final inspection in U.S. distribution facility

the line supervisor and ultimately with the worker to develop a plan for bringing the operation back "under control." Managers said the approach was based on looking "at systems and procedures as opposed to just focusing on product."

The firm believed this method was superior to random inspections or end-of-the-line sampling, since it allowed problems to be traced to a particular work station. It permitted continuous monitoring of the performance of each operator over time, gave each operator immediate feedback, and generated a chart as "visual" evidence of poor performance. The company developed two pilot programs, one in Colombia and the other in Indonesia. Based on results in these sites, it decided to expand the program to other suppliers. By late 1999 the company produced 85 percent of its apparel using statistical process control, involving 98 of its 250 suppliers. It reported a 33 percent reduction in shipments that failed to meet quality standards from 1996 to 1999 and an additional 33 percent reduction during 1999. The firm believed these measures would allow it to produce goods that met its quality standards virtually anywhere in the world. The apparel press covered the initiative prominently, with headlines such as "Liz Launches Global Quality Coup" and "Navigating New Terrain," featuring photographs of the managers in charge of SPC programs posed playfully on the cover.

Despite the more intensive supervision required, the higher percentage of first-quality garments produced and the reduction in the number of operatives led managers to see statistical process control as a way to reduce costs. Managers believed that its successful implementation would allow factories to reduce their workforce, largely by eliminating the need to rework garments. They cited the example of a factory in El Salvador that was able to reduce its workforce from 900 sewing machine operators to 600.

Hearing these comments reminded me of the angst that some Tultex managers experienced when they closed their sewing shops, and of the angry confrontations between workers and their former bosses in high-school cafeterias when the main plant closed. It appeared far easier to make such decisions from an office suite in New Jersey, without knowing much about the workers who would lose their jobs and without ever having to meet them face-to-face.

Building a Brand

A fourth key to Liz Claiborne's success had been its development of a strong brand within the fashion industry. The company had accrued significant "brand name rents" from the image it had been able to project to consumers, which targeted working women and emphasized clean lines and bold colors in traditional styles.[33] Moving into the 1990s, the firm's branding strategies required updating as well. Throughout the 1980s, it had found its market in upscale department stores. While it marketed its core lines as designer products, it priced them for a broader market. The 1990s presented a competitive environment in which businesses had to grow larger to succeed on Wall Street, and this created pressure on the firm to diversify. Its response was to spin off brands directed to new market segments that could be sold in a wider range of retail contexts at a broader range of prices.

Through the 1980s, the company had operated with a small set of key brands. Beginning in 1994 it sought to diversify its brand "portfolio," and by 2002 it was marketing clothing under twenty-seven brand names. It captured the cachet of strong design houses such as Sigrid Olsen and Ellen Tracy through purchase and that of potential competitors—such as Donna Karan and Kenneth Cole—through licensing agreements. It purchased small companies that were reaching more contemporary markets (Laundry by Shelli Segal) and younger consumers (Lucky Brand Dungarees). It developed a plus-size line and a men's line. Most boldly, perhaps, it expanded what it called a "special markets" division, which produced garments for JC Penney, Sears, Wal-Mart, and other low-price or discount stores under purchased brand names such as Russ, Villager, and Crazy Horse. These acquisitions gave the firm steady growth through the decade. At its annual shareholders' meeting in November 2000, the company's CEO was able to boast twenty consecutive quarters of sales growth and twenty-four consecutive quarters of growth in earnings per share.

33. Gereffi, "International Trade and Industrial Upgrading," 44.

While apparel firms needed to embrace a growth strategy based on acqui-sitions and licensing agreements in order to succeed on Wall Street, their collective adoption of this approach created contradictions within the over-all market. A company manager explained the dilemma:

> What's happening is, Wall Street is forcing Liz Claiborne, Jones, Ralph Lauren, anyone that's on Wall Street to have top line growth and bottom line growth. . . . So you have a lot of activity designed to increase our growth. We add divisions. We try to increase our sales. And this goes on across all of apparel. The only way you can drive those sales is to mark down the product. So in apparel in the USA, you really have a defla-tion. . . . But if you go to the Far East, you have a lot of inflationary things happening because demand [at the wholesale level] is going up. But it's only going up because it's being driven by needing to get top line sales growth . . . not because consumer demand is increasing.

Liz Claiborne's radical increase in its brand portfolio took place in this com-petitive arena—where large manufacturers were competing to increase their market share in a glutted and deflationary consumer market.

Maintaining a brand's integrity is a tricky proposition. While it is normal for a firm to want to expand its market as much as possible, selling a brand too broadly will erode its appeal. Kitty Dickerson notes that it is anathema to sell identical merchandise to department stores and discount stores un-der the same brand name, since the product will lose its appeal in the higher-price market as soon as it appears in discount stores.[34] Consultants to the apparel industry advise taking labels to new markets overseas for expansion, if possible, to avoid the "traditional dilemma, namely that by expanding sales they risk losing the mystique that lets them charge a for-tune for clothes." Designers like Calvin Klein and Ralph Lauren are seen as having expanded their lines as far downscale as they can without "devaluing the brand."[35] Executives at major firms refer to decisions about how and where to place brands as "brand stewardship." This was the risk Liz Claiborne took in expanding into moderate and mass markets, but it appeared to pay off for the company, at least in the short run. The company's strategy was bolstered by expenditures of over $1 million a year on consumer research and $40 million to $50 million on advertising campaigns.

If Tultex Corporation epitomized a nationally based knitwear firm that came to global production late and with little expertise, Liz Claiborne Incor-porated was the epitome of a successful globally organized apparel concern.

---

34. Dickerson, *Textiles and Apparel in the Global Economy*, 255.
35. "Couture Ordinaire," *Economist*, October 14, 1995, 79–82.

It had begun producing and procuring garments overseas when few other U.S. firms were doing so. It developed relationships with key factories and suppliers and established a presence through regional offices. It was well positioned to take advantage of trade policies such as the Multi-Fiber Arrangement, to draw benefits from an established network of overseas partners, and to trade on the strengths of a well-established brand. Relying on these assets, the firm expanded and achieved growth that made it a success on Wall Street during the frenetic expansion of the 1990s.

The strategies that appear to be unqualified successes from the vantage point of glass and chrome offices in New Jersey, however, look more complex from the perspective of the shop floor. Initiatives like supplier certification and statistical process control are not just abstract programs but ways of shaping relationships with factory owners and workers in far-off places. Understanding the costs and benefits, routines and contradictions of their daily application requires us to travel to the regions where factories are located and the shop floors where clothing is produced, and to listen to perspectives from these locations. The contending voices of workers and owners that engaged one another in the community spaces of Martinsville are, in the new logic of global production, distributed across geographic space, national boundaries, and language. In the next chapter we will travel to Aguascalientes, Mexico, where both Tultex and Liz Claiborne subcontracted some of their production. We will look at the ways the firms' different global strategies structured shop floor production and at the consequences for labor relations in those plants. In this way we will trace the implications that the companies' programs to reduce labor costs, ensure quality, and enable quick response had for the individuals who made their clothes.

5

ON THE SHOP FLOOR IN AGUASCALIENTES

Labor vulnerability . . . travels without a passport.

—MICHAEL STONE AND GABRIELA WINKLER, TRANSLATORS'
FOREWORD TO *BEAUTIFUL FLOWERS OF THE MAQUILADORA*[1]

Aguascalientes' Apparel Industry

Shifting our focus to the Mexican factories where Tultex and Liz Claiborne have produced garments lets us ask several comparative questions. First, what are the differences in the "offshore" labor processes of the two firms, and what can this tell us about the direction of job change in the industry? Second, for a firm like Tultex that operated both within the United States and abroad, what are the key differences between labor relations in its home community and its relations with Mexican workers? By looking at differences between firms and across places, we can understand how competitive pressures lead to particular labor processes and how the enactment of those processes is shaped by the spatial distribution of relationships and local traditions of the work sites. In addition, looking closely at production practices in all of these sites reveals how gender becomes a pivotal tool for

1. Michael Stone and Gabriela Winkler, translators' foreword to *Beautiful Flowers of the Maquiladora: Life Histories of Women Workers in Tijuana,* by Norma Iglesias Prieto (Austin: University of Texas Press, 1997), xiii.

managers mapping a new global division of labor and segmenting a new global workforce.

About 320 miles north of Mexico City, on the central plateau of Mexico, lies the city of Aguascalientes, capital of the state of the same name (fig. 5.1). This rapidly growing town of half a million people was home to more than 130 apparel factories in 2000, with 140 additional firms providing inputs to the industry. Among them were Confitek, an apparel factory that formerly assembled knitwear for Tultex Corporation, and Burlmex, a subsidiary of the U.S.-based textile firm Burlington Industries, which produced under contract to Liz Claiborne. We can learn much about the way the two case study firms function in the global economy from an investigation of these two factories where they produced clothing.

Aguascalientes is an industrial city, though it does not have the sprawl that is often seen in the rapidly growing towns of the U.S.-Mexico border. Its industrial base dates to the early twentieth century, and many historians attribute the region's tranquillity during the Mexican Revolution to its high rate of factory employment in that period.[2] Because of its location in the center of national territory and on major highways and rail lines, Aguascalientes has developed a diversified economic base, and no single industry dominates the region's economy. In the 1990s local businesses engaged in food processing, fabricated metal products, textiles, and ceramics, and provided services to the region's farms and ranches. Because they had close connections to officials of the Institutional Revolutionary Party (PRI), members of the regional elite of Aguascalientes were able to ensure a steady stream of federal investment in infrastructure that supported development. They secured improvements such as highways and electricity at midcentury, an industrial park in 1975, and a garment industry emporium (Plaza Vestir) in 1977. The region's industries weathered the transition from a national policy of import substitution industrialization to one of export-led industrialization, making it through the economic difficulties of the 1970s and 1980s with one of the highest growth rates in the country.[3] By the mid-1990s the area boasted a regional rate of growth

2. Víctor Manuel González Esparza, *Jalones modernizadores: Aguascalientes en el siglo XX* (Aguascalientes: Instituto Cultural de Aguascalientes, 1992); Alan Knight, "Caudillos y campesinos en el México revolucionario: 1910–1917," in *Caudillos y campesinos en la Revolución mexicana* (Mexico City: Fondo Cultura Económica, 1985), 44.

3. Fernando I. Salmerón Castro, *Intermediarios del progreso: Política y crecimiento económico en Aguascalientes* (Mexico City: Centro de Investigaciones y Estudios Superiores en Antropología Social, 1996).

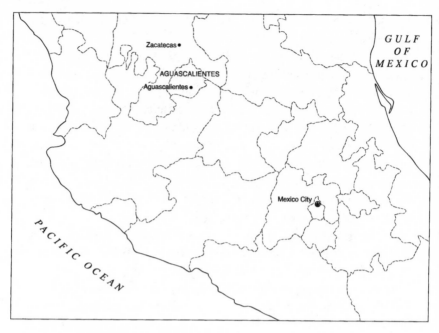

Figure 5.1. Map showing Aguascalientes, Mexico.

twice the national average, with unemployment hovering around 2 percent.[4]

Small garment factories in Aguascalientes had produced for the regional market since the early twentieth century. But as table 5.1 shows, employment in apparel and textile factories rose from 25 percent of the labor force in 1960 to over 45 percent in 1989. More than sixty small shops closed between 1989 and 1992, but most of those that stayed in business made the transition to maquiladora production (assembly for export). Whereas in 1970 the region's apparel factories employed an average of twelve workers per plant, by 1989 that number had risen to fifty-seven.[5] In 1990 the region had fewer textile and apparel firms than food processing plants, but the apparel sector was the largest employer, with more than 12,000 workers.[6]

Aguascalientes' regional elite had a long history of ties to the PRI, which governed Mexico from 1917 to 1990. In the 1980s and 1990s, however, they

4. Aguascalientes State Council for Economic and Trade Development, *Mexico OnLine*, 2000. www.mexonline.com/aguacal.htm.

5. Salmerón Castro, *Intermediarios del progreso*, 140.

6. Instituto Nacional de Estadística, Geografía e Informática, *Aguascalientes hoy* (Aguascalientes: INEGI, 1993).

Table 5.1. Growth in employment in the
apparel-textile sector, Aguascalientes

Year	Percentage of region's employment
1960	25.6
1965	32.0
1970	32.8
1975	34.1
1981	47.6
1985	45.1
1989	45.6

Source: Data from tables 21 and 34 in Fernando I. Salmerón
Castro, *Intermediarios del progreso: Política y crecimiento económico en Aguascalientes* (Mexico City: Centro de Investigaciones y Estudios Superiores en Antropología Social, 1996).

also developed strong relationships with foreign firms. Local officials developed Web sites and other promotional materials to lure investors, and they
supported trade fairs hosted by industry associations. The town's hotels did
a brisk business serving the representatives of transnational companies.
Partly as a result of this new export-oriented development strategy, by the
mid-1990s many of the region's industrialists had shifted their allegiance
to the pro-business, right-of-center National Action Party (PAN). The PAN
won its first municipal elections in the state in the mid-1990s, and its candi-
date was elected mayor of the city of Aguascalientes in 2001.[7]

Over the decades of the twentieth century, Aguascalientes developed a
reputation as a region with a compliant labor force. Most unionized employees in the region were members of the Federation of Workers of Aguascalientes (FTA), which was affiliated with the powerful Confederation of Mexican Workers (CTM). As in many other regions of Mexico, the leaders of the
FTA had close ties to government officials. They were committed to "social
peace" secured through collaboration between the union, management, and
the state. They saw the exclusion of competing unions as an important
condition of this peace. Union officials signed what have come to be called
in Mexico "protection contracts" (in the sense of protecting employers from
union militancy). Under these contracts, strikes were illegal. When a new
factory came to Aguascalientes, its "union officials" signed the contract
before the first workers were hired. The FTA's slogan was, "For workers there
is no worse company than one that closes."[8]

7. *La Reforma,* "Adelanta PAN en Aguascalientes," August 5, 2001.
8. Eugenio Herrera Nuño, *Aguascalientes: Sociedad, economía, política y cultura* (Mexico
City: Universidad Nacional Autónoma de México: Centro de Investigaciones Interdisciplinarias en Humanidades, 1989), 88.

To protect this arrangement, local officials initially established policies prohibiting foreign firms operating in the region from bringing in migrant labor, hoping to prevent the entrance of workers with more radical labor traditions. They loosened this policy, however, as increased foreign investment absorbed a growing proportion of the region's workforce in the 1990s.[9] In the latter part of that decade, the government of Aguascalientes could boast that its employers had not seen a strike in thirty years. While this system of corporatist unions was oppressive to workers, its effects on the apparel sector were not large, since the workforce was more than 80 percent female and the rate of unionization was only 12 percent.[10]

The Growth of Mexico's Export Apparel Industry

Mexico's apparel industry grew rapidly in the last two decades of the twentieth century in a context of changing national economic policies and international trade law. Before the 1960s, national firms producing for the domestic market dominated the Mexican apparel industry, with most factories located in and around Mexico City.[11] Beginning in the 1960s, however, the industry developed more export production. From that time forward Mexican policies regarding foreign investment, and trade pacts established between the United States and Mexico, shaped its growth.

The Mexican government launched its well-known Border Industrialization Program in 1965. The United States had just ended the "bracero program," which it had used to recruit Mexican workers for temporary job contracts between 1942 and 1964. Mexican policymakers sought to reabsorb some of the labor surplus created by return migration.[12] The Border Industrialization Program, which established an "export zone" on a 12.5-mile strip along the U.S.-Mexico border, was part of a systematic effort to encourage foreign investment to create jobs. It permitted the duty-free import of raw materials, machinery, and parts to this zone as long as the investor purchased a bond guaranteeing that the assembled product would be

9. Salmerón Castro, *Intermediarios del progreso*, 181.

10. Ibid., 169.

11. Gordon H. Hanson, "Industrial Organization and U.S.-Mexico Free Trade: Evidence from the Mexican Garment Industry," in *Global Production: The Apparel Industry in the Pacific Rim*, ed. Edna Bonacich, Lucie Cheng, Norma Chinchilla, Nora Hamilton, and Paul Ong (Philadelphia: Temple University Press, 1994).

12. María Patricia Fernández-Kelly, *For We Are Sold, I and My People: Women and Industry in Mexico's Frontier* (Albany: State University of New York Press, 1983), 26.

reexported.[13] The "in-bond" plants producing under these rules came to be known as maquiladoras. They included wholly owned transnational subsidiaries, jointly owned factories, and Mexican-owned subcontracted facilities. In 1972 the Mexican government extended the program from the border region to the rest of Mexico, excluding only those already industrialized areas around Mexico City, Guadalajara, and Monterrey.[14]

The maquiladora system grew up in tandem with Item 807 of the U.S. Tariff Code, which was established in 1963. Item 807 allowed U.S. firms to produce goods made of U.S. components abroad and to reimport them while paying duties only on the value added. Thus investors received tariff breaks not only on equipment and materials they sent out of the country, but on the finished goods they brought back. By 1987 Mexico had become the leading developing country supplying Item 807 imports.[15]

Mexico's maquiladora program has always been extremely sensitive to currency fluctuations, since these affect the cost of its labor to U.S. firms. In periods of economic crisis, the Mexican state has used peso devaluations to attract foreign currency.[16] In the late 1970s the government devalued the peso several times in response to economic crises. While this doubled the amount that an investor's dollar could buy, the minimum wage in Mexico also rose. This led industry representatives to complain that labor was becoming too expensive and precipitated a decline in the number of maquiladoras in the early 1980s.[17]

In 1982, in response to a generalized crisis in the Mexican economy, President López Portillo began a series of sharp currency devaluations that were continued by his successor Miguel de la Madrid. By 1988 the exchange rate was 2,257 pesos to one U.S. dollar, and the cost of labor had dropped to well below a dollar an hour.[18] The government imposed new ceilings on the minimum wage to keep it at this level despite inflation in the economy as a whole. The real minimum wage thus declined throughout the 1980s; the consequent decline in workers' living standards was

---

13. Susan Tiano, *Patriarchy on the Line: Labor, Gender and Ideology in the Mexican Maquila Industry* (Philadelphia: Temple University Press, 1994), 18.

14. Fernández-Kelly, *For We Are Sold, I and My People,* 33.

15. Tiano, *Patriarchy on the Line,* 20.

16. James D. Cockcroft, *Mexico: Class Formation, Capital Accumulation and the State* (New York: Monthly Review Press, 1983).

17. Leslie Sklair, *Assembling for Development: The Maquila Industry in Mexico and the United States* (Boston: Unwin Hyman, 1989), 63; Tiano, *Patriarchy on the Line,* 20.

18. Sklair, *Assembling for Development,* 63.

made worse by government cuts in public expenditures on health and edu-cation.[19]

While these events affected its dynamic, the maquiladora sector contin-ued to grow at an average of 10 percent a year between 1974 and 1993. By 2000, investors had established a total of 3,703 factories. Over time, these plants spread throughout the nation. Whereas 88 percent of maquiladoras clustered along the U.S.-Mexican border in 1981, by 1994 that figure had dropped to approximately 66 percent as the government provided more in-centives for investment in states to the south; this figure remained the same in 2001.[20]

A little over 10 percent of all maquiladoras established under the Border Industrialization Program were apparel plants. In 1991 the "textile" sector (which included apparel) was responsible for nearly 10 percent of Mexico's gross domestic product.[21] Apparel maquiladoras employed 43,830 workers and produced US$236.8 million in value added.[22] This growth accelerated after the passage of the North American Free Trade Agreement (NAFTA) in 1994, and in 1997 Mexico surpassed China as the primary exporter of apparel to the United States.[23]

Mexican maquiladora employment practices also shifted over the 1980s. By 1990 there were many more male workers, up to one-quarter from only 16 percent a decade before.[24] Workers were older (averaging twenty-six years old). More than half of all workers were married, and more than a third had children. The amount of time workers had spent at their jobs averaged 3.5 years.[25]

Because of the terms of Item 807 of the U.S. Tariff Code, apparel maquila-doras could perform only a limited array of tasks. The code said that facto-ries could only assemble clothing made from fabrics "formed and cut" in the United States. This prevented Mexican firms from producing textiles for

19. Tiano, *Patriarchy on the Line*, 23.

20. Jorge V. Carrillo, "The Apparel Maquiladora Industry at the Mexican Border," in *Global Production: The Apparel Industry in the Pacific Rim*, ed. Edna Bonacich, Lucie Cheng, Norma Chinchilla, Nora Hamilton, and Paul Ong (Philadelphia: Temple Univer-sity Press, 1994), 219; "Slower Growth in Maquilas," *Mexican Labor News and Analysis* 6, no. 5 (2001).

21. Mexico Investment Board, *The Textile Industry in Mexico* (Distrito Federal: Mexico Investment Board, 1993).

22. Carrillo, "Apparel Maquiladora Industry," 220. Amounts of money are given in U.S. dollars throughout.

23. Joanna Ramey and Scott Malone, "House to Get CBI Parity Bill—Again," *Women's Wear Daily*, March 2, 1999.

24. Carrillo, "Apparel Maquiladora Industry"; Tiano, *Patriarchy on the Line*, 24.

25. Carrillo, "Apparel Maquiladora Industry," 223.

the goods they exported to the United States. It also meant that Mexican firms could not perform more lucrative design tasks. Thus Item 807 posed a significant obstacle to the development of a system of "full package" production, in which Mexican factories took charge of all aspects of manufacturing.

This situation changed with the passage of NAFTA in 1994. Under NAFTA, the United States and Mexico began staged reductions of import duties and removed import quotas for goods that satisfied certain "rules of origin." In the case of apparel, the agreement specified a "yarn forward rule," meaning that the garments had to be made of fabric formed in North America (i.e., one of the three signatory states, including Mexico) and of yarn made in the region. This opened the door to the expansion of textile production in Mexico. Large U.S. mills such as Burlington, Cone, and Guilford began establishing Mexican operations almost immediately. The legislation expanded the possibilities for full package production of apparel.

After the passage of NAFTA, the annual rate of growth in apparel imports from Mexico increased from 20 to 27 percent per year. Thus the legislation quickened, but did not create, a trend toward the production of U.S. apparel in Mexico. Interpreting NAFTA's role in increasing imports is made more difficult by the fact that the Mexican peso crisis of 1994 led to a devaluation that reduced the cost of Mexican labor by nearly half. The cheapening of labor also had an important effect on firms that were considering relocating their production to Mexico.[26]

Confitek: Manufacturing Mass Market Knitwear

The Confitek plant, which produced knitwear for Tultex Corporation from 1995 to 1998, was located in a warehouselike building in downtown Aguascalientes that was dark and cramped. The manager who provided a tour of the plant apologized and commented that the company planned to install more lights in the near future. The owners of Confitek ran three other factories in the state of Aguascalientes, but two were outside the city. By setting up plants closer to rural communities, the firm had hoped to circumvent the intense competition for labor in the urban area. In this particular site, Confitek employed about sixty workers. Approximately 85 percent were women, and the workers' ages ranged from seventeen to twenty-eight. Unlike some other apparel plants, all the workers here remained seated at their

---

26. Brenda Jacobs, "Mexico Promises to Remain Number One for Production Sharing," *Bobbin*, March 1998, 22.

stations during most of the workday, with very little movement about the plant.

A group of Mexican investors started Confitek in 1995 to accept production contracts from transnational firms. In 2000, its workers sewed knitwear for Sara Lee, Pluma, Hanes, and Highlander among other labels. Until 1998 the firm had sewed for Tultex Corporation. Managers described the work done in the plant as "pure assembly." "They send us the raw materials, and all we do is assemble and return them."[27] The products themselves—mostly sweatshirts and "golf" shirts—were not particularly complicated, and styles did not change a great deal. "This firm has always worked with a very similar pattern," the general manager said. "The fabric is the same, and it is a very uniform style."

The assembly process at the plant began when a retailer or branded marketer placed an order and shipped the cut parts. Managers logged in the materials and instructed workers to set up the machines for the weight and type of fabric. They sent the cut pieces to the preassembly room, where seamstresses attached various small pieces to the shirt—hoods, pockets, or collars were sewn to the body, and cuffs were attached to the sleeves. In the main assembly area, workers stitched the panels of the body together and attached sleeves and other components. At the end of the line, inspectors checked the garments for quality, and workers folded and packed them for shipment back to the United States.

The plant's general manager noted that although the work was routine, every new order had a learning curve. In the early stages of a run, the factory might experience defect rates as high as 30 percent, but they were usually able to reduce this to 6 to 8 percent over time and had set a goal of 4 percent. Inspectors examined every garment at the end of the line. When they found a defect, they returned the bundle to the operator who had sewn it and asked her to rework it. This interrupted production and slowed the line. Inspectors then checked it again. The manager mentioned that one of their new clients had asked them to supplement this procedure with in-line inspection, in order to identify and correct problems earlier, before whole bundles were spoiled. For that client, the factory was attempting in-line inspection of eight out of twelve garments. At each work station in the Confitek factory, the quality control inspector kept bar

---

27. Greta Krippner, a graduate student in the Department of Sociology at the University of Wisconsin, Madison, traveled to Mexico to conduct observations and interviews in March 2000. She taped all interviews and I (JC) transcribed and translated them.

graphs drawn in pink marker that showed each worker's productivity. An upward-sloping black line plotted the expected efficiency, with operators' performance falling either above or—in most cases—below the programmed level.

Workers at Confitek assembled garments according to the progressive bundle system. A *chico de bultos* or "bundle boy" moved stacks of twelve sweatshirts from worker to worker. Line managers gave workers a ticket for every bundle of twelve they completed and calculated their income based on how many tickets they held at the end of the day. They paid a bonus to workers whose quality ratio was 90 percent—that is, who produced nine out of every ten bundles without defects.

In previous years, managers had flirted with the idea of modular, or team-based, production because they thought it might speed production, reduce inventories, and improve work flows. But they claimed that the "mentality of the workers" posed an obstacle. Sewing workers were accustomed to working individually, they argued. " 'I make my thousand [shirts] and I earn my money,' no?" They did not believe workers would accept a system where their wage was pegged to the performance of a group. The factory had conducted a brief experiment with the system in 1998 but ended it because productivity dropped. It was not clear whether this decline was related to inefficiencies in the system that had not been worked out or to what Devon Peña has called *tortuguismo*—workers resisting the new system by working "at the pace of a turtle" on the line.[28]

Given the rapid growth of the industry and the tightening labor market in Aguascalientes, managers listed the main requirements for new workers as "good health, good eyesight, and no criminal record." They did not require experience or prior knowledge of sewing. One supervisor described the training program for new workers:

> First the theory. What is a needle? What is the machine? How does it work? Policies of the firm. This is a period of two days. Then the worker begins with the machine—not in production, but in a practice setting where she learns about the machine, her other work instruments, and then begins specific exercises to learn to use the equipment. This takes about a week. But workers don't leave the training area until they achieve 50 percent efficiency [can produce 50 percent of quota]. When they reach that level they go out on the shop floor.

28. Devon Peña, *The Terror of the Machine: Technology, Work, Gender and Ecology on the U.S.-Mexico Border* (Austin: Center for Mexican-American Studies, 1997), 14.

While line managers did not consider the work at Confitek highly skilled, it required dexterity, attention, and care. As Angela Coyle has said of mass production sewing work, "the ability to work at high speed is a skill itself, inadvertently created by deskilling."[29] More than that, however, sewing knit fabric is inherently tricky, requiring the operator to maintain accurate machine settings and not stretch the extremely malleable fabric.

Confitek fit the pattern of a traditional maquiladora. Its workers assembled garments from fabric that other workers had knit and cut in the United States. Partly because of the simplicity of its operations, it made few investments in training, infrastructure, or machinery. But such investments were also constrained by the availability of credit. The director of the local branch of the National Apparel Industry Chamber of Commerce argued that firms like Confitek found it difficult to modernize their production because of a lack of funds. He suggested that for this reason they were slow to establish new systems for quick response production or better quality control, or even to improve industrial hygiene and labor conditions. While transnational firms had access to capital in their home countries, Mexican firms had few credit options. This is why, he conjectured, "siguen maquilando"—they continued operating as maquiladoras.

The National Apparel Industry Chamber of Commerce (CANAIVE) provided some assistance to its member firms. In 2000, the organization had signed an agreement with the secretary of labor and social provision for a special program in industrial hygiene. Under this program, the federal government suspended inspections and sanctions for violations for a given period for any factory that would willingly embark on a course of improvement. It could receive assistance in bringing its operation closer to federal standards in industrial hygiene, health, and safety. No matter how bad its existing violations, it would not face inspections, fines, or closing while it was engaged in reform. The Aguascalientes chapter of the chamber advertised this program prominently to its member firms.[30]

The Aguascalientes branch of CANAIVE also organized a labor skills certification program that served apparel companies in the region. It recruited new entrants into the workforce, provided them with a one-month training program, then sent them to plants that had openings. In the 1990s CANAIVE and the State Development Agency were still touting the quiescence of the region's workers. "The state is one of the most stable in terms of worker-

29. Angela Coyle, "Sex and Skill in the Organization of the Clothing Industry," in *Work, Women and the Labour Market,* ed. Jackie West (London: Routledge, 1982), 15.

30. CANAIVE [Camara Nacional de la Industria del Vestido], "Higiene y seguridad laboral," *Informe: Delegación Aguacaliente* 2, no. 1 (2000): 4–5.

employer relations," a Web site for potential investors boasted, "as evidenced by the fact that not a single strike has taken place in the last two decades."[31]

Burlmex: Putting Fashion on an Industrial Basis

Burlmex, which produced apparel under contract for Liz Claiborne, was a subsidiary of Burlington Industries. The facility opened in 1999 in an industrial park about twenty minutes from the center of Aguascalientes. The factory complex included two large buildings and an office suite. The buildings were unadorned, well-lighted, and clean. Workers dressed casually in jeans or slacks and T-shirts. There was not a lot of talking in the plant, since the machines were very loud.

Burlington Industries is a textile firm with a long history of production in the southern United States. It was started by textile baron Spencer Love in 1923 in Burlington, North Carolina. The first plant employed 200 people and wove cotton fabric for flags, dresses, and diapers. Love introduced rayon production in 1924, and the firm became a leading producer of rayon fabrics.[32] In 2000, the company did over $1.6 billion in sales and employed nearly 18,000 people. Its operations were spread throughout the United States as well as in India and Mexico.[33] The difficult competitive conditions of the 1990s took their toll, however. In November 2001 Burlington Industries declared Chapter 11 bankruptcy to reorganize its operations, and in January 2002 it closed the Burlmex plant as part of this reorganization.

Burlington was one of those U.S. mills that had moved into Mexico soon after NAFTA opened the doors to the use of Mexican cloth in apparel assembly. Once textile operations were in place, large contractors like Liz Claiborne put pressure on these mills to integrate forward into garment production, either by establishing their own factories or by developing strategic alliances with other firms. As Robert Zane, vice president for manufacturing and sourcing at Liz Claiborne, said, "We have met with the owners of various mills, domestic and foreign, and met with the principals of various apparel manufacturing companies and suggested the concept of getting together with someone on the other side of the supply chain to be able to offer us

31. Aguascalientes State Council for Economic and Trade Development, "Aguascalientes," *Mexico OnLine,* December 2000.

32. Jacqueline Dowd Hall, James Leloudis, Robert Korstad, Mary Murphy, Lu Ann Jones, and Christopher Daly, *Like a Family: The Making of a Southern Cotton Mill World* (New York: Norton, 1987), 246.

33. Burlington.com.

a total package." He continued, "We like the one-vendor concept. It enables the one party to be more responsive. They know exactly what we want to pay for merchandise, and they can look at it from the perspective of fabric as well as manufacturing."[34]

Mill owners expressed some discomfort with this "concept." One executive complained that his firm's entry into the sewing business was being driven by apparel companies that had decided to focus their energies on marketing and design and to reduce their investments in manufacturing. He implied that the apparel companies were divesting themselves of the least lucrative and riskiest parts of the process. Mill owners were also afraid of alienating the apparel firms who were their customers by moving into competition with them.[35] Despite their hesitancy, they were urged on by executives of firms like Liz Claiborne. As a manager responsible for one of that firm's key divisions noted, the shift "may not be profitable in the beginning, but mills need to ask themselves 'do I want to be part of the future?'" This executive spoke critically of Burlington's first moves in the direction of apparel production, noting that the "mill didn't have its own apparel plants at first. They were subcontracting. I could do that myself." Burlington subsequently acquired several plants of its own, including the Burlmex factory in Aguascalientes.[36]

The factory in Aguascalientes produced "fashion" jeans for Liz Claiborne and Calvin Klein as well as more basic jeans for Levi-Strauss and Rocky Mountain. Liz Claiborne used a company based in Mexico City to oversee its operations in the plant. That firm—Aztex Trading—stationed an agent permanently in the factory to oversee operations. Burlmex ran a separate line for each of its contractor firms, with two for Liz Claiborne. Each of these were "small" lines of approximately 50 operators. It also maintained one larger, more traditional line of 150–200 seamstresses. The company employed a little over 1,000 production workers in the year 2000, and approximately 85 percent of those workers were women.

Like Confitek, Burlmex did not require a particular level of schooling or experience for its sewing workers, although it did for those in quality control. Managers said they assigned workers who had experience to more difficult jobs (like attaching waistbands) and specifically to the Liz Claiborne line, where the product was more complicated and control ranges stricter.

34. Scott Malone, "Mills Move to Sewing Machines," *Women's Wear Daily*, April 6, 1999, 12.
35. Ibid, 14.
36. Ibid., 17.

New employees went through a period of mostly on-the-job training. When they achieved 50 percent efficiency at a particular task, they passed to the regular line. Depending on the task, this could take from two to six weeks.

In 2000, Burlmex was in the process of automating its preassembly operations, where pockets, tabs, and other small pieces were attached to larger panels. These had started out as women's jobs, but when managers introduced machines, they hired men to run them. While automation arguably made the work less skilled, those who ran the machines earned higher pay. Managers explained that because the system was new and they were still working out the kinks, they wanted to avoid the "distraction" of mixed gender groups and thus did not offer these jobs to women.

Burlmex made jeans for several of its customers from fabric produced in its mill in Yecapixtla, Morelos. For these jobs, operators cut the fabric in a newly automated cutting room. Liz Claiborne had not approved this fabric for its products, however, so fabric for its jeans arrived already cut from the United States. The cut parts entered the preproduction process just described, then moved on to assembly. As at Confitek, the lines at Burlmex used the progressive bundle system. Workers moved bundles of fifty jean parts from station to station as they completed each task. It took thirty discrete operations to finish each pair of jeans. They hemmed the pants, stitched side seams, attached waistbands, inserted zippers, formed buttonholes, and attached buttons. After assembly, other operators packaged the jeans for shipment to Chihuahua, where Burlington operated a laundry for softening and bleaching them.

Interspersed among the workers assembling jeans were four control stations. These stations were key to statistical process control, the method of quality management that Liz Claiborne required of its contractors. While Claiborne was the only contractor who demanded it, Burlmex had implemented the method on all five of its smaller lines. Statistical process control is different from earlier methods in that it measures the accuracy of sewing rather than the adequacy of the final product. As one manager explained it, "The quality control department is no longer responsible for quality— the operator is." Traditional methods, such as those used at Confitek, examined a sampling of items from each bundle, or from a sampling of bundles, at the end of the line. The stringency of the measures was associated with the size of the sample. Firms with the highest quality standards examined 100 percent of the garments. Under this system, managers sent bundles with defective garments back to operators to be fixed. They calculated operators' efficiency ratios based on how many good bundles they produced as a proportion of their total output.

With statistical process control, sampling was based on time. Every hour, inspectors would examine the garments emerging from every work station. Each was assessed based on several attributes; some were "visual," or qualitatively assessed, and others were "variable," or quantitatively measured. An example of a visual attribute might be whether a seam was puckered. A variable attribute would be the depth of a seam. An inspector at each of the four stations made these measurements and graphed them on a chart. She discussed the results with a line supervisor, who provided feedback to the operator. While the engineers who adapted statistical process control to the requirements of the garment industry had recommended that inspectors sample 40 to 60 percent of the work at each station, managers at Burlmex were not yet comfortable with the system and claimed they still examined every garment.

Every control station prominently displayed each worker's "SPC" chart (fig. 5.2). The managers in charge of quality control calculated limits for each operation by taking the average of twenty-four readings (over twenty-four hours) and calculating a "tolerance range" of 0.01 around that number. They then graphed the operator's hourly performance in relation to these limits (fig. 5.3). If it consistently fell outside the range, the manager would speak to the line operator, who approached the worker about corrective action or took disciplinary measures. Managers emphasized that the charts provided information in a form that was accessible to workers. One said, "Before, the information was very dry, nothing but numbers, or x's to indicate defects that had occurred. But now any person who looks at the graph can understand it without reading numbers or data. It's so easy that everyone can see when there's a problem."

According to managers, statistical process control was an improvement over earlier methods of quality control because it signaled an "unstable situation"—an operation that was being performed outside control limits—and they could correct the problem immediately. They could provide feedback to workers the same hour they made the mistake rather than at the end of the day. In addition, inspectors did not simply review the garment to see if it "looked right" but made and recorded a large number of measurements. Managers described the process as "controlling critical variables" on the line rather than checking garments after the fact. "This statistical process control is making us very preventive in our approach," one said. "If our graphs are bad, we can attack the problem the very next hour." On the back of the SPC chart, the inspector documented the specific corrective

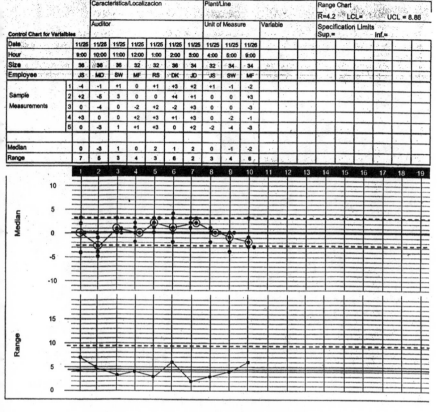

Figure 5.2. Statistical process control chart from Burlmex plant.

actions taken to bring the process into control. At the end of the line, the final inspection station produced summary charts for that line.

At the same time that managers at Burlmex were implementing statistical process control, they were also using a "garment sewing data" system to calculate the time that should be allotted to each operation. This system specified the optimal sequence of movements for each sewing task and the standard allocated minutes it should require. It determined the number of garments an operator needed to process in order to be operating at 100 percent efficiency. Managers said that operators might start a new job at 30 percent efficiency, but they would be expected to reach 100 percent within a few months. For workers at Burlmex, the need to meet the quality standards that were part of statistical process control while simultaneously adhering to standards for speed and efficiency established under the garment sewing data system created tremendous stress on the job.

Figure 5.3. Worker at statistical process control station, Sara Lee International, Colombia (Liz Claiborne subcontractor).

Recruitment, Hours, and Wage Levels at the Plants

Although the Mexican government opened the interior of the country to in-bond plants, or maquiladoras, beginning in the early 1970s, the vast majority of industry remained on the border for years after that. As late as 1987, investors had established only 120 maquiladoras in the "deep" interior of Mexico (defined as nonborder states). About this time, however, firms began what Leslie Sklair has called "the long march to the interior." Labor shortages and rising costs along the border led investors to look seriously at other regions of Mexico. In 1985, while wages in the border region averaged 76¢ an hour, the average for sites in nonborder states was 60¢.[37]

Companies moved to the interior to reduce their wage costs, but also to improve their bargaining position with workers. They believed that the border's tight labor market also contributed to high turnover and absenteeism, since workers assumed they could find another job whenever they wished. Reports of "job hopping" and of workers' playing "musical maquiladoras" had emerged in border states by the late 1980s.[38] In addition, Jefferson Cowie quotes managers in these states who said that workers' produc-

37. Sklair, *Assembling for Development,* 143, 152.
38. Ibid., 142.

tivity dropped and their absenteeism increased after their second year of employment. These managers said they would rather absorb substantial costs of rehiring and retraining than allow wages to rise or workers to acquire "dangerous" levels of commitment to their jobs.[39] In seeking inexperienced workers in less developed labor markets—what have been called "greenfields" labor practices—managers were looking for tractability as well as lower wages.[40]

Aguascalientes' emergence as an export platform for apparel began in the early 1990s, as firms sought new production opportunities in the less costly cities of central Mexico. The town presented the advantages of good transport opportunities, good infrastructure, a location north of Mexico City, and a strong industrial elite that devoted itself to building industrial parks and to accommodating investors. It also combined a resident population of approximately 500,000 with access to a hinterland of small rural communities. By the late 1990s, as the labor market within the city of Aguascalientes itself began to tighten, both Confitek and Burlmex recruited most of their workers from rural areas of the state of Aguascalientes and neighboring Zacatecas.

Both firms recruited workers from villages as far as two hours away, driving trucks with loudspeakers through settlements to advertise good wages and "free dining" and leaving leaflets with local officials and store owners describing employment opportunities. One manager at Burlmex noted that the cost of transporting these workers to and from the plant added significantly to the firm's labor costs. "Many times when there is overtime," he said, the cars leave to take them home at ten o'clock at night, and they live two hours from here, so they arrive at home very late, and nevertheless they have to leave home again extremely early the next day. It costs a lot to cover this transportation." While the cost to the firm was undoubtedly significant, such hours must have also affected the health and well-being of workers. As one worker (a single mother with three children) in a knitwear plant in another region noted, "You have no energy after work. I get home by 6:30, but I have to wake up again at 5:30 in the morning. In the smaller towns, some get home at 8:30 and have to wake up at 3:00 or 4:00 in the morning."[41]

---

39. Jefferson Cowie, *Capital Moves: RCA's Seventy Year Quest for Cheap Labor* (New York: New Press, 1999), 161.

40. Huberto Juárez Núñez, *Rebelión en el Greenfield* (Puebla: Benemérita Universidad Autónoma de Puebla and American Federation of Labor–Congress of Industrial Organizations, 2002).

41. This interview was conducted by Molly McGrath, undergraduate student at the University of Wisconsin, Madison, in Atlixco, Puebla, Mexico, December 2001.

In 2000, the minimum wage in Mexico was about $3.50 a day. A study of the purchasing power of this wage, conducted in three regions of Mexico that same year, found that a family of four would require the minimum wages of four to five workers to meet their most basic needs.[42] Ruth Rosenbaum, the author of this study, developed a purchasing power index based on the costs of food, housing, and other necessities in specific regions. She argued that the minimum wage established by the Mexican government, and widely accepted by maquiladoras as the appropriate wage for workers, did not meet the nutritional needs of workers and their families and would not pay for adequate housing. As one former maquiladora worker associated with the study reported: "In community after community, maquiladora workers can afford only to live in makeshift houses without water or electricity, and even to talk about nutritious diets for themselves and their children is a luxury. . . . They work long, productive hours for the world's biggest corporations and still cannot provide the most basic needs for their families."[43]

While it is difficult to determine wage scales at firms that pay workers by piece rate, most apparel factories in Aguascalientes appear to have set those rates so that a worker of average productivity could earn the legal minimum wage. There is some evidence that factories in a given region, particularly when there is a tight labor market, coordinate their wage scales to slow movement between plants.[44] When workers left the training program organized by the local branch of CANAIVE, for example, their entry-level wage did not vary depending on the enterprise they were sent to. What did vary among firms was the accuracy of their record keeping, their willingness to pay bonus rates for overtime, and their tendency to run up bills for back wages. While, particularly in the 1990s, many transnational firms placed pressure on their subcontractors to adhere to a "code of conduct" in labor relations that had been developed by the U.S. Department of Labor under the Clinton administration, their willingness and capacity to monitor those factories varied tremendously.

If we compare these indicators of prevailing wage standards in the region

42. Ruth Rosenbaum, *Making the Invisible Visible: A Study of the Purchasing Power of Maquila Workers in Mexico* (Hartford, Conn.: Center for Reflection, Education and Action, 2000).

43. Martha Ojeda, quoted in "Landmark Study Shows Mexican Maquila Workers Not Able to Meet Basic Needs on Sweatshop Wages," *Mexican Labor News and Analysis* 6, no. 6 (2001).

44. Cowie, *Capital Moves*, 160; Altha Cravey, "Cowboys and Dinosaurs: Mexican Labor Unionism and the State," in *Organizing the Landscape: Geographical Perspectives on Labor Unionism*, ed. Andrew Herod (Minneapolis: University of Minnesota Press, 1998), 85.

with what companies themselves said they were paying in 1999–2000, the discrepancies are not large. Apparel industry trade publications in that year said that wages of "average line workers" in regions of Mexico outside the border area were "$40 for a forty-eight-hour week." While this figure is a good bit higher than the minimum wage of $3.50 a day, it still amounts to a little over 80¢ an hour, or about half of what Rosenbaum calculates to be an adequate wage.

Factory Discipline and Workplace Relations

If a worker at Confitek or Burlmex wanted to speak to her employer, she would first need to figure out who that was, and this was not a small task. Workers at Confitek, for example, had only an abstract idea that they worked for Tultex Corporation. Tultex, Hanes, and Fruit of the Loom were names on the labels they sewed into garments. From the perspective of workers on the shop floor, shifting labels signified small changes in production protocols: a different set of the sleeve, a plastic versus a metal zipper. It was not immediately clear that these shifts also entailed changing bosses, from a family-managed Virginia knitwear firm (Tultex), to a multinational conglomerate producing thousands of consumer products (Hanes, a division of Sara Lee), to a large but failing knitwear conglomerate (Fruit of the Loom). Workers at Burlmex faced a similar question: Which large U.S.-based multinational was their employer? Was it Burlington Industries, which owned and ran the Aguascalientes plant, or was it Liz Claiborne, which certified its operations, provided fabric, specified the labor process, and branded and sold the product? It was not impossible for workers to trace these relationships, but it required access to information that was not immediately available to them. Rather than engaging in daily face-to-face relations with the firm's owner, a worker had to conduct what amounted to a research project to identify the individuals who had responsibility for conditions of work. As Norma Iglesias Prieto has said, "Workers in the maquiladoras . . . cannot find out for whom they work, the use of the product they manufacture, or the value it might have. These conditions have grave implications for efforts to organize labor and raise worker consciousness."[45]

For the employees of some apparel factories, relations with the owners of subcontracting firms were more face-to-face and personal than those with

45. Norma Iglesias Prieto, *Beautiful Flowers of the Maquiladora: Life Histories of Women Workers in Tijuana* (Austin: University of Texas Press, 1997), 18.

the branded marketer.[46] At Confitek and Burlmex, however, these proprietors were as invisible as the firms that owned the labels. They did not show up on the shop floor and were not involved in the day-to-day affairs of the plant. The highest level of administration workers had access to was the general manager, or *gerente,* of the plant.

In many apparel firms of Mexico or Central America, general managers were expatriates from the United States or East Asia. At both Confitek and Burlmex, however, this position was filled by a Mexican national. General managers occupied a strategic position between the local workforce and the U.S. headquarters. They were intermediaries between speakers of English and speakers of Spanish, and between foreign-born executives schooled in U.S. business practices and Mexican-born managers with local education and training. These managers interacted regularly with executives of the U.S. corporations they produced for, negotiating contracts, planning, and trouble-shooting. They experienced every day the work of translating between two languages, cultures, sets of business practices, and regimes of labor law. When this work was not successful, resulting in misunderstandings or failed expectations, higher-level managers often laid the blame on their shoulders.

While general managers worked to bridge this gulf in corporate culture, there was also a gulf of class and education between them and the workers. Managers at this level were all university educated. As in Martinsville, most were members of elite families. Unlike the situation in Martinsville, however, their relations with workers were unlikely to involve personal acquaintance through church and community organizations. This was in part because Aguascalientes was a much bigger town than Martinsville. It was also partly because the factories recruited workers from such a wide hinterland. In general, higher levels of management did not know workers by name and rarely interacted with them.

Sewing operators did have personal interactions with their line supervisors and auditors. These were positions that a sewing worker could move into once she acquired experience. It was not unusual, therefore, for a seamstress to share kin ties with her line supervisor or inspector or to live in the same neighborhood. Unlike the one-dimensional and arm's-length relations between workers and higher levels of management, these relations combined personal and professional elements and were multistranded.

46. See Caitrin Lynch, "The 'Good Girls' of Sri Lankan Modernity: Moral Orders of Nationalism and Capitalism," *Identities* 6, no. 1 (1999): 55–89, for a description of close relations between owners and workers in a Sri Lankan firm.

Relations among workers themselves were shaped by several factors. Many observers of the Mexican political situation had hoped that the ascendance of the National Action Party (PAN) to national governance in 2000 might open new opportunities for independent workers' organizations.[47] During the period of PRI dominance, two state-sponsored labor federations had dominated the national scene. The Confederation of Mexican Workers (CTM) was formed in 1936 under President Lázaro Cárdenas and grew to be the dominant labor organization in the country. Historians and political scientists have widely perceived the CTM as trading radical demands and democratic governance for strong ties to administration and state subsidies. The Revolutionary Confederation of Workers and Peasants (CROC) was established in 1952 under President Miguel Alemán. While critical of the CTM's servility to the ruling party, the CROC was also strongly allied with the PRI. Both federations secured their survival and strong national presence through loyalty to the state, but at the cost of the ability to act independently in defense of workers' rights.[48]

While opportunities for independent unions appeared to increase with the defeat of the PRI in 2000, the legacy of the old unions was strong, and the prospect of building autonomous organizations where no such tradition existed was daunting. Workers in the apparel sector faced an additional challenge—they were predominantly female. Official unions in Mexico have historically excluded women, and thus women workers did not emerge from the PRI period with much experience in those institutions. In addition, women in Mexico—as in many other parts of the world—face a double day. They return home from work to perform an additional day's work cooking, cleaning, and caring for their families. It is hard for any worker to find time to attend meetings after a ten-hour day, especially if they have a two-hour commute ahead. It becomes even more difficult if one returns home to additional hours of labor. While this is less of an issue for single women, in 1990 over half of Mexico's apparel workers were married.[49]

Despite these obstacles, on a number of occasions women in Mexico's apparel sector have organized themselves into collectives advocating for their rights, though they generally have not worked through the official (and male-dominated) union structure. The Center for the Orienta-

47. "Will Fox Allow Independent Unions in Mexico's Maquilas?" Maquila Solidarity Network Update, December 2001. Maquilasolidarity.org/resources/maquilas/fox_dec2001.htm.

48. James D. Cockcroft, *Mexico's Hope: An Encounter with Politics and History* (New York: Monthly Review Press, 1998); Cowie, *Capital Moves*, 120–21;

49. Carrillo, "Apparel Maquiladora Industry," 223.

tion of Women Workers (COMO) began in 1968 to support women working in the maquiladoras of the northern border, providing educational and consciousness-raising programs and organizing cooperatives as well as encouraging organizing efforts on the shop floor.[50] Drawing together workers from many companies and across sectors of the economy, COMO addressed the special problems of women workers—including health care, domestic violence, the double day, child care concerns, and environmental health issues such as clean water–in ways that traditional unions had not done.[51]

In other examples, workers at Acapulco Fashions in Ciudad Juárez organized a wildcat strike over wages, and they formed an independent union in 1978. But the strike ultimately failed, since the shop simply closed down rather than give in to workers' demands.[52] In the aftermath of the 1985 earthquake in Mexico City, garment workers there organized the independent "Nineteenth of September" union, challenging the CTM for control of unions in garment firms and advocating for autonomous and democratic labor representation.[53] The obstacles to taking independent action have been formidable, however, and such actions have remained exceptional.

The women working at the Burlmex and Confitek factories in Aguascalientes were not members of traditional corporatist unions, nor had they developed their own forms of workers' associations. This may have been due in part to the relatively recent entry of apparel maquiladoras to the region. Garment factories producing for export had begun to move into the region only in the late 1980s and early 1990s, once labor markets along the northern border tightened. Confitek had been open for only four years and Burlmex for one. Another problem for worker organizations was the strength of CANAIVE, the local branch of the National Apparel Industry Chamber of Commerce, which organized and represented the region's apparel factory owners. Like local government, this group took a strong antiunion stance. A third factor making union activity difficult was that factory owners recruited workers from such a broad area. While some workers in the plants lived in municipalities of Aguascalientes, others were from rural communities of the state or from the neighboring state of Zacatecas. This meant that workers did not necessarily live in the same neighborhoods and communities, and it made sharing information and meeting informally outside the

50. Peña, *Terror of the Machine,* chap. 5.

51. Cowie, *Capital Moves,* 157–60.

52. Ibid., 121; Peña, *Terror of the Machine,* 122, 352.

53. Teresa Carrillo, "Women, Trade Unions and New Social Movements in Mexico: The Case of the 'Nineteenth of September' Garment Workers Union" (Ph.D. diss., Stanford University, 1990).

workplace more difficult. It also meant that some workers added four hours in travel time to their day, leaving very little time to eat, sleep, do household chores, and restore themselves before the next working day.

Conditions in the Confitek and Burlmex plants did not differ greatly. Wages, hours, and opportunities for workers to come together and organize were largely the same. The Burlmex plant was larger, its factory was more modern, and a Liz Claiborne agent monitored conditions there. The Confitek plant looked more like the popular image of a sweatshop. But the stress of work at Burlmex—under the newly introduced system of statistical process control—was far greater than at Confitek. The following chapter will present a more detailed comparison of the two plants as well as comparing the Confitek plant with its counterpart in Martinsville, Virginia. It will also examine the way gender shaped the routines and practices of both workplaces.

6

LOCAL LABOR
AND GLOBAL CAPITAL

*It is not regions that interrelate, but the social relations of
production which take place over space.*

—DOREEN MASSEY, *SPATIAL DIVISIONS OF LABOR*[1]

Place, Space, and Power

The globalization that took place in the apparel industry in the 1990s entailed not only a geographic movement but a reorganization of production
relations in and around the workplace. A company that moved production to
Mexico needed to do more than invest $5 million in a factory or $30 million in
the information technologies necessary to manage dispersed facilities. Firms
that made these financial investments also needed to create a social infrastructure that would support their business. They needed to engage local
institutions in order to recruit, control, and reproduce a labor force.

Geographers and other social scientists have on occasion argued that
capitalist firms relate to their sites of operation through a calculus of
profitability, seeing them as one-dimensional locations for realizing certain
purposes. They have suggested that corporations relate to locality as *space,*
whereas workers develop more multidimensional relations to *place,* which

---

1. Doreen Massey, *Spatial Divisions of Labor: Social Structures and the Geography of
Production,* 2d ed. (New York: Routledge, 1995), 118.

they fill up with the institutions of daily life. Huw Beynon and Ray Hudson have argued that space is "a domain across which capital is constantly searching in pursuit of greater profits," while place refers to "the meaningful situations established by labor."[2] Jamie Peck argues even more provocatively that neoliberal policies, by privileging the agendas of capitalist firms, represent "an attempt to reduce place to space."[3]

This formulation contains both a profound insight and a crucial error. The error is to suggest that firms can operate in a purely economic dimension, independent of more multivalent social connections. However fervently neoliberal ideology may try to construe labor relations as purely market transactions, they are always more than that. Labor is always, in Karl Polanyi's words, "a fictive commodity." "It is not produced for sale," Polanyi said. "It is only another name for human activity that goes with life itself."[4] Wherever workers enter into production, they bring with them their needs for subsistence, the needs of their families, their commitments to affairs outside the workplace, and their ideas of what is right and fair. Because of this, in every site where production touches down, it is instantiated differently. It must work through local institutions and establish the necessary web of social relationships to get the job done.

Accounts that refer to capital's use of space and labor's relation to place also contain an important insight, however. They recognize that firms can develop different degrees of connection to their production sites and that those connections can sometimes be quite thin. Reframing the question in this way opens up an area of empirical inquiry. This area includes questions about how different kinds of firms embed themselves differently in local institutions, how their operations are shaped by local culture, and how law and specific forms of economic organization condition different degrees of connection to workers and foster or inhibit the development of strong workplace communities. Setting up the question in this way allows us to view the strategies of firms as existing on a continuum, with production activities that are densely embedded in local social life at one end and thinly constituted, singularly focused, and more ephemeral relations at the other. The continuum runs between localization and deterritorialization, between high-road and low-road employment relations, and between long-term commitment and the short-term outlook of fly-by-night firms.

2. Huw Beynon and Ray Hudson, "Place and Space in Contemporary Europe: Some Lessons and Reflections," *Antipode* 25, no. 3 (1993): 182.

3. Jamie Peck, *Work-Place: The Social Regulation of Labor Markets* (New York: Guilford Press, 1996), 238.

4. Karl Polanyi, *The Great Transformation* (New York: Rinehart, 1944), 72.

In considering the localization decisions of companies like Liz Claiborne and Tultex, three arenas emerge as especially important. These are not simply domains of corporate decision making but are arenas of struggle, as workers confront the arrangements that arise from corporate plans. The first is the workplace itself, where firms craft production practices, with attendant expectations of skill and knowledge. In doing so, they make "human relations" decisions about the duration and solidity of the employment relation and about relations of hierarchy and control within the factory. A second arena is the web of relations between the firm and the communities where their workers live. It includes the firm's decisions about social investments, its labor recruitment practices, and the way it is regulated by, or circumvents, local political structures and laws. A third set of questions concerns the firm's contribution to the social reproduction of the workforce. This arena encompasses not only the issue of a living wage but also the ways workers make ends meet in the absence of that wage—the community-based livelihood strategies that subsidize poorly paid factory work and make it possible. Each of these arenas is a site of profound contradictions, and all are permeated by gender.

The three sections that follow draw on the cases of Tultex and Liz Claiborne and on production practices in Martinsville and Aguascalientes to address each of these questions about localization and deterritorialization. They examine differences in the ways the two case study firms have structured relations within the workplace; the distinct kinds of social relations Tultex developed in the communities surrounding its plants in the United States and Mexico; and the ways both firms relied on subsidies from the local economy to reproduce their labor force. The picture that emerges from these contrasts is one where firms have deliberately minimized their investments in what David Harvey calls the social infrastructure of production, while workers have sought to expand the sphere of corporate responsibility—that is, where deterritorialized production practices have ironically become a "site" of struggle. The story is also one of gender conflict, as firms seek to construct a workforce around traditional expectations about women workers, while the experience of these women inside and outside the factory leads them to develop new forms of resistance.

Reinventing Taylorism in Mexico: Manufacturing Fashion and Commodity Apparel

Theorists of labor market segmentation have raised important questions about the kinds of investments firms make in the production process and in workers. Writing in the 1970s and 1980s, they distinguished what they called primary- and secondary-sector firms. In the primary sector, firms offered high wages and secure employment to workers with whom they expected to have a long-term relationship. In the secondary sector, smaller, less-capitalized firms offered lower wages and poorer working conditions to a less privileged segment of the workforce.[5] By the 1990s these distinctions had begun to look somewhat antiquated. As all firms sought to enhance their flexibility by casualizing employment relations, the features that had distinguished a primary sector eroded. The vocabulary for referring to these corporate strategies also changed. Analysts began to speak of "flexible specialization" as a kind of high-road flexibility that involved training and retraining workers and using their creative input and multiple skills to meet rapidly changing product requirements and the demand for just-in-time production. Firms that continued to combine routinized, low-skilled work with low pay and insecure employment contracts were characterized as employing low-road strategies.

As we have seen, many commentators have argued that when garment orders need to be turned around quickly in response to changing fashion cycles, or when the products need to be of high quality, traditional mass production methods are inadequate to the task, and some authors have claimed it is difficult for U.S. companies to produce these garments "offshore." The theory behind these predictions is that short runs of high-quality goods require skilled workers—that they can best be managed by recombining mental and manual labor. With the growth of the mass market for apparel in the late nineteenth century, the creative work of the tailor's shop gave way to mass production methods like the progressive bundle system. Except—these accounts claim—for production at the top of the fashion pyramid. For these goods, perhaps not single tailors but teams of workers operating according to the principles of flexible specialization will continue to construct whole garments with patience and care.

This vision of the structure of the industry and its implications for jobs has been widely disseminated and adopted by the popular press, and in particular by U.S. communities seeking to respond to the loss of apparel jobs that they associate with NAFTA. In its more general form, this argument implies that the superior skills of U.S. workers will keep certain jobs in the country. This is a proposition that analysts like William Greider have questioned, noting the dissemination of skilled and high-tech jobs, as well

---

5. Richard Edwards, *Contested Terrain* (New York: Basic Books, 1979).

as simple assembly jobs, throughout the world.[6] It is an argument that is also belied by the rapid shift of production of high-end fashion merchandise to the developing world in the 1990s and by the presence, in a single Mexican town, of factories producing sweatshirts for Tultex and designer clothing for Liz Claiborne.

Comparing the shop floor conditions at Confitek and Burlmex reveals important parallels and divergences in workers' experiences. In terms of its layout, lighting, and cleanliness, Burlmex—the factory that subcontracted for Liz Claiborne—was undeniably a more pleasant place to work (fig. 6.1). And because of the emphasis Liz Claiborne placed on adherence to a corporate code of conduct for labor relations and the constant presence of that firm's agent in the plant, it was less likely to violate labor law. With regard to the organization of the labor process, however, there were surprisingly few differences between the firms. Both relied on the progressive bundle system to direct the flow of materials through the plant. Neither had instituted modular production or other forms of workplace organization that claim to use workers' skills and expertise more intensively. With the exception of the automated preassembly section at Burlmex, the machines workers used were fundamentally the same.

The idea that production for the bottom and top of the "fashion pyramid" would have to be organized in radically different ways was contradicted by this basic similarity. Workers at Burlmex received no more training and were asked to demonstrate no greater array of skills than those at Confitek, even though they were working on more intricate garments. They used the same technology to assemble clothing in the same methodical and repetitive way that workers have done since the late nineteenth century. The only significant difference in the work organization of the two plants was in supervisors' control over the operations and the scrutiny that work received. As described earlier, the pace and intensity of the work at Burlmex were shaped by the firm's use of statistical process control.

Both companies paid workers by piece rate based on the number of tickets they accumulated for bundles completed during the day. At Burlmex, however, in addition to trying to sew as quickly as possible, workers were concerned to keep their operations within a "control range." While piece rates have always measured the productivity of apparel workers, the graphs of statistical process control made it possible to attach new numbers to the

---

6. William Greider, *One World, Ready or Not: The Manic Logic of Global Capitalism* (New York: Simon and Schuster, 1997), 20.

Figure 6.1. Burlmex plant, Aguascalientes, Mexico.

quality of the work. Making quota thus became a more complex task, requiring the worker to manage two variables at the same time.

From their corporate offices in New Jersey, Liz Claiborne managers described statistical process control as "a method, or tool, for continually monitoring a process and reacting to situations that create instability in that process." It requires inspectors to measure quality in a statistical sampling of garments as they come off a particular operation, hour by hour. At stations near the critical operations, the inspectors

> visually check a garment's appearance and measure the garment's critical points, such as pocket placement, to determine whether the operation was performed within upper and lower control limits. . . . Calculating the level of variance between the target specification measurement and the measurement taken of the in-process garment, the inspector then plots his or her findings. Upon noticing variances away from the control limits, or a consistent trend toward out-of-control work, the inspector works with the line supervisor and the operator to identify the cause of the problem.[7]

On the shop floor in Aguascalientes, this meant that workers not only performed repetitive tasks as quickly as they could, but they learned to sew seams and attach pockets within a tolerance range of 0.01. As styles changed—the innovation that was frustrating workers in March 2000 was a new kind of elastic waistband—workers had to quickly bring themselves

7. Kathleen DesMarteau, "Liz Launches Global Quality Coup," *Bobbin*, July 1999, 34–38.

up to expected speed and accuracy levels. This created stress levels far higher than at the Confitek plant.

In contrast to theory, then, the quality of the Liz Claiborne merchandise produced in Aguascalientes was not achieved by tapping the skills and creativity of "tailorlike" workers or by organizing the production process on "making-through" principles. Instead, quality was "controlled in" through intensive supervision. Managers measured production values that were formerly unmeasurable and held workers to more difficult standards than any imposed in the industry to date. Quality was achieved not by developing workers' skills, but by intensifying control.[8]

The production regime at Burlmex thus represented a deepening and extension of Frederick Taylor's principles of scientific management, promulgated in the early years of the twentieth century. In searching for and enforcing the "one best way" to perform tasks, Taylorism extended managerial control and permitted the speedup of work.[9] While it has been argued that firms in the United States, Western Europe, and Japan moved away from such highly standardized work regimes in the late twentieth century, they were being reinvented in many contexts in the developing world. Alain Lipietz has referred to this as "primitive Taylorization" and characterizes it as a nineteenth-century solution to twentieth- and twenty-first-century problems.[10]

Statistical process control has been widely disseminated in the manufacture of products as diverse as small appliances, telecommunications equipment, computer components, and silicon chips. The machines that workers in electronics factories use to produce components often measure the variance of critical processes from one item to another. Statistical process control charts are thus generated for each worker automatically and can be read by managers in their offices.[11] In the high-end apparel industry of the 1990s, inspectors made these measurements manually and charted them with colored markers, but the idea that quality could be controlled in by monitoring and disciplining workers rather than by relying on their creativity and skill was the same.

As scholars analyzing transitions in work have argued, a labor process cannot be examined in isolation from its larger political context. In addition

8. Jane L. Collins, "Flexible Specialization and the Garment Industry," *Competition and Change* 5, no. 2 (2001): 165–200.

9. John Tomaney, "A New Paradigm of Work Organization and Technology?" in *Post-Fordism: A Reader,* ed. Ash Amin (Cambridge: Blackwell, 1994), 158.

10. Alain Lipietz, *Mirages and Miracles* (London: Verso, 1987), 74–78.

11. Business Week, "Brave New Factory," July 23, 2001, 75–78; Steven C. McKay, "Securing Commitment in an Insecure World: Power and the Social Regulation of Labor in the Philippine Electronics Industry" (Ph.D. diss., University of Wisconsin, 2001).

to being shaped by technology, quality requirements, and scheduling demands, it will reflect both state policies regulating work and the balance of power between management and labor. Daniel Leborgne and Alain Lipietz have predicted that new Taylorist labor processes will emerge where unions and state regulation are weak.[12] As the manufacturing of fashion apparel moves into new parts of the world, managers innovate to find new ways to produce high-quality goods in a timely fashion. While such goods *can* be produced through small teams of multiskilled workers, their production can also be organized through piece rate payment, intensive surveillance, and direct control. In the absence of state regulation or strong and organized labor movements, there is little to prevent firms from choosing this low road.

What Leborgne and Lipietz do not address is the way gender shapes the dissemination of Taylorist work regimes. Just as women have always been overrepresented in the secondary sector, they are more likely to find employment in factories that adopt the low-road strategies of the new economy. But more to the point, the reinvention of Taylorism in developing nations presupposes a female workforce. Workers do not easily tolerate the combination of tedium and stress and the practices of direct control that are at issue here. As so many feminist ethnographers have shown, factory owners in many settings buy into and reproduce the idea that women are more docile and compliant and thus more appropriate workers for these conditions. It is not coincidence, but gendered power relations, that leads managers to institute practices like statistical process control in areas where a largely female workforce is available.

Teamwork and multiskilling require a long-term relationship with individual workers, entailing opportunities for training and advancement, attainment of seniority, and provision of benefits. Surveillance-based measures are built on an expectation of high worker turnover, since individuals are highly replaceable within the framework of monitoring and control. This kind of system makes no provision for advancement or retraining, does not reward seniority, and offers only the legally mandated minimum of benefits. Indeed, as some observers have noted, such systems *generate* high turnover because of the levels of stress created by constant monitoring and piece rate production.

Technology and forms of work organization are not dictated by competitive pressures. They can vary greatly from one place to another, and even

12. D. Leborgne and Alain Lipietz, "New Technologies, New Modes of Regulation: Some Spatial Implications," *Environment and Planning, D: Society and Space* 6 (1988): 263–80.

from one firm to another, and still allow companies using diverse strategies to achieve the average rate of profit within the industry. As David Harvey has said, "There are more ways to make a profit than to skin a cat."[13] In the 1990s, with global competition driving deflation in apparel prices and information and telecommunications technologies facilitating the organization of global production regimes, few apparel firms were opting for high-road approaches. Statistical process control provided an alternative means to attain high-quality production—one that did not require long-term investments in workers but tapped the skills of female workers under a new Taylorist work regime.

Subcontracting as Deterritorialization: Tultex in the United States and Mexico

Firms do not invest only in the workplace itself. They must also build what Harvey has called "the social infrastructure which supports life and work."[14] Transnational corporations must develop ways to operate within the political and legal context of each nation where they produce. They must recruit workers in regional labor markets and function within the norms and practices of local communities. They make a multitude of decisions in constructing this social infrastructure. They may choose to relocate their managers from headquarters or to hire local personnel, and each choice has different implications for relations with workers. They may house workers on their premises, as in some export processing zones, or they may transport them daily from distant communities. They can invest in day care, open an infirmary, and provide meals in a cafeteria, or they can leave workers to obtain these services on their own. These choices are often influenced by what goes on in the broader labor market. In both Martinsville and Aguascalientes, employers came together in formal and informal associations to decide what benefits they would offer workers in addition to the going wage. Each of these choices makes the tie between worker and employer multistranded and more complex or thinner and more unidimensional. Each alters the sense of commitment and engagement on both sides, as well as the working definition of what is right and fair.

As Harvey has pointed out, however, the social infrastructure that evolves around a production site is not "a mirror reflection of capital's needs, but the locus of powerful and potentially disruptive contradic-

13. David Harvey, *The Limits to Capital* (New York: Verso, 1999), 116.
14. Harvey, *Limits to Capital,* 98.

tions."[15] Dense and multistranded connections between the firm and its workers generate loyalty; they may also inhibit workers' freedom to resist by putting in jeopardy not only their wages but also their housing or other basic needs. Workers with fragile relationships to individual firms may feel free to move from job to job but may have no other defense against unfair treatment. They may experience their employer as little more than a shadowy presence and find their ties to other workers short-lived. Localized and deterritorialized relations to community and region create very different constraints and opportunities for workers and give rise to different forms of resistance.

Comparing the Tultex Corporation's relations with its workers in Virginia and those it established with subcontracted workers in Mexico requires a full appreciation of the contradictory nature of paternalism. The paternalist labor practices that Tultex had fostered in its Virginia plant were complicated in their implications for workers. Although Martinsville, Virginia, was not "owned" in the same way that pre-1930s mill villages had been, the economists at the Virginia Employment Commission in the 1990s continued to call it a "company town" because of the way a single firm dominated its economy.[16] As historians of paternalism in the industrial South have argued, the system was premised on a balance of consent and force. The firm's public face of largesse, its cultivation of a sense of personal connection between workers and owners, and its provision of occasional assistance and favors were balanced by a lack of options for workers to participate in decision making of any kind and their commitment to support the owners by making concessions when asked. If the paternalist relations between workers and owners in mill towns represent a kind of social capital, Michael Schulman and Cynthia Anderson have argued that they are its "dark side."[17]

However complex and contradictory the nexus of relationships in which Tultex's Martinsville employees found themselves in the period before the plants closed down, it was quite different from the relations that governed Tultex's transnational production. Specifying these differences is difficult because Mexican workers were separated from the company's owners and managers both by space and by layers of subcontracting. These arrangements challenge many of our ideas about what social relationships and community mean. They require us to recognize relationships where the two

15. Ibid., 403.

16. Page Boinest Melton, "How Global Trade and NAFTA Hit a Vital Virginia Business," *Virginia Business,* August 2000.

17. Michael D. Schulman and Cynthia Anderson, "The Dark Side of the Force: A Case Study of Restructuring and Social Capital," *Rural Sociology* 64, no. 3 (1999): 355.

parties involved may not know each other—may not even know of each other. They force us to recognize geographically dispersed communities of workers whose fates are linked to the success or failure of a single firm.

The practice of subcontracting shapes the labor relations of the apparel industry in many ways. Contract shop owners serve as intermediaries between branded manufacturers and workers and organize the labor process on behalf of "absentee" apparel firms. In reality, there are often several "layers" of subcontracting involved. When Confitek and Burlmex had more orders than they could handle, their owners would contract with smaller shops in the region. Or as in the case of Liz Claiborne's East Asian operations, headquarters would contract with Fang Brothers, who might offer to produce the garments in a factory they owned or might contract with shops they knew in Indonesia, Malaysia, or the Philippines. In these cases, several layers of bureaucracy (and profit taking) separated workers from their "true" employers.

Edna Bonacich and Richard Appelbaum argue that practices of subcontracting benefit apparel firms in several ways. First, they externalize risk, allowing the company to expand and contract production without maintaining the operations necessary to do so. When demand slackens, it is the contractor—not the lead firm—that must lay off workers and bear the cost of an idle factory. Second, subcontracting lowers the cost of labor because contractors must bid for jobs. "Each attempts to offer the manufacturer a better deal than the next guy can, bidding down the price of labor." Third, these authors suggest that contracting inhibits union organizing. Manufacturers can simply refuse to do business with unionized shops, at no cost to themselves. "Contractors can truthfully tell their workers," they argue, "that if they unionize, their shop will be boycotted . . . and will not receive the work it needs to remain in business." In addition, the financial constraints faced by contractors trying to make low bids for jobs make them notoriously hostile to union activity.[18]

Bonacich and Appelbaum also note that manufacturers rely on subcontracting to shield themselves from legal responsibility for labor conditions in the plants where their goods are produced. The issues surrounding legal responsibility are complex and are under contest in the courts of several nations. In the United States, the standard used for determining the employer of record varies according to the purpose of the determination. Courts use different standards, for example, to define an employer under

---

18. Edna Bonacich and Richard Appelbaum, *Behind the Label: Inequality in the Los Angeles Apparel Industry* (Berkeley: University of California Press, 2000), 136–39.

the Fair Labor Standards Act, under the Americans with Disabilities Act, for Social Security purposes, for workers' compensation, and so forth. Existing law applies a variety of tests that examine such factors as who owns the property and the materials on which the work is performed, who has the discretion to hire and fire, and who bears the losses for unsatisfactory merchandise.[19]

Apparel manufacturers were shocked in 1999 when a U.S. district court for southern New York found an apparel manufacturer jointly liable for its contractor's failure to pay overtime to employees. The trade press noted that the decision "dramatically impacts the core structure of the garment industry's traditional contracting system—whereby manufacturers or jobbers are relieved of any direct responsibility for their contractors' production employees, and any liability for violations of labor standards is generally assumed by the contractor."[20] This analyst noted that "the decision comes at a time when contracting is playing an increasingly important role in the apparel supply chain, as more manufacturers seek to streamline overhead, gain seasonal flexibility, and focus more on functions such as marketing and customer service, without the burden of managing their own manufacturing operations."[21]

In the United States, several states have sought to define their own more stringent standards for manufacturers' responsibility. In 1996 the state of New York passed a "hot goods law" that allowed the state's attorney general to prosecute the shipment, sale, or purchase of goods produced by firms that failed to adhere to state wage and hour laws.[22] The attorney general was able to use this measure to prevent manufacturers from shipping goods produced by subcontractors found to be in violation of labor law.[23] In 1998 the state of New York also passed a joint liability law (AO 6685) that held manufacturers and their contractors jointly responsible for back wages. Using this law, the state commissioner of labor could require firms with a

19. The three tests of employment relationship used in 2000 were the "common law control" test, the "economic reality/economic dependency test," and the "suffer or permit to work" test. See Bruce Goldstein, Marc Linder, Laurence E. Norton II, and Catherine K. Ruckelshaus, "Enforcing Fair Labor Standards in the Modern American Sweatshop: Rediscovering the Statutory Definition of Employment," *University of California at Los Angeles Law Review* 46, no. 4 (1999): 983–1164.

20. Alan Rolnick, "Labor Law Liability: Where Does the Buck Stop? Lopez Case Shakes U.S. Manufacturer-Contractor Paradigm," *Bobbin*, April 1999, 64.

21. Ibid.

22. New York State, Office of the Governor, Press Release: Governor Signs Law Adding Another Tool to Fight Sweatshops, August 10, 1998.

23. New York State, Office of the Attorney General, Press Release: Garment Manufacturers Cited under "Hot Goods Law," July 19, 1998.

history of violating wage laws to post up to $50,000 bond to ensure that workers' wages would be paid.[24]

Similarly, in 1999 the California state assembly passed a bill (AB 633) making manufacturers liable for labor law violations committed by their subcontractors. The law was designed to hold manufacturers responsible for paying wages if the contractor could not. The assembly passed the bill on a wave of concern over the proliferation of sweatshops in the state. But strong lobbying from the West Coast fashion industry subverted the bill's original goals. The legislation entered a year-long regulatory process in which the state labor commissioner determined how it should be applied. It emerged with draft regulations saying that for manufacturers to be held liable, they must "purchase the piece goods, own them through the manufacturing process and convert them into finished product." Under this narrow definition, few if any manufacturers faced liability. Labor organizations, which had worked hard to support passage of the original bill, were frustrated and angered by this unintended outcome.[25]

The measures available to hold apparel firms legally responsible for the conditions their workers experienced were thus complex and contested, even when all parties operated within the United States.[26] No such remedies were available where subcontractors produced abroad. Although labor groups had pressed for side agreements to NAFTA that might have created such a framework, the provisions that were added provided few if any protections.[27] Thus workers in plants like Confitek and Burlmex could make no legal claims on the firms whose labels they stitched into garments.

If we compare the relationship between employers and workers at the Confitek plant with those in Martinsville in the era of the union, it is clear that at Confitek there were no established practices by which workers could govern themselves. There were no grievance procedures, no contract, and no institutions through which they could come together to discuss their situation and take action. Within the context of the plant in Aguascalientes, prospects for a union were dimmed by the concerted opposition of local industrialists. Workers and managers had not developed a common language

24. New York State, Office of the Governor, Press Release.

25. Kristi Ellis and Kristin Young, "Who Pays? Liability Debate Rages On," *Women's Wear Daily*, January 29, 2001, 18–19.

26. This included its territories and protectorates. In 1999, lawsuits were brought against manufacturers whose subcontractors violated U.S. labor law in Saipan, Northern Mariana Islands.

27. Jefferson Cowie and John D. French, "NAFTA's Labor Side Accord: A Textual Analysis," *Latin American Labor News* 9 (1993-94): 5–8.

and set of expectations with regard to workplace fairness. Given that the turnover rates of the workforce were as high as 100 percent annually,[28] and given the tenuous nature of subcontracting commitments, it was not clear that they would do so.

Even if we look back to the preunion era at Tultex, however—to the times of paternalism and "management by personal appearance"—workers' ability to make claims on their employers was stronger than at the Confitek plant. While it bound workers to an agenda and a set of rules wholly determined by factory owners, paternalism could be understood as a kind of moral economy within which workers could declare certain acts unfair; it provided an agreed-on language to express their complaints.

Contracting relationships make it difficult for workers to know and make claims on the corporations they produce for, but they may also find it difficult to engage in interactions with the owners and managers of the factory sites where they work. This is especially true when those managers are expatriates, but it may also be true when supervisors are required to conform to an externally imposed set of rules and regulations and are discouraged from interacting face-to-face with workers in the plant. Melissa Wright has documented a case in which maquiladora workers in northern Mexico waged a slowdown to demand that a particular line supervisor be promoted to production manager in their plant. This woman knew all the workers, the neighborhoods they came from, their class background, family status, and reputation. Wright notes that she had developed an elaborate social network of insiders and outsiders and a strong patronage system extending "through the supervisors to the section leaders and down to the operators." She used this system "to oust rivals to her authority at all levels."[29] To workers she had confidence in, this manager would give days off when they were ill, advances on their wages, or even personal loans. She summarily fired workers who were disloyal or caused her trouble. When management passed her over for promotion and gave the position to a much less engaged and less accessible Mexican man, the entire shop stopped working in protest. This altercation was not so much about the personality of an individual supervisor as about the workers' desire to interact with the people who made the rules and controlled their fate. In an employment situation where there was so little accountability, they struggled to maintain a point of access.

28. Mercedes Cortázar, "El pulso de la industria: Alianzas progresistas en Aguascalientes," *La Bobina,* August 2001.

29. Melissa Wright, "Crossing the Factory Frontier: Gender, Place and Power in the Mexican *Maquiladora,*" *Antipode* 29, no. 3 1997): 289.

Saskia Sassen, Aihwa Ong, and others have written of the dilemmas of deterritorialization that immigrant workers face as they change locations within the global economy.[30] It seems straightforward to think of workers who move as experiencing disruptions of cultural and social networks. But concepts of deterritorialization are also relevant to understanding the experiences of workers in developing nations who are employed by transnational firms. Although the workers themselves do not move, the mobility of firms, and their construction of radically deracinated production processes, creates new kinds of relations between workers and their employers.[31]

What happens to moral economies of work and their rhetorical frameworks when the labor market in question becomes global, and when employers and workers are broadly separated by geographic space and layers of subcontracting? When Tultex began subcontracting its sewing operations in Mexico, it had no ties to the communities where these new workers lived. Corporate executives knew little about the town where production took place and less still about its workers. In addition, they had no legal responsibility, in the courts of Mexico or the United States, for working conditions. In these circumstances, firms made headway toward the neoliberal goal of reducing employment to a simple labor market transaction in which their responsibilities began and ended at the factory door.

Workers have contested such deterritorialization in ways that reveal its gendered dimensions, and particularly the rigid lines its practices draw between public and private. When the firm construes its circle of responsibility narrowly, it declares many domains of life to be the private responsibility of workers or, alternatively, the burden of the Mexican state. But many workers live in communities where factory effluents (from processes like bleaching denim) spoil the water supply. They carry home in their bodies the effects of exposure to glues and lint and the eyestrain from detail work in poor lighting. And they the face the struggle to feed children on inadequate wages. The women's organizations that have sprung up around the maquiladoras—discussed later in this chapter—have challenged the idea that what happens in the factory is separate from what happens in the community and that the company's responsibility does not extend beyond the factory gate.

Male-dominated unions have historically given health, reproductive free-

30. Aihwa Ong, *Flexible Citizenship: The Cultural Logics of Transnationality* (Durham, N.C.: Duke University Press, 1999); Saskia Sassen, *Globalization and Its Discontents: Essays on the New Mobility of People and Money* (New York: New Press, 1998).

31. Jane L. Collins, "Deterritorialization and Workplace Culture," *American Ethnologist* 29, no. 1 (2002): 151–71.

dom, and environmental concerns short shrift, preferring to focus on "traditional" workplace issues such as wages. But women's organizations have argued that corporations' production practices affect all these areas, and they have tried to hold firms accountable. While older models of community unionism have sought to establish *alliances* between labor and community groups, these new organizations recognize that factory workers are *the same people* who live in communities and that activism can spill over from one site to the other. In addressing this expanded set of issues, organizations of women workers have sought to construct a new discursive framework. They have insisted that workers have bodies, and that these bodies are sometimes female. They have challenged traditional notions of public and private and new neoliberal projects to reinscribe them. And they have demanded an expanded sphere of corporate responsibility at a time when corporations themselves are trying to shrink it.

Deterritorialization is not an inevitable part of globalization. It is always in tension with its opposite—tendencies to localize, to draw on locally specific labor market advantages, to embed production in local networks. As discussed earlier, there is a continuum between localization and deterritorialization, along which we can locate the strategies of transnational firms. These strategies are shaped not simply by the administrative decisions of firms themselves, but also by the laws and policies of host nations and regions. In Sri Lanka, for example, Caitrin Lynch has described the ways a government initiative called the "Two Hundred Garment Factories Program" influenced the labor practices of apparel factories in the 1990s. This program, which the government developed in response to a period of rural unrest, encouraged investors to provide social services to workers. The government used tax breaks and other financial incentives to shape investors' behavior in ways that served its development goals.[32] The Mexican context contrasts sharply with this situation. In Mexico, the ability of the state or regional government to require such investments, or to regulate the behavior of firms beyond existing labor law, is severely limited by NAFTA. Under NAFTA's Chapter 11, foreign investors from Canada, Mexico, and the United States can sue a national government if their assets, including expected profits, are damaged by laws or regulations.[33]

32. Caitrin Lynch, "Thy 'Good Girls' of Sri Lankan Modernity: Moral Orders of Nationalism, Gender, and Globalization in Village Garment Factories" (Ph.D. diss., University of Chicago, 2000).

33. William Greider, "The Right and U.S. Trade Law: Invalidating the Twentieth Century," *Nation* 273, no. 11 2001): 21. Since 1997, a number of cases have been filed with the tribunals established under NAFTA to arbitrate such claims.

If the owners of a subcontracted factory have close ties to the regions where they operate, they are more likely to adhere to locally grounded ways of doing business. In his research with electronics firms operating in free trade zones of the Philippines, Steven McKay found that companies managed by local entrepreneurs tapped long-standing patronage networks to recruit new women workers from rural communities. These firms authorized officials from rural areas to conduct preliminary interviews with young women and to make lists of those eligible to work. It also relied on them to "guarantee" the workers' behavior, thus creating dense networks of responsibility and control. These practices were very different from those McKay observed among more transnationally oriented firms.[34]

Managers at both Confitek and Burlmex used the kin networks of existing workers to recruit new employees from local villages. Upper-tier managers relied on the social networks of line managers to enhance their capacity for shop floor control–relying on them to know the difference between "troublemakers" and workers in whom they could have confidence, and allowing them to grant favors in return for loyalty. But in the context of their subcontracting relationships and the neoliberal deregulation fostered by NAFTA, the opportunities for such embedding and localization were simply not large.

When large apparel firms choose where they will "source" their goods, they do not do so blindly or randomly. They make these decisions with regard to quota availability, transport costs, the cost of labor, how quickly an order can be filled, and the capabilities associated with particular factories. They are able to draw advantage from locality without "locating" there to any significant degree. Even where state policy supports local investments and transnational firms tap local business practices, subcontracting diminishes the investments firms make in locations where they have factories. It tends to reduce multidimensional employment contracts to singledstranded wage transactions, to minimize long-term commitments, to keep labor a truly "variable" cost, and to enhance the flexibility of the firm at the expense of the security of workers.

At the same time, the firm's ability to pick and choose among contracting factories provides an additional tool—the hegemonic despotism Michael Burawoy has written about.[35] The threat that the manufacturer will choose another locale is ever present—always lurking as the consequence that will follow from asking for higher wages or voting for a union. While firms seek

---

34. McKay, "Securing Commitment in an Insecure World."
35. Michael Burawoy, *The Politics of Production* (London: Verso, 1985).

competitive advantage through their spatial decision making, their ability to choose so costlessly throws workers into competition as well. They compete not just against their peers in a local labor market but against workers in other locations, whose currency may be weaker against the dollar, whose labor laws may be less strict, or whose minimum wage is lower.

Contrasting Tultex's operations in the Confitek plant with its factory in Martinsville suggests that spatially dispersed production regimes and casual bonds between employers and workers make it difficult for local conventions and practices to structure and regulate employment. They make it hard for moral economies of work to come into play. It is perhaps ironic that both the fraught conventions of paternalism and the bonds of unionism rely on dense networks within a place. As workers at Tultex moved from one to the other they had the advantage of operating within a densely articulated and shared social space. Both factory regimes required more durable connections than current global sourcing patterns provide.

The practices that constitute localization and deterritorialization are sites of struggle. We saw one example when the workers Wright describes fought to retain a manager and the clientelistic work culture she fostered. In these struggles, workers sometimes seek points of access and leverage, preferring "negative social capital" to no access. In these cases we are in the realm of Marx's dilemma when he observed that the Indian village life uprooted by British colonialism was no bed of roses.[36] The women's organizations that operate in many areas of Central America and Mexico have asked if another path is possible—one that is preferable to both of these alternatives. Outside the narrowly circumscribed agendas of traditional unions, they have worked to expose the many ways that corporations draw subsidies from and affect the regions where they locate, and to construct new moral economic frameworks within which they can hold firms accountable.

Social Reproduction in a Global Labor Market

The kind of relationship a firm establishes with its production site has implications for the social reproduction of the workforce. Part of what has been called the Fordist bargain, struck in the United States in the mid-twentieth century, established that workers should be paid enough for their families to live on. The wage was supposed to be sufficient to allow them to educate

---

36. Karl Marx, "The British Rule in India: Surveys from Exile," in *Political Writings* (London: Penguin, 1973), 2:306–7; Michael Hardt and Antonio Negri, *Empire* (Cambridge: Harvard University Press), 2000, 119.

their children and to purchase the consumer goods they themselves produced in the factory. As Peck has noted, in transnational production regimes "the ties that under the Keynesian welfare state bound the reproduction of labor power to the medium-term profitability of capital within national spaces" have been broken.[37] Mexican auto workers will never be able to buy the Volkswagens and GM Suburbans they manufacture. But more poignantly, the apparel workers who sew a hundred pairs of $100 jeans a day will never be able to afford a single pair.[38]

The question is even more dire, however, than whether workers in new zones of apparel production can constitute a market for certain kinds of consumer goods. Mexico is a relatively high-wage area for transnational firms compared with China or Bangladesh. But studies of wage levels among maquiladora workers show that the minimum wage paid in Mexico falls far short of meeting a family's needs.[39] According to the most comprehensive survey of the relation between wage levels and cost of living, conducted in fifteen sites in Mexico, most maquiladora workers were forced to make decisions about whether to pay rent or buy food and were not able to provide adequately for their families. The money they earned from maquiladora work was far from what this study called a "sustainable living wage"—one that meets the basic needs of a family, enables them to participate in culturally required activities, and lets them set aside a small savings. While most workers received the legal minimum wage plus some bonuses, most took home less than 30 percent of the income required to meet basic needs.

Workers at apparel factories like Confitek and Burlmex, like their peers throughout the world, live and restore themselves in households and communities. It is through the social relations of these family and community networks that they find care for their children while they work and are cared for themselves when they are sick. It is through these networks that they pool resources in ways that allow them to afford housing, food, and other necessities. These relationships sustain workers and reproduce the labor force.

When branded marketers of apparel subcontract their production in the developing world, they tap the resources of these communities. By paying less than a living wage, they require them to supplement and subsidize the

---

37. Peck, *Work-Place,* 237.

38. Huberto Juárez Núñez, *Rebelión en el Greenfield* (Puebla: Benemérita Universidad Autónoma de Puebla and American Federation of Labor–Congress of Industrial Organizations, 2002).

39. Ruth Rosenbaum, *Making the Invisible Visible: A Study of the Purchasing Power of Maquila Workers in Mexico* (Hartford, Conn.: Center for Reflection, Education and Action, 2000).

work that is done in the factory.[40] This is the secret of the low-cost labor of the developing world—that families where wage earners make so little sustain themselves by putting together a range of other kinds of income: the wages of additional family members, transactions in the informal economy, rent, transfers, and a range of self-provisioning activities.[41]

Maquiladora workers deal with the inadequacy of the wage in a variety of ways. Huberto Juárez Núñez has noted that when transnational industry moved into the Mexican interior in the 1990s, it tended to prefer zones where out-migration to the United States was high.[42] The factories employed family members of migrants—those who remained at home. In other words, labor migration and maquiladora work became, for many families, part of an intertwined strategy of social reproduction, made necessary by the insufficiency of the wage paid by factories. Migration is not an option for every household, and certainly not for single mothers. But for all apparel workers, the factory wage must be combined with income from other sources, including the earnings of other family members or the sale of goods and services in the informal economy.

The contradictions of paying workers less than a living wage become evident over time. Jobs in the apparel industry require long hours. Women who do these jobs cannot invest much time in other income-earning endeavors or in self-provisioning. If the pooled resources of their households are insufficient, they must try to increase their wages through working faster or longer, or they must look for another kind of job. While manufacturers sometimes complain about high turnover, it is not at all clear that they want to change this situation. Workers do not build up enough time in one plant to develop expectations that their wages should be raised. They do not develop the close ties with other workers that would allow a collective response to poor conditions. Those who have grievances "vote with their feet." Workers who want to increase their earnings move to another plant where they hope that better equipment or the nature of the new task will allow them to work faster and make more on piece rate.[43]

40. Michael Burawoy, "The Functions and Reproduction of Migrant Labor: Comparative Study of California and South Africa," *American Journal of Sociology* 81, no. 5 (1976): 1050–66.

41. Joan Smith and Immanuel Wallerstein, "Households as an Institution of the World Economy," in *Creating and Transforming Households*, ed. Joan Smith and Immanuel Wallerstein (New York: Cambridge University Press, 1992), 7.

42. Juárez Núñez, "Rebelión en el greenfield."

43. María Patricia Fernández-Kelly, *For We Are Sold, I and My People: Women and Industry in Mexico's Frontier* (Albany: State University of New York Press, 1983); Norma Iglesias Prieto, *Beautiful Flowers of the Maquiladora: Life Histories of Women Workers in Tijuana,*

In the cruelest of ironies, gender ideologies permit managers to use the insufficiency of the maquiladora wage against women workers. Factory owners have pointed to the fact that household members pool their incomes to argue that women's earnings in the maquiladora are only "supplemental." The irony here is that the necessity-driven practice of pooling income becomes a justification for paying less than a living wage. This irony is experienced most harshly by single mothers with young children, who often do not have access to the supplements that are supposedly their lot as women and that are the justification for their low wage.

Given gender relations in the United States and Mexico, it is probably accurate to see women's roles in families as shaping their labor force participation. But the way that happens is not as straightforward as the managers' logic presumes. In fact, managers use contradictory arguments to justify paying low wages. As Ruth Rosenbaum has noted: "Some argue that many workers are not married, and that a woman's take-home wage needs to support only the worker. Others argue that the worker is married and therefore the take-home wage should be half of what is needed to support the family. The reality is that persons are not paid according to family size."[44]

Women's responsibilities within households and families vary widely. While apparel companies moving into a new region of Mexico may hope to recruit younger, unmarried women, as demand for labor increases they must turn to workers in a broader range of situations, including married women with children, single mothers, and in some cases men. Some employers argue that women with children are more stable employees, in part because they need the job more. Family status alone does not adequately determine women's responsibilities. The husbands of married women may be unemployed or may earn too little to feed the family. As noted earlier, women may be married to men who have migrated to work in the United States. In this case the timing and amount of remittances may be unpredictable. Like those of male workers, women's economic responsibilities are heterogeneous. Yet the tendency that Alice Kessler-Harris has identified to pay a female worker for "what she is" rather than "what she does" remains.[45] The story is an old and familiar one, but it takes on new force as women in poor nations struggle to demand a living wage from some of the world's wealthiest corporations.

trans. Michael Stone and Gabrielle Winkler (Austin: University of Texas Press, 1997); Susan Tiano, *Patriarchy on the Line: Labor, Gender and Ideology in the Mexican Maquila Industry* (Philadelphia: Temple University Press, 1994).

44. Rosenbaum, *Making the Invisible Visible,* 5.

45. Alice Kessler-Harris, *A Woman's Wage: Historical Meanings and Social Consequences* (Lexington: University Press of Kentucky, 1990), 15–17.

Gender and the Construction of a Global Labor Market

The labor practices of Tultex and Liz Claiborne vividly illustrate Nancy Fraser's claim that gender is never a single issue but runs "like pink and blue threads" through our institutions of work and citizenship.[46] Gender is implicated in how firms imagine and design work processes and in how they structure jobs and the employment relationship. As companies begin to recruit workers from a labor market that is global in scope, gender also shapes the way they think about this endeavor. Gender ideologies inform their definition of the job and its skills, their understanding of the characteristics of new groups of workers, and their mapping of appropriate and inappropriate pools of labor.

When I interviewed managers at both Liz Claiborne and Tultex, I asked pointed questions about how they decided to produce different kinds of garments in different parts of the world, hoping to elicit information about when and why they moved into new regions and tapped new populations of workers. I understood that a range of economic criteria affected these decisions—from transport costs to trade law. And I believed that insofar as labor entered into their decision making, it would be as a cost—that is, that firms would consider the cost of labor as one factor in their choices. I was surprised, therefore, that when I asked managers at both Tultex and Liz Claiborne to explain their sourcing decisions, they spoke about skill. Individuals charged with sourcing decisions at both companies claimed that one of the key reasons they were producing "offshore" was to access skills that had become scarce in the United States.

At first glance, these claims appear to contradict an understanding that the movement of production was driven by cost competition and the search for low wages. In the case of women's labor, however, the apparent contradiction was resolved by naturalizing the skills involved. According to the managers' logic, women's location within the family economy and their inexperience with labor markets—those factors that garnered a low wage—were also the guarantee of their sewing skills.

In the discourse of managers, skill thus became a useful device for mapping a low-wage global workforce. The concept of skill has always been more than a way of assessing the technical requirements of jobs. Historically, it has been a dense nexus of claim making in which workers assert and attempt to defend claims that certain capabilities are scarce and valuable while em-

46. Nancy Fraser, *Unruly Practices: Power, Discourse and Gender in Contemporary Social Theory* (Minneapolis: University of Minnesota Press, 1989), 127.

ployers accept or refute that claim. Discussions of skill have been an important means of establishing hierarchies among types of work and providing a framework for determining rewards.

When discussing the characteristics they sought in workers, managers at both of the case study firms made statements that on the surface seemed paradoxical. The CEO at Tultex made the following comment about sewing positions: "They're hard jobs; they require some skill. Our sewing workforce is aging, and young people are not coming into these jobs. Not everyone can sew at a productive rate, so these jobs are probably best done somewhere else."[47] This view, so at odds with the way the industry historically has devalued sewing skills and with broader cultural evaluations of sewing work, was echoed by the vice president for sourcing. He asserted, "To get an operator—a beginner person that's never sewn before—to full speed probably could take eight or nine months or a year. It's a pretty difficult skill to master. . . . Sewing is the most difficult part of the process." These sentiments were further elaborated on and explained by the company's vice president for operations. He noted, "The workforce is getting older every year that goes by, and the people that sewed are gradually aging out of the market. And the new ones—the twenty-year-old sewing people—just are nonexistent. . . . In those areas that we have that require more skills— sewing, for example— . . . we move outside the U.S. The cost of paying labor for those high-skilled jobs is too great."

This manager not only argued that sewing work was skilled but suggested that the skill was becoming scarce among U.S. workers. He argued that the cohort of workers who possessed the necessary skills were aging and that younger women were not filling their jobs. He suggested that this was an important reason for moving jobs offshore.

Managers at Liz Claiborne made it clear that the cost of labor, quality, and performance were their three primary criteria in assigning work to a factory. But they saw this as linked in many ways to the global distribution of sewing skills. Managers there also commented on the erosion of sewing skills among the U.S. workforce, attributing it to a late twentieth-century job market where women had a broad range of employment options and where their wage work meant they no longer had time to sew or to teach their daughters to sew. "It is a specialized skill," one manager said. "And in my opinion, we've lost the ability to sew in America."

These statements contained three interlinked propositions about skill:

---

47. "With a Name Like Tultex, You've Got to Be Good," *Apparel Industry Magazine*, December 1997.

sewing is skilled work; the necessary skills are growing increasingly scarce in the United States; therefore it is necessary to seek these skills elsewhere. Taken together, these propositions form an argument about why it is necessary to move sewing jobs overseas. This argument not only presents the move as economically necessary and appropriate but attributes that necessity to a flaw, or lack, in the U.S. workforce. It relies on a paradigm of "naturalization of skill" that says sewing skills are found in a local population in the same way that a natural resource is discovered. According to such a paradigm, women do not acquire skills through training programs or learn them on the job. Believing them to be cultivated through socialization within the family, we do not see them as capacities forged through "public work." Rather, the paradigm portrays them as practices brought into the public realm from the family economy.

The first proposition—that sewing is skilled work—is surprising, given the difficulty sewing operators have had in pressing claims to skill throughout the history of the garment industry. As described in chapter 2, the high proportion of women in the industry and the structure of unions historically have made it hard for seamstresses to gain recognition for their difficult and intricate work. Managers' statements were even more surprising, however, because they were contradicted by the ways sewing was handled within the firms in question. Jobs that are highly skilled generally have long training periods and specific requirements. They command high wages, and these workers have bargaining power. None of these features characterized sewing jobs at Tultex Corporation. As noted earlier, the *Qualifications Book* that contained job descriptions for positions at the company listed the requirements for a sewing operator only as "good hand and finger dexterity; basic math ability; ability to follow written and oral instructions; lifting up to 30 pounds; standing; sitting."

The training period for the job was the shortest listed for any position— sixty days. There was no mention of familiarity with any particular type of sewing equipment, of the ability to perform specific operations, or of experience. Starting wages for sewing workers were approximately $2 an hour less than those for operators of knitting machines, dye jets, or cutting machines.

Evidence also contradicted the second proposition—that sewing skills were scarce. Certainly, managers at Tultex had no trouble filling these positions. In fact, because of the decision to locate its sewing shops in small, employment-starved rural U.S. communities, the firm was able to maintain waiting lists for these jobs. But managers implied that the larger problem was that young women were not entering the workforce with the same sewing skills their mothers had because they were not getting the training at home. They attributed the loss of these skills to a late twentieth-century job market where women had a broad range of employment options and where their wage work meant they no longer had time to sew or to pass the skill to their daughters.

On the surface, this argument about the scarcity of sewing skills made some sense. The U.S. workforce is, in fact, aging, and sewing skills in general have been declining among the population.[48] But workers were quick to take issue with this logic. A union organizer at Tultex who had worked as a sewing machine operator for most of her adult life responded to management's assertion that girls weren't leaving school knowing how to sew by saying, "That's bullshit! People don't come out of high school knowing how to operate a dye jet either." Her response revealed the gendered workings of the naturalization paradigm. Nearly all positions in the plant required training, from sixty days to six months. Every job required workers to become familiar with a machine, learn a complicated series of operations, and exercise discretion and care in performing them. Only with sewing did managers presume that workers entered the job with prior training, provided at home or in home economics classes in school. By pointing to the ways management's statements made sewing machine operators and dye-jet operators incommensurable, she uncovered the way that naturalization of skill allowed the firm to pay less for sewing work.

The third proposition, that the scarcity and cost of skill made it necessary for the firm to move to Mexico, is in many ways the most complex of the three. It presented Mexico (and developing economies more generally) as places where sewing skills were both abundant and cheap. If the United States is a place where women's homemaking skills have been lost to modernization and labor force participation, managers portrayed Mexico as a place where that has "not yet happened." This contrastive strategy implied that, although lost in the West, remnants of sewing cultures "still" exist in other parts of the world, to be discovered and tapped by resourceful entrepreneurs. In the 1990s, as the infrastructure and labor force of Mexican border regions became overtaxed, the apparel industry's trade fair recommended "seeking out new areas of the Mexican interior which had agricultural economies and cottage industries."[49] In these regions, the domestic

48. In 1998, the Bureau of Labor Statistics moved sewing machines from the "apparel and upkeep" category of consumer spending to "recreation" to take account of the fact that so few people make or mend their clothes. See Peter T. Kilborn, "Prosperity Builds Mounds of Cast-off Clothes," *New York Times*, July 19, 1999, A1.

49. Scott Malone, "Flying South? It's Time to Go," *Women's Wear Daily*, November 9, 1999, 8.

(womanly) skills "lost" by U.S. workers were conceptualized as intact, linked to the "simpler" ways of life that pertained there.[50]

Such a proposition needs to be evaluated in its multiple dimensions. First, it clearly overstates the ease with which new workers acquire necessary sewing skills. While some women in the rural areas where apparel factories relocate may have learned hand sewing or embroidery as children, they are not likely to be familiar with industrial sewing machines.[51] In the 1990s, labor productivity in the apparel factories of rural Mexico stood at approximately 55–65 percent of U.S. levels,[52] and Tultex management estimated their productivity levels in Mexico at 50 percent. The same vice president who claimed that sewing was skilled work and that those skills were growing increasingly scarce in the United States explained that "in Mexico and Jamaica we started out with very basic products. . . . The skill of the workforce was not . . . up to the level of the States." In the third quarter of 1997, company reports noted that substandard work performed in Mexican factories had affected profits. Improving the work quality and productivity of Mexican sewing operators took some time, suggesting that the skills involved were indeed substantial, but that they were learned, not found.[53]

While at the level of fact management's account of skill decline had numerous problems, at the level of ideology it was powerful and compelling. Workers and analysts have long noted the way a paradigm of skill naturalization can be used to depress wages by arguing that the abilities in ques-

50. Johannes Fabian has described the tendency in Western discourse to portray other cultures as representing the past of the West; see *Time and the Other: How Anthropology Makes Its Object* (New York: Columbia University Press, 1983).

51. The lack of transferability between industrial and home sewing (and the faultiness of the presumption that all women know how to sew) is vividly illustrated by the fact that one Honduran nongovernment organization serving maquila workers established workshops to teach women to sew their own clothes. In describing this program Mendez notes, "Ironically, though these workers labor all day at sewing, the piecemeal way in which labor is organized in the factories means that women lack the skills for sewing an entire article of clothing from start to finish." See Jennifer Bickham Mendez, "Creating Alternatives from a Gender Perspective: Transnational Organizing for Maquila Workers' Rights in Central America," in *Women's Activism and Globalization: Linking Local Struggles and Transnational Politics,* ed. Nancy A. Naples and Manisha Desai (New York: Routledge, 2002), 129.

52. Josephine Bow, "Made in Merida: The Next Hot Mexican Label," *Women's Wear Daily Global,* August 1999, 8.

53. Jane L. Collins, "Mapping a Global Labor Market: Gender and Skill in the Globalizing Garment Industry," *Gender and Society* 16, no. 5 (2002): 921–40. On the difficulties of learning the skills involved in industrial sewing, see Louise Lamphere, *From Working Daughters to Working Mothers: Immigrant Women in a New England Industrial Community* (Ithaca, N.Y.: Cornell University Press, 1987), 304–5.

tion are neither scarce nor acquired at much cost to the worker.[54] Managers here drew on a related strand of argument generated by the paradigm. They claimed that naturalized skills, because they are innate or the product of early socialization, cannot be acquired through training programs or on the job. This claim worked to strip agency from workers, who were assumed (as already fully socialized adults) to be unable to acquire or improve sewing ability. It placed agency in the hands of managers, who could search out, discover, and map new repositories of skill.

Managers' accounts played with a paradox that is generated by a paradigm of naturalized skill. If women reproduce certain skills through their domestic labor and transmit them through socialization in the home, how are those skills to be preserved once women are in the workforce? If women's labor market participation undermines both their home sewing and their ability to teach their daughters to sew, then by drawing women into the workforce, the apparel industry depletes its skill base. According to this view, as factories employ new populations of women, they undermine the reproduction of skill in the labor market.

This line of argument provides a justification for greenfields employment practices, where employers seek new populations of workers without labor market experience. It creates a linkage between what managers are willing to call skill and the vulnerability of these new populations of workers— that is, the paradigm links workers' skill to their *lack* of labor market experience. This paradoxical framing of skill makes women's "disadvantages" in the labor market at least a temporary advantage.[55] By defining sewing skill as "learned at home," managers are downplaying the importance of previous employment and justifying recruitment in regions with few labor market alternatives.

While managers claim it is the reproduction of "skill" that is being damaged by women's labor market participation, there is no real evidence that women's ability to sew is changing. What *does* change as women enter the labor market is the ability of the naturalization paradigm to effectively delegitimize their skill claims. As women gain experience with wage work, they come to realize the market value of their skills and their comparability to other skills that may be more highly remunerated. Working side by side

54. Diane Elson, "Nimble Fingers and Other Fables," in *Of Common Cloth: Women in the Global Textile Industry,* ed. Wendy Chapkis and Cynthia Enloe (Amsterdam: Transnational), 1983; Kessler-Harris, *Woman's Wage.*

55. Lourdes Arizpe and Josefina Aranda, "The 'Comparative Advantages' of Women's Disadvantages: Women Workers in the Strawberry Export Agribusiness in Mexico," *Signs* 7, no. 2 (1981): 453–73.

with other workers, developing more experience in—and options within— the labor market, perhaps participating in union activities, their sense that the work they do is skilled eventually comes to exceed management's claims that it is not.

Labor Activism and New Forms of Community

Not only are the apparel workers of places like Aguascalientes geographi- cally separated from their employers, but firms have constructed a social infrastructure where the connections between the worker and the work- place, and therefore among workers themselves, are tenuous and short- lived. The dense webs of social connection and shared experience out of which labor activism grows do not have much chance to emerge in these contexts. Workers themselves are actively responding to the difficulties— by scrambling to make ends meet, seeking out alternative sources of in- come, changing jobs, and in some cases developing new practices for con- fronting their employers about the terms and conditions of their work.

Given the daily realities of deterritorialized work regimes, it is not sur- prising that the locus of struggle among apparel workers has been not the shop floor but the community. The most important examples of this form of organizing come from the northern border region where, in the 1960s, the Center for the Orientation of Women Workers (COMO) emerged to sup- port women workers in their health and safety concerns and ultimately to link factory struggles with community organizing in more comprehensive ways. COMO, which was born out of labor mobilizations at the RCA electron- ics plant in Ciudad Juárez, provided a context for workers to discuss and analyze problems they confronted in the workplace.[56] It supported the for- mation of an independent union and the strike at Acapulco Fashions in Ciudad Juárez in 1978. But it was not primarily a workplace-based organiza- tion. It offered courses on a variety of topics and sponsored literacy and health campaigns. It also organized cooperatives among women working in the informal sector. Organizations like COMO were made necessary by the way state-run unions like the Confederation of Mexican Workers (CTM) and the Revolutionary Confederation of Workers and Peasants (CROC) dominated the Mexican labor movement, and by the way these groups marginalized women workers.[57] But the community was also an important site of organi-

56. Devon Peña, *The Terror of the Machine: Technology, Work, Gender and Ecology on the U.S.-Mexico Border* (Austin: Center for Mexican-American Studies, 1997), 149.

57. Jennifer Mendez ("Creating Alternatives," 127) has written that most organiza- tions in the Central American Network of Women in Solidarity with Women Workers in the

zation because of the transience of workers' ties to any one employer and the difficulty of forging connections on the shop floor.

A second community-based organization that supported apparel workers was the Border Committee for Women Workers (CFO), organized in the 1990s to promote improvements in working conditions in the maquiladoras and to inform workers of their rights. Edmé Dominguez has called the CFO "a workers organization without being a trade union," and she argues that this form of organization is necessary because of the difficulties trade unions have working in the maquiladora area.[58] While it provided support for workers in negotiating with specific companies, the Border Committee also organized against actions of the Mexican state (such as peso devaluations) and conducted more general programs in worker education.

A third organization of this type is the Casa de la Mujer—Factor X, established in 1989 in Tijuana. The Casa de la Mujer is renowned for combining its organizing around labor issues with initiatives in support of women's health and reproductive freedom. It sponsors workshops in sexuality, contraception, and domestic violence as well as on environmental conditions in the workplace and their effects on women's health. Casa de la Mujer insists that these issues are interconnected, supporting women's autonomy as workers and as people.

These organizations, and others like them, were built on principles of community unionism that emphasized alliances with other groups and linked labor's struggles to other community issues. But they also represent a gendered model of community unionism that recognizes the specific ways women negotiate the relationship between work, home, and community, the difficulties of operating through male-dominated political institutions, and the gender-specific concerns of women workers. As women who work in maquiladoras have invented their own forms of organizing, they have brought issues from what society has construed as the private domain into the zone of public discussion.

Because women who work in maquiladoras live and restore themselves in households and communities, and because of the nature of the family responsibilities they shoulder, it is not surprising that their activism spills over from where they work to where they live. When maquiladora workers

---

Maquilas were formed as a direct result of gender conflicts within unions or organizations of the Left.

58. Edmé Dominguez, "Regionalism from the People's Perspective: Mexican Women's Views and Experience of Integration and Transnational Networking," paper presented at the forty-first annual meeting of the International Studies Association, Los Angeles, March 14–18, 2001, 6.

have come together in organizations, they have been just as likely to address concerns about urban services, clean water, and day care as about their wages. Working outside traditional unions has meant that women in these organizations have not had to argue with their male colleagues about whether birth control and reproductive health were appropriate topics for discussion or whether child care was a priority. They have not been constrained by charters or agendas from deciding that fighting the effluents from the factory that poison the community's water supply is more important than demanding a better wage. Mexican maquiladora workers have confounded existing definitions of what is properly contestable by labor, pushing the historical boundary between public and private spheres.[59] In a similar way, new organizations of export sector workers in Central America "are not just concerned with traditional labor issues" but "work to empower women and improve their daily lives. . . . Their programs and strategies cut across the public/private divide by addressing women's social positions at home, in the workplace and in society in general."[60] These groups run programs on domestic violence and sexual abuse and other educational programs as well as administering credit and job training programs.

Another response to the deterritorialization of globalized production regimes has been the development of transnational organizing and solidarity work in support of apparel factory workers. The United Electrical, Radio, and Machine Workers of America (UE), a U.S.-based independent union started in 1936, and the Authentic Workers' Front (FAT), an independent federation of unions founded in Mexico in 1960, have been pioneers in cross-border labor organizing in the era of NAFTA. Since the mid-1990s, the UE and the FAT have maintained a strategic organizing alliance. They have conducted a number of cross-border actions, including filing complaints under NAFTA's labor-side agreements and holding demonstrations at work-

59. In 1999 the University of Wisconsin held a series of forums on the university's newly developed code of conduct for the sourcing of its collegiate apparel. At the second of these events, students who were involved in the national antisweatshop movement presented a number of new points that they wanted to see incorporated in the code. One of these was the demand that firms that produce collegiate apparel respect the rights of women workers, and specifically that they not subject them to pregnancy tests, fire them for being pregnant, or allow sexual harassment on the shop floor. Both the university administration and representatives of organized labor seemed puzzled about how these issue had gotten onto the agenda and what they had to do with labor rights. But the demand emerged directly out of communications between the student movement and the nongovernment organizations supporting Mexican apparel workers, and it reflected the concerns that came out of the nonunion labor activism of these groups.

60. Mendez, "Creating Alternatives," 129.

places and shareholders' meetings. The unions began these campaigns in the automobile and electronics sectors but later extended them to apparel. The alliance has involved UE members from the United States traveling to Mexico to support the FAT, but also FAT members traveling to Milwaukee and Chicago to support union drives there. In addition to specific organizing efforts, the alliance has held conferences, conducted joint mural projects, and run educational campaigns.

One of the most visible examples of transnational solidarity is the Coalition for Justice in the Maquiladoras, a group of religious, environmental, labor, and women's organizations in the United States, Mexico, and Canada. The Coalition has pressured transnational corporations that operate in maquiladoras to adopt socially responsible practices. A number of similar organizations sprang up in the 1990s. Some—like the Maquila Solidarity Network and the Maquiladora Health and Safety Support Network—focused specifically on maquiladoras in Mexico but did not limit their work to apparel factories. Others—like Sweatshop Watch, the Clean Clothes Campaign, United Students Against Sweatshops, and Behind the Label—monitored conditions in apparel factories worldwide. This antisweatshop movement, which operated on college campuses, in unions, in urban social movements, and as part of religious organizations, has created a kind of nongeographic community to monitor and publicize the practices of transnational firms. Activist groups have sought to build globally dispersed communities of accountability through public campaigns that bring workers' concerns to a broader community.

One example of how such community can operate occurred in 1999, when workers at a Phillips–Van Heusen factory in Guatemala voted for a union. This was the first time any of the country's more than two hundred export apparel factories had waged a successful union drive. Although it had signed the Clinton administration's Apparel Industry Partnership—formed to promote voluntary compliance with fair labor practices—Phillips–Van Heusen immediately shut the factory down, claiming that orders for shirts had fallen. The factory closing not only allowed the company to avoid dealing with the union at the plant in question but served as a warning to workers at plants throughout Central America that a union vote would place their jobs in jeopardy. In response to these events, United Students Against Sweatshops, The AFL-CIO's Labor Education in the Americas Project, and the People of Faith Network conducted an on-site investigation of the plant. They interviewed workers and managers and reviewed shipping records and other documents. Their report, which was posted on the Internet and covered by the *New York Times* and other national media, showed that Phillips–Van Heusen's official rationale for closing the plant was a coverup and that its actions had violated both Guatemalan labor law and the terms of the Apparel Industry Partnership.[61] Two other organizations, the Clean Clothes Campaign and Sweatshop Watch, organized a letter-writing campaign directed to corporate executives and shareholders. The company did not reopen the plant, but it was forced to recognize that its actions in Guatemala were not invisible in the United States and that they had consequences for its public image and ultimately for the value of its shares.

An even more dramatic example occurred in 2001, when workers at a Mexican factory (then Kukdong, now Mexmode) that produced athletic apparel for Nike and Reebok were fired for protesting the food they were served. United States students and solidarity workers responded by pressuring the athletic apparel manufacturers to have the plant rehire the workers and permit them to form an independent union. The apparel companies complied, and the workers established the first independent union in the Mexican apparel sector. They negotiated a bargaining agreement that significantly improved their wages and benefits. Even with these increased costs, Nike committed itself to continue doing business with the factory.[62]

In a final example, workers at two Guatemalan factories producing for Liz Claiborne held union votes in 2001. When managers responded with violence and threats against union members, an independent monitoring group hired by Liz Claiborne reported on these events. In response, CEO Paul Charron sent workers a letter affirming their right to choose a union, and the company pressured the factory owners to stop the harassment. In both of these cases, a community of accountability constituted of grassroots organizing efforts brought far-off events to public awareness, put names and faces on corporations, and exposed labor practices to scrutiny and evaluation. This response to the deterritorialization of production regimes allowed firms to be held responsible in the court of public opinion when they could not be in courts of law.

One weakness of these transnational alliances has been their tendency to rely on a narrow definition of what constitutes a labor movement. Jennifer Mendez reports that in Central America, northern-based solidarity organizations have tended to ally themselves with local trade union federations but have excluded autonomous women's organizations from their initiatives. She suggests that this has hampered projects to monitor the application of

61. Steven Greenhouse, "Union Criticizes Plant Closing in Guatemala," *New York Times,* February 28, 1999.

62. Ginger Thompson, "Mexican Labor Protest Gets Results," *New York Times,* October 8, 2001.

corporate codes of conduct in apparel factories. She argues that these attitudes have also made it difficult for women's groups like the Women Workers
and Unemployed Women's Movement María Elena Cuadra in Nicaragua to
gain access to "transnational political spaces such as summits of Central
American Ministers of Labor" or conferences sponsored by the International
Labor Organization or the U.S. Department of Labor.[63]

The comparative cases examined in this chapter teach us several things.
The first is that manufacturing sophisticated, high-quality products does
not automatically generate a more humane work process. The small-batch
production of high-quality fashion garments can be organized in ways that
rely on Taylorist control rather than principles of flexible specialization.
Where labor organizations and state regulation are weak, firms are unlikely
to invest in high-road alternatives.

Second, geographic distance and subcontracting arrangements tend to
deterritorialize the social relations of work. While firms' ties to the places
where they do business vary in complexity and strength, in general subcontracting weakens accountability. In the preface I mentioned the story of
Rumpelstiltskin, which Jane Schneider argues was a potent parable through
which workers conveyed their ambivalence about the first wave of textile
industrialization. In the fairy tale, Rumpelstiltskin struck a bargain with a
young woman. He would help her spin straw into gold if she would give
him her firstborn child in return. But in most versions of the story the
young woman would be allowed to keep the child if she could guess her
helper's name. For maquiladora workers, as for the rest of us, knowing the
names of things is an important source of power. In contexts of global subcontracting, it is a daunting challenge for workers to obtain the basic information necessary to defend their rights and interests. It is sometimes difficult for them even to know their employer's name.

The gender relations in maquiladoras, and gendered ideologies of work
and skill, create additional obstacles to organizing for change. Managers
use ideologies of skill to justify seeking out inexperienced workers. They
use time-honored preconceptions about women's role in families to justify
paying a low wage. At the same time, women's multiple responsibilities,
and their exclusion from traditional labor organizations, make it difficult
for them to organize. And yet they do, inventing radical new forms of activism that challenge our notions of public and private, of what work is, and
of what a social movement can be.

63. Mendez, "Creating Alternatives," 135, 137.

7

FROM GILDED AGE
TO NEW DEAL?

By the end of the 1990s, there was broad agreement among scholars and policymakers that the labor market in the apparel industry had become global in scope. As the International Labor Organization (ILO) proclaimed:

> The textile, clothing and footwear (TCF) industries are global: global inasmuch as production activities are worldwide and connected through various arrangements and strategic decisions to serve the world market; global insofar as trade, which is expanding more rapidly than the average of the manufacturing sector, is highly influenced by the changing conditions of international competitiveness and the relocation strategies implemented by global companies; and global because the geographical distribution of world employment is affected by the rapid changes in production and

The chapter title refers to Tom Hayden and Charles Kernaghan, "Pennies an Hour, and No Way Up," *New York Times*, July 7, 2002, A27; the authors say that improved conditions for workers in the United States resulted because they "fought their way out-marched for economic justice, built unions, voted and finally forced the Gilded Age to become the New Deal."

trade. TCF industries can be regarded, accordingly, as a "one world em-ployer."[1]

Ajit Singh and Ann Zammit have suggested that this integration of the industry has altered workers' rights, the terms and conditions of their work, and "indeed their whole lives." They argue that collective bargaining within one country must now take account of developments elsewhere and that "the mobility of investments by multinationals poses a continual threat to workers everywhere, changing the power relations at the bargaining table."[2] Apparel firms have regularly used the threat of relocation to discipline workers in all their production sites. Singh and Zammit note that while "it is widely agreed that the ability of multinationals to move their investment anywhere, North or South, weakens the bargaining power of labor in ad-vanced countries and is inimical to its interests . . . the same threat can be used against Southern workers."[3] In fact, the use of relocation threats against workers has become so common throughout the world that the ILO has classified it as a pervasive form of harassment and noted that it was particularly pernicious since workers had no legal grounds for redress.[4]

By 2002, Mexican workers were experiencing an onslaught of relocation threats and job loss in the export sector. In late spring of that year the *New York Times* announced, "Latest Data Dampens Mexico's Hopes," and *Women's Wear Daily* proclaimed, "Mexico's Shine Fades."[5] Between mid-2001 and mid-2002, the Mexican maquiladora sector lost over 240,000 jobs, or one-fifth of its workforce.[6] Analysts attributed the job loss to the downturn in the U.S. economy and the strong Mexican peso. But the most important factor in the apparel sector, everyone agreed, was competition from China and other very low wage countries, as quotas established under the Multi-Fiber Arrangement entered the third stage of their phase-out. From 2000 to 2001, China's share of apparel and textile imports rose 3 percent, to $9.5 billion, while Mexico's proportion of these imports declined 6 percent, to $9.6 billion. In the first three months of 2002, China surpassed Mexico as

1. International Labour Organization, "Labour Practices in the Footwear, Leather, Tex-tiles and Clothing Industries," Report for discussion at the Tripartite Meeting on Labour Practices in the Footwear, Leather, Textiles and Clothing Industries, Geneva, October 16–20, 2000, 6.

2. Ajit Singh and Ann Zammit, *The Global Labour Standards Controversy: Critical Issues for Developing Countries* (Geneva: South Centre, 2000), 77.

3. Ibid., 78.

4. Ibid., 77.

5. Graham Gori, "Latest Data Dampens Mexico's Hopes," *New York Times*, April 12, 2002; Joanna Ramey, "Mexico's Shine Fades," *Women's Wear Daily*, May 12, 2002, 19.

6. Gori, "Latest Data Dampens Mexico's Hopes."

the primary source of U.S. imports of textiles and apparel for the first time since 1997.[7] As one industry analyst reported, "Companies are almost frantically preparing for the end of quotas by moving sourcing offices . . . into Shanghai and building relationships with Chinese factories. . . . That sucking sound you hear on January 1, 2005 is going to be China taking in the world's sourcing."[8]

According to the *Washington Post*, the problem was that wages in Mexico had been rising faster than inflation for several years. Mexican workers were "paying for their success," the headline read. Although wages in the maquiladora sector were still below subsistence levels, workers were losing their jobs because their wages "were no longer considered low in the world economy."[9] As Mexican managers considered the wreckage left behind by the loss of corporate contracts, one noted flatly, "T-shirt factories do not stimulate economic expansion. . . . A textile plant can open and close in a week."[10]

As conditions have shifted, workers of both global North and global South have sought to move beyond an understanding of their condition as one of competition. They have sought to build, in Harvey's words, "a movement that reaches out across space and time . . . to confront the universal and transnational qualities of capital accumulation."[11] They have examined the ways that multinational investment decisions, international mergers and acquisitions, and the corporate pursuit of shareholder value create coincidences of interest[12] and have sought to develop an alternative vision of globalization that includes regulation and social provision.

Despite the undeniable connections between workers in places like the United States, Mexico, China, and Bangladesh, many economists have persisted in using evolutionary or developmental frameworks to deny the "coevalness" of workers in different parts of the world.[13] These accounts

---

7. Data are from OTEXA (Office of Textiles and Apparel), U.S. Department of Commerce, International Trade Administration, "Textile and Apparel Trade Balance Report, 2001–2002."

8. Thomas Cunningham, "The China Syndrome," *DNR*, May 27, 2002.

9. Mary Jordan, "Mexican Workers Pay for Success," *Washington Post*, June 20, 2002, A1.

10. Ginger Thompson, "Mexico Is Attracting a Better Class of Factory in Its South," *New York Times*, June 29, 2002. Unfortunately the story reported on the opening of only one airplane parts factory, in the face of the closure of 350 maquiladoras.

11. David Harvey, *Spaces of Capital: Toward a Critical Geography* (New York: Routledge, 2001), 390.

12. Singh and Zammit, *Global Labour Standards Controversy*, 78.

13. The term is used by Johannes Fabian to describe arguments that frame poorer nations as "further back in time"; see *Time and the Other: How Anthropology Makes Its Object* (New York: Columbia University Press, 1983).

present the situation in developing nations today as parallel to Europe at the dawn of the Industrial Revolution. According to these arguments, apparel is a starter industry and is particularly appropriate to countries with abundant unskilled labor. It provides a way for nations with few other resources to begin to accumulate capital. This process will eventually lead to a "transition" from low to higher-skill and higher-wage jobs and to improved levels of development.[14] Such arguments ignore the fact that the key actors in the industry are multinational corporations operating from cities like New York, Seoul, and Los Angeles. These firms have no long-term commitment to the places where they produce apparel and have been quite vocal about their willingness to relocate if wage levels rise. Far from committing themselves to the development of a region, they play off and draw advantage from the differences among regions. In the words of a recent ILO report: "This constant challenge to international competitiveness . . . means that jobs created in any one country cannot be regarded as a long-term gain. . . . The countries that suffer most as a result of this instability are those with limited development alternatives."[15]

Some economists have suggested that criticism of wages and working conditions in apparel factories of developing nations is ethnocentric in imposing the standards of wealthy nations on poor ones. Jagdish Bhagwati has argued, for example, that "wages paid to workers in the developing world are considered 'too low' because they are measured against developed world standards."[16] Critics of antisweatshop activism have also argued that attempting to improve these conditions may have a negative impact. Well-known economists who came together in response to antisweatshop endeavors on U.S. campuses have noted that multinational corporations "commonly pay their workers more on average in relation to the prevailing market wage for similar workers . . . [and] in cases where subcontracting is involved, workers are generally paid no less than the prevailing market wage." Furthermore, they expressed concern that "if MNCs are persuaded to pay even more to their apparel workers . . . the net result would be shifts in employment that will worsen the collective welfare of the very workers in poor countries who are supposed to be helped."[17] Or as Paul Krugman

14. Linda Lim, summary of sweatshop discussion, University of Michigan Business School, http://www.spp.umich.edu/rsie/acit/Documents/LimStanfordSlides.pdf.

15. ILO, "Labour Practices," 31.

16. Jagdish Bhagwati, "Nike Wrongfoots the Student Critics," *Financial Times*, May 2, 2000.

17. ACIT (Academic Consortium on International Trade), *Anti-Sweatshop Letter*, July 29, 2000.

has written, "The facts of global trade are not always pretty. If you buy a product made in a third-world country, it was produced by workers who are paid incredibly little by Western standards and probably work under awful conditions. . . . But the anti-globalization movement has a remarkable track record of hurting the very people and causes it claims to champion. . . . Even what looks to us like bad jobs at bad wages are almost always much better than the alternatives."[18] These critics have suggested that the desire to improve apparel industry working conditions represents the misinformed impulses of First World activists who are "captive to unions" like UNITE.[19]

There is a troubling contradiction here between the claim that the garment industry can provide a good starting point for development and the assertion that improvements in wages or working conditions will lead to the withdrawal of investment. How is development to be achieved if workers do not struggle for better conditions? Advances such as the forty-hour week, the minimum wage, and health and safety rules did not simply evolve in the industrialized nations, and they were not the result of the largesse of industry leaders. They resulted from workers' protest and national dialogue about what was right and fair. If workers in developing country cannot express their desire for better wages and working conditions without fear of capital flight, how is social progress to be achieved?

Kimberly Ann Elliott and Richard B. Freeman have responded to the argument that campaigns to improve wages and working conditions may actually harm workers. They contend that First World apparel workers who join movements in solidarity with their Third World peers do not harbor the "illusion that low wage apparel or shoe manufacturing jobs will return to the United States, although they may want to slow the decline," and they point out that the antisweatshop movement has been outspoken in opposing protectionism.[20] They acknowledge that if wage targets are determined "by outside activists with strong ideological stances rather than by local NGOs or unions," they may risk setting standards so unrealistic as to cause firms to close shop.[21] The solution, they argue, is not to do nothing, but to actively make use of local information to develop realistic goals while advocating for core labor rights such as freedom of association and collec-

18. Paul Krugman, "Hearts and Heads," editorial, *New York Times,* April 22, 2001.

19. Bhagwati, "Nike Wrongfoots the Student Critics."

20. Kimberly Ann Elliott and Richard B. Freeman, "White Hats or Don Quixotes? Human Rights Vigilantes in the Global Economy," paper presented at National Bureau of Economic Research Conference on Emerging Labor Market Institutions, August 2000, 21.

21. Ibid., 22.

tive bargaining. As described in chapter 6, labor and its affiliated movements have also sought to create "communities of accountability" within which firms that move operations in response to workers' activism will be called on publicly to account for those actions.

Political economist Jeffrey Winters has responded to the claims that multinationals pay better than local firms and that any jobs are better than no jobs by arguing, "Should American students be any less outraged just because Nike positions itself slightly higher than some of the exceptionally bad local Indonesian or Vietnamese producers?" Some of these jobs with multinationals are good only in relation to horrible prevailing conditions, he suggests. Given high rates of unemployment and underemployment, "Indonesians would line up outside a slave plantation if they could be sure they got regular food and a roof over their head."[22] But would that make it right for multinationals to employ them as slaves?

Within a more general frame, Nobel laureate Amartya Sen has suggested that to ask whether workers are better off as a result of globalization is to pose the wrong sort of question. "Even if the poor were to get just a little richer," he writes, "this would not necessarily imply that [they] were getting a fair share of the potentially vast benefits of global economic interrelations. . . . One cannot rebut the criticism that a distributional arrangement is unfair simply by noting that all parties are better off than they would be in the absence of cooperation."[23] Sen goes on to argue for the construction of democratic institutions within which the poor can claim economic rights and freedoms. For workers this would entail establishing key rights to association and bargaining.

Global activism has not yet been very successful in gaining these "enabling rights" for workers where states have not wished to provide them.[24] The ILO has attempted to assess what it calls "Fundamental Principles and Rights at Work" for the apparel industry. Relying on responses to questionnaires that were provided by governments and their social partners, the picture that emerges is not encouraging. Formal sector labor regulation in many nations is undercut by large underground sectors and homework. In some countries, firms operating in specially designated export processing zones are exempt from national labor law. Unions, where they exist, are not always fully democratic but are frequently affiliated with an employer

22. Quoted in Liza Featherstone and Doug Henwood, "Clothes Encounters: Activists and Economists Clash over Sweatshops," *Lingua Franca* 11, no. 2 (2001): 1–6.

23. Amartya Sen, "How to Judge Globalism," *American Prospect,* special supplement, "Globalism and Poverty," Winter 2002, A5.

24. Elliott and Freeman, "White Hats or Don Quixotes?" 23.

or with the state or dominant political parties. Rights to collective action and free association and institutional mechanisms for workers to exercise a voice remain an important domain of struggle.[25]

The argument that "25 cents an hour is better than nothing at all"[26] also forecloses discussion of the kinds of jobs and workplace community that are being created by the apparel industry as it relocates production around the globe. If any job is better than none (ignoring, for the moment, the question whether "none" is the true alternative), then we cannot distinguish between jobs that impose new regimens of quality control and more traditional processes. We cannot address the question of how subcontracting alters the relation between workers and employers, affecting the prospects for collective bargaining or any resolution of grievances. Social scientists and activists need to move from blunt questions of whether workers are somewhat better off to address how work and working conditions are changing in response to competitive pressures and investment strategies. While the market for apparel labor is global, production is instantiated through different social relations and practices in different contexts. We need to focus more attention on the methods corporations use to recruit, train, and discipline workers and through which they institute particular labor processes, and on the ways workers seek autonomy and improved conditions within these arrangements.

What this book contributes to such an understanding is twofold. First, it has disproved the contention of economists and sociologists in the 1980s that producing fashion goods requires greater skill and a more participatory labor process (with the attendant expectation that this would remain a First World specialty). Production of high-quality fashion apparel on a quick response base is now common throughout the world. It is accomplished not through flexible work practices and new skills but by intensifying Taylorist techniques of measurement and control. These practices have not undermined the traditional forms of organizing production such as the progressive bundle system and its remuneration by piece rate, but they have been applied in conjunction with these methods, creating new levels and kinds of stress for workers.

Second, subcontracting and casualization of employment relations have been shown to erode the basis on which workers can make claims on their employers. The paternalist system of labor relations in southern U.S. gar-

25. ILO, "Labour Practices."

26. Daniel L. Jacobs, "A Sweatshop Is Better Than Nothing," Los Angeles Times, April 25, 2001, B9.

ment factories like that run by Tultex was harsh and unfair, and its demise was duly celebrated by workers with the advent of the union and the era of "rule and contract." But *both* of these systems offered workers more voice and more recourse than the systems of subcontracting in place in the factories studied in Mexico. Workers there had no contract—formal or informal—with their employer. They had very little knowledge about the firm. And perhaps most important, they had no institutional means to bring claims, to grieve ill treatment, or to otherwise challenge the conditions of their labor. If rights to association and collective bargaining are the crucial first step in achieving gains for workers, how are they to be exercised in the context of such deterritorialized work regimes?

Workers at plants like Burlmex and Confitek are not laboring in a nascent industry in a nation that is taking its first steps toward economic development. They are working for multinational corporations in a globally organized production process that, in the case of Liz Claiborne, encompasses thirty-two countries. The fate of the workers in those thirty-two nations is linked through the firm's investment strategies. It is also linked, as activists have argued, to the attitudes and demands of consumers (and shareholders) in industrialized nations. New international communities of accountability, focused on particular firms and their brands, can support workers in their attempts to negotiate improved conditions.

If new forms of globally organized community can provide certain kinds of support to apparel workers, so can new forms of community-based unionism. While community or social movement unionism has been envisioned as a set of alliances between labor movements and other interests within a locality or region,[27] women workers—who have frequently been excluded from unions, or marginalized within them—have developed new models of how this can be accomplished. Their organizations support members as whole persons, whose health and reproductive activity affect their work and whose work sustains (or fails to sustain) their families. They address the ways that power relations within the workplace intersect with hierarchies of race, ethnicity, and gender outside its boundaries. And they create contexts for workers to discuss grievances and problems and to learn about existing rights and labor law. If there is hope that workers can devise ways of confronting highly mobile, geographically distant, and legally removed firms, it is through some combination of these new forms of global and local organizing.

27. Kim Moody, *Workers in a Lean World: Unions in the International Economy* (New York: Verso, 1997).

REFERENCES

Scholarly Works

Abernathy, Frederick H., John T. Dunlop, Janice H. Hammond, and David Weil. *A Stitch in Time: Lean Retailing and the Transformation of Manufacturing; Lessons from the Apparel and Textile Industries*. New York: Oxford University Press, 1999.

Adler, William M. "A New Day in Dixie." *Southern Exposure* 12, no. 1 (1994): 17–27.

———. *Mollie's Job: A Story of Life and Work on the Global Assembly Line*. New York: Scribner, 2000.

Amin, Ash, ed. *Post-Fordism: A Reader*. Cambridge: Blackwell, 1994.

Amin, Ash, and Anders Malmberg. "Competing Structural and Institutional Influences on the Geography of Production in Europe." In Amin (1994), 227–48.

Anderson, Benedict. *Imagined Communities: Reflections on the Origin and Spread of Nationalism*. London: Verso, 1983.

Appelbaum, Richard, and Gary Gereffi. Power and Profits in the Apparel Commodity Chain. In Bonacich et al. (1994), 42–62.

Arizpe, Lourdes, and Josefina Aranda. "The 'Comparative Advantages' of Women's Disadvantages: Women Workers in the Strawberry Export Agribusiness in Mexico." *Signs* 7, no. 2 (1981): 453–73.

Arrighi, Giovanni. *The Long Twentieth Century: Money, Power and the Origins of Our Times*. New York: Verso, 1994.

Ashbaugh, Carolyn, and Dan McCurry. "On the Line." *Southern Exposure* 4, nos. 1–2 (1976): 30–39.

Bean, Susan S. "Gandhi and Khadi, the Fabric of Indian Independence." In *Cloth and Human Experience*, ed. Annette B. Weiner and Jane Schneider, 355–76. Washington, D.C.: Smithsonian Institution Press, 1989.

Belussi, Fiorenza. "Benetton, Italy: Beyond Fordism and Flexible Specialization; The Evolution of the Network Firm Model." In *Computer-Aided Manufacturing and Women's Employment: The Clothing Industry in Four EC Countries*, ed. Swasti Mitter, 73–91. London: Springer-Verlag, 1992.

Berger, John. *The Look of Things*. New York: Viking Press, 1974.

Beynon, Huw, and Ray Hudson. "Place and Space in Contemporary Europe: Some Lessons and Reflections." *Antipode* 25, no. 3 (1993): 177–90.

Bhagwati, Jagdish. *Free Trade Today*. Princeton: Princeton University Press, 2002.

Billings, Dwight. *Planters and the Making of a "New South": Class, Politics and Development in North Carolina, 1865–1900*. Chapel Hill: University of North Carolina Press, 1979.

Blauner, Robert. *Alienation and Freedom: The Factory Worker and His Industry*, 1964. Chicago: University of Chicago Press.

Bluestone, Barry, and Bennett Harrison. *The Deindustrialization of America: Plant Clos-*

ings, Community Abandonment and the Dismantling of Basic Industry. New York: Basic Books, 1982.

Bonacich, Edna, and Richard Appelbaum. *Behind the Label: Inequality in the Los Angeles Apparel Industry.* Berkeley: University of California Press, 2000.

Bonacich, Edna, Lucie Cheng, Norma Chinchilla, Nora Hamilton, and Paul Ong, eds. *Global Production: The Apparel Industry in the Pacific Rim.* Philadelphia: Temple University Press, 1994.

Bonacich, Edna, and David V. Waller. "Mapping a Global Industry: Apparel Production in the Pacific Rim Triangle." In Bonacich et al. (1994), 21–41.

Boyte, Harry. "The Textile Industry: Keel of Southern Industrialization." *Radical America* 6, no. 2 (1972): 4–49.

Buni, Andrew. *The Negro in Virginia Politics, 1902–1965.* Charlottesville: University Press of Virginia, 1967.

Burawoy, Michael. "The Functions and Reproduction of Migrant Labor: Comparative Study of California and South Africa." *American Journal of Sociology* 81, no. 5 (1976): 1050–66.

———. *The Politics of Production.* London: Verso, 1985.

Byerly, Victoria. *Hard Times, Cotton Mill Girls: Personal Histories of Womanhood and Poverty in the South.* Ithaca, N.Y.: ILR Press, 1986.

Carrillo, Jorge V. "The Apparel Maquiladora Industry at the Mexican Border." In Bonacich et al. (1994), 217–29.

Carrillo, Teresa. "Women, Trade Unions and New Social Movements in Mexico: The Case of the 'Nineteenth of September' Garment Workers Union." Ph.D. diss., Stanford University, 1990.

Cash, Wilbur J. *Mind of the South.* New York: Alfred A. Knopf, 1941.

Castells, Manuel. *The Informational City.* Oxford: Blackwell, 1989.

———. *The Rise of Network Society.* Vol. 1. Oxford: Blackwell, 1996.

Chandler, Alfred D., Jr. *The Visible Hand: The Managerial Revolution in American Business.* Cambridge: Harvard University Press, 1977.

———. *Scale and Scope: The Dynamics of Industrial Capitalism.* Cambridge: Harvard University Press, 1990.

Chapkis, Wendy, and Cynthia Enloe. *Of Common Cloth: Women in the Global Textile Industry.* Washington, D.C.: Transnational Institute, 1983.

Chazen, Jerome. "Notes from the Apparel Industry: Two Decades at Liz Claiborne." *Columbia Journal of World Business* 31, no. 2 (1996): 40.

Cleal, Dorothy, and Hiram H. Herbert. *Foresight, Founders and Fortitude: The Growth of Industry in Martinsville and Henry County, Virginia.* Bassett, Va.: Bassett Printing, 1970.

Cockburn, Cynthia. *The Machinery of Dominance: Women, Men and Technical Know-How.* London: Pluto Press, 1985.

Cockcroft, James D. *Mexico: Class Formation, Capital Accumulation and the State.* New York: Monthly Review Press, 1983.

———. *Mexico's Hope: An Encounter with Politics and History.* New York: Monthly Review Press, 1998.

Collins, Jane L. "Flexible Specialization and the Garment Industry." *Competition and Change* 5, no. 2 (2001): 165–200.

———. "Deterritorialization and Workplace Culture." *American Ethnologist* 29, no. 1 (2002): 151–200.

———. "Mapping a Global Labor Market: Gender and Skill in the Globalizing Garment Industry." *Gender and Society* 16, no. 5 (2002): 921–40.

Cowie, Jefferson. *Capital Moves: RCA's Seventy Year Quest for Cheap Labor.* New York: New Press, 1999.

Cowie, Jefferson, and John D. French. "NAFTA's Labor Side Accord: A Textual Analysis." *Latin American Labor News* 9 (1993–94): 5–8.

Coyle, Angela. "Sex and Skill in the Organization of the Clothing Industry." In *Work, Women and the Labour Market,* ed. Jackie West, 10–26. London: Routledge, 1982.

Cravey, Altha. "Cowboys and Dinosaurs: Mexican Labor Unionism and the State." In Herod (1998), 75–98.

Cunningham, Thomas. "The China Syndrome." DNR, May 27, 2002.

Dicken, Peter. *Global Shift: Transforming the World Economy.* 3d ed. New York: Guilford, 1998.

Dickerson, Kitty. *Textiles and Apparel in the Global Economy.* 2d ed. Englewood Cliffs, N.J.: Merrill, 1995.

Dominguez, Edmé. "Regionalism from the People's Perspective: Mexican Women's Views and Experience of Integration and Transnational Networking." Paper presented at the forty-first annual meeting of the International Studies Association, Los Angeles, March 14–18, 2001.

Dublin, Thomas. *Women at Work.* New York: Columbia University Press, 1979.

Dudley, Kathryn Marie. *The End of the Line: Lost Jobs, New Lives in Postindustrial America.* Chicago: University of Chicago Press, 1994.

Edelson, S., and A. D'Innocenzio. "Seminar's Focus: Megafirm's Clout." *Women's Wear Daily,* March 26, 1998.

Edwards, Richard. *Contested Terrain.* New York: Basic Books, 1979.

Elger, Tony, and Paul K. Edwards. "Introduction." In *The Global Economy, Nation-States and the Regulation of Labour,* ed. Paul K. Edwards and Tony Elger, 1–41. London: Mansell, 1999.

Elson, Diane. "Nimble Fingers and Other Fables." In *Of Common Cloth: Women in the Global Textile Industry,* ed. Wendy Chapkis and Cynthia Enloe, 5–14. Amsterdam: Transnational, 1983.

Encarta (Microsoft). Liz Claiborne. *Distinguished Women of Past and Present,* 1995. Distinguishedwomen.com/biographies/claibor.html.

Enloe, Cynthia. *Bananas, Beaches and Bases.* Berkeley: University of California Press, 1989.

Ewen, Stuart, and Elizabeth Ewen. *Channels of Desire: Mass Images and the Shaping of American Culture.* New York: McGraw-Hill, 1982.

Fabian, Johannes. *Time and the Other: How Anthropology Makes Its Object.* New York: Columbia University Press, 1983.

Fernández-Kelly, María Patricia. *For We Are Sold, I and My People: Women and Industry in Mexico's Frontier.* Albany: State University of New York Press, 1983.

Frankel, Linda. "Southern Textile Women: Generations of Survival and Struggle." In *My Troubles Are Going to Have Trouble with Me: Everyday Trials and Triumphs of Women Workers,* ed. Karen Brodkin Sacks and Dorothy Remy, 39–60. New Brunswick, N.J.: Rutgers University Press, 1984.

———. "'Jesus Leads Us, Cooper Needs Us, the Union Feeds Us': The 1958 Harriet-Henderson Textile Strike." In Leiter, Schulman, and Zingraff (1991), 101–20.

Fraser, Nancy. *Unruly Practices: Power, Discourse and Gender in Contemporary Social Theory.* Minneapolis: University of Minnesota Press, 1989.

Frederickson, Mary. "'I Know Which Side I'm On': Southern Women in the Labor Movement in the 20th Century." In *Women, Work and Protest: A Century of U.S. Women's Labor History,* ed. Ruth Milkman, 156–80. Boston: Routledge, 1985.

Freeze, Gary. "Poor Girls Who Might Otherwise Be Wretched: The Origins of Paternalism in North Carolina's Mills, 1836–1880." In Leiter, Schulman, and Zingraff (1991), 21–32.

Garson, Barbara. *Money Makes the World Go Around: One Investor Tracks Her Cash through the Global Economy, from Brooklyn to Bangkok and Back.* New York: Viking, 2001.

Gaventa, John. "From the Mountains to the Maquiladoras: A Case Study of Capital Flight and Its Impact on Workers." In *Communities in Economic Crisis: Appala-*

chia and the South, ed. John Gaventa, Barbara Ellen Smith, and Alex Willingham, 85–95. Philadelphia: Temple University Press, 1990.

Genovese, Eugene. *Roll, Jordan, Roll: The World the Slaves Made.* New York: Random House, 1976.

Gereffi, Gary. "The Organization of Buyer-Driven Global Commodity Chains: How U.S. Retailers Shape Overseas Production Networks." In Gereffi and Korzeniewicz (1994), 95–122.

———. "International Trade and Industrial Upgrading in the Apparel Commodity Chain." *Journal of International Economics* 48 (1999): 37–70.

Gereffi, Gary, and Miguel Korzeniewicz, eds. *Commodity Chains and Global Capitalism.* Westport, Conn.: Praeger, 1994.

Gereffi, Gary, Miguel Korzeniewicz, and Roberto P. Korzeniewicz. "Introduction." In Gereffi and Korzeniewicz (1994), 1–14.

Ghadar, Fariborz, William H. Davidson, and Charles S. Feigenoff. *U.S. Industrial Competitiveness: The Case of the Textile and Apparel Industries.* Lexington, Mass.: D. C. Heath, 1987.

Glenn, Susan A. *Daughters of the Shtetl: Life and Labor in the Immigrant Generation.* Ithaca, N.Y.: Cornell University Press, 1990.

Goldstein, Bruce, Marc Linder, Laurence E. Norton II, and Catherine K. Ruckelshaus. "Enforcing Fair Labor Standards in the Modern American Sweatshop: Rediscovering the Statutory Definition of Employment." *University of California at Los Angeles Law Review* 46, no. 4 (1999): 983–1164.

González Esparza, Víctor Manuel. *Jalones modernizadores: Aguascalientes en el siglo XX.* Aguascalientes: Instituto Cultural de Aguascalientes, 1992.

Green, Nancy L. "Women and Immigrants in the Sweatshop: Categories of Labor Segmentation Revisited." *Comparative Studies in Society and History* 38, no. 3 (1996): 411–33.

———. *Ready-to-Wear and Ready-to-Work: A Century of Industry and Immigrants in Paris and New York.* Durham, N.C.: Duke University Press, 1997.

Greider, William. *One World, Ready or Not: The Manic Logic of Global Capitalism.* New York: Simon and Schuster, 1997.

Hall, Jacqueline Dowd, James Leloudis, Robert Korstad, Mary Murphy, Lu Ann Jones, and Christopher Daly. *Like a Family: The Making of a Southern Cotton Mill World.* New York: Norton, 1987.

Hammond, Janice H. "Quick Response in Retail/Manufacturing Channels." Research Paper, Harvard University Center for Textile and Apparel Research, 1993.

Hamrick, Karen S., Stephen A. MacDonald, and Leslie A. Meyer. International Trade Agreements Bring Adjustment to the Textile and Apparel Industries. *Rural Conditions and Trends* (U.S. Department of Agriculture) 11, no. 1 (2000): 31–41.

Hanson, Gordon H. "Industrial Organization and U.S.–Mexico Free Trade: Evidence from the Mexican Garment Industry." In Bonacich et al. (1994), 230–46.

Hardt, Michael, and Antonio Negri. *Empire.* Cambridge: Harvard University Press, 2000.

Harrison, Bennett. *Lean and Mean: Why Large Corporations Will Continue to Dominate the Global Economy.* New York: Guildford, 1994.

Harvey, David. The *Condition of Post-modernity.* Cambridge: Blackwell, 1989.

———. *The Limits to Capital.* New York: Verso, 1999. (Originally published 1982.)

Helfand, Judith. "Sewing History." *Southern Exposure* 22, no. 1 (1994): 42–44.

Herod, Andrew, ed. *Organizing the Landscape: Geographical Perspectives on Labor Unionism.* Minneapolis: University of Minnesota Press, 1998.

Herrera Nuño, Eugenio. *Aguascalientes: Sociedad, economía, política y cultura.* Mexico City: Universidad Nacional Autónoma de México, Centro de Investigaciones Interdisciplinarias en Humanidades, 1989.

Hill, Judith. *A History of Henry County, Virginia.* Baltimore: Regional Publishing, 1983.

Hodges, James. "J. P. Stevens and the Union Struggle for the South." In *Class and Com-*

munity in Southern Labor History, ed. Gary M. Fink and Merl E. Reed, 53–64. Tuscaloosa: University of Alabama Press, 1994.

Hopkins, Terence, and Immanuel Wallerstein. "Commodity Chains in the World Economy prior to 1800." *Review* 10, no. 1 (1986): 157–70.

Iglesias Prieto, Norma. *Beautiful Flowers of the Maquiladora: Life Histories of Women Workers in Tijuana.* Translated by Michael Stone and Gabrielle Winkler. Austin: University of Texas Press, 1997.

Janiewski, Dolores. "Southern Honor, Southern Dishonor: Managerial Ideology and the Construction of Gender, Race and Class Relations in Southern Industry." In *Work Engendered,* ed. Ava Baron, 47–69. Ithaca, N.Y.: Cornell University Press, 1991.

Jennings, J. Rhyne. *Some Cotton Mill Workers and Their Villages.* Chapel Hill: University of North Carolina Press, 1923.

Jones, Gareth Stedman. *Languages of Class: Studies in English Working Class History, 1832–1982.* New York: Cambridge University Press, 1983.

Juárez Núñez, Huberto. *Rebelión en el Greenfield.* Puebla: Benemérita Universidad Autónoma de Puebla and American Federation of Labor–Congress of Industrial Organizations, 2002.

Kessler-Harris, Alice. "Organizing the Unorganizable: Three Jewish Women and Their Union." In *Class, Sex, and the Woman Worker,* ed. Milton Cantor and Bruce Laurie, 144–65. Westport, Conn.: Greenwood Press, 1977.

———. *Out to Work: A History of Wage Earning Women in the United States.* New York: Oxford University Press, 1982.

———. "Problems of Coalition-Building: Women and Trade Unions in the 1920s." In *Women, Work and Protest: A Century of U.S. Women's Labor History,* ed. Ruth Milkman, 110–38. New York: Routledge, 1985.

———. *A Woman's Wage: Historical Meanings and Social Consequences.* Lexington: University Press of Kentucky, 1990.

Kidwell, Claudia B., and Margaret C. Christman. *Suiting Everyone: The Democratization of Clothing in America.* Washington, D.C.: Smithsonian Institution Press, 1974.

Klein, Naomi. *No Logo: Taking Aim at the Brand Bullies.* New York: Picador, 1999.

Knight, Alan. "Caudillos y campesinos en el México revolucionario: 1910–1917." In *Caudillos y campesinos en la Revolución mexicana,* ed. David A. Brading. Mexico City: Fondo Cultura Económica, 1985.

Korzeniewicz, Miguel. "Commodity Chains and Marketing Strategies: Nike and the Global Athletic Footwear Industry." In Gereffi and Korzeniewicz (1994), 247–65.

Lahne, Herbert J. *The Cotton Mill Workers.* New York: Farrar and Rinehart, 1944.

Lamphere, Louise. *From Working Daughters to Working Mothers: Immigrant Women in a New England Industrial Community.* Ithaca, N.Y.: Cornell University Press, 1987.

Latour, Bruno. *We Have Never Been Modern.* Cambridge: Harvard University Press, 1993.

Leborgne, Daniel, and Alain Lipietz. "New Technologies, New Modes of Regulation: Some Spatial Implications." *Environment and Planning, D: Society and Space* 6 (1988): 263–80.

Lee, Ching Kwan. *Gender and the South China Miracle: Two Worlds of Factory Women.* Berkeley: University of California Press, 1998.

Leiter, Jeffrey, Michael D. Schulman, and Rhonda Zingraff, eds. *Hanging by a Thread: Social Change in Southern Textiles.* Ithaca, N.Y.: Cornell University Press, 1991.

Lipietz, Alain. *Mirages and Miracles.* New York: Verso, 1987.

Louie, Miriam Ching Yoon. *Sweatshop Warriors: Immigrant Women Workers Take on the Global Factory.* Boston: South End Press, 2001.

Lynch, Catrin. "The 'Good Girls' of Sri Lankan Modernity: Moral Orders of Nationalism and Capitalism." *Identities* 6, no. 1 (1999): 55–89.

———. "The 'Good Girls' of Sri Lankan Modernity: Moral Orders of Nationalism, Gender, and Globalization in Village Garment Factories." Ph.D. diss., University of Chicago, 2000.

Marcus, George. "Ethnography in/of the World System: The Emergence of Multi-sited Ethnography." *Annual Review of Anthropology* 24 (1995): 95–117.

Marx, Karl. *Capital*. Vol. 1. New York: Vintage, 1954. (Originally published 1886.)

———. "The British Rule in India: Surveys from Exile." In *Political Writings*, vol. 2. London: Penguin, 1973.

Massey, Doreen. *Spatial Divisions of Labor: Social Structures and the Geography of Production*. 2d ed. New York: Routledge, 1995.

McHugh, Cathy. *Mill Family: The Labor System in the Southern Textile Industry*. New York: Oxford University Press, 1988.

McKay, Steven C. "Securing Commitment in an Insecure World: Power and the Social Regulation of Labor in the Philippine Electronics Industry." Ph.D. diss., University of Wisconsin, 2001.

Mendez, Jennifer Bickham. "Creating Alternatives from a Gender Perspective: Transnational Organizing for Maquila Workers' Rights in Central America." In *Women's Activism and Globalization: Linking Local Struggles and Transnational Politics*, ed. Nancy A. Naples and Manisha Desai, 121–40. New York: Routledge, 2002.

Mishel, Lawrence, Jared Bernstein, and John Schmitt. *The State of Working America, 2000-01*. Washington, D.C.: Economic Policy Institute, 2000.

Mitchell, Broadus. *The Rise of the Cotton Mills in the South*. Baltimore: Johns Hopkins University Press, 1921.

Mohanty, Chandra Talpade. "Cartographies of Struggle: Third World Women and the Politics of Feminism." In *Third World Women and the Politics of Feminism*, ed. Chandra Talpade Mohanty, Ann Russo, and Lourdes Torres, 1–50. Bloomington: Indiana University Press, 1991.

———. "'Under Western Eyes' Revisited: Feminist Solidarity through Anticapitalist Struggles," *Signs* 28, no. 2 (2003).

Feminism without Borders. Durham, N.C.: Duke University Press, 2003.

Moody, Kim. *Workers in a Lean World: Unions in the International Economy*. New York: Verso, 1997.

NACLA [North American Congress on Latin America]. "Capital's Flights: The Apparel Industry Moves South." *NACLA Report on the Americas* 11 (1977): 1–33.

Ong, Aihwa. *Spirits of Resistance and Capitalist Discipline: Factory Women in Malaysia*. Albany: State University of New York Press, 1987.

———. *Flexible Citizenship: The Cultural Logics of Transnationality*. Durham, N.C.: Duke University Press, 1999.

Orlove, Benjamin. *Alpacas, Sheep and Men: The Wool Export Economy and Regional Society in Southern Peru*. New York: Academic Press, 1977.

Peck, Jamie. *Work-Place: The Social Regulation of Labor Markets*. New York: Guilford Press, 1996.

Peña, Devon. *The Terror of the Machine: Technology, Work, Gender and Ecology on the U.S.–Mexico Border*. Austin: Center for Mexican-American Studies, 1997.

Piore, Michael J., and Charles F. Sabel. *The Second Industrial Divide: Possibilities for Prosperity*. New York: Basic Books, 1984.

Polanyi, Karl. *The Great Transformation*. New York: Rinehart, 1944.

Porter, Michael. *The Competitive Advantage of Nations*. New York: Free Press, 1990.

Rabach, Eileen, and Eun Mee Kim. "Where Is the Chain in Commodity Chains? The Service Sector Nexus." In Gereffi and Korzeniewicz (1994), 123–41.

Rise, Eric. *The Martinsville Seven: Race, Rape and Capital Punishment*. Charlottesville: University Press of Virginia, 1995.

Roediger, David. *The Wages of Whiteness: Race and the Making of the American Working Class*. New York: Verso, 1991.

Rosenbaum, Ruth. *Making the Invisible Visible: A Study of the Purchasing Power of Maquila Workers in Mexico*. Hartford, Conn.: Center for Reflection, Education and Action, 2000.

Ruggie, John. "Territoriality and Beyond: Problematizing Modernity in International Relations." *International Organization* 47, no. 1 (1993): 139–74.

Sabel, "Flexible Specialization and the Re-emergence of Regional Economies." In Amin (1994), 101–56.

Safa, Helen. "Runaway Shops and Female Employment: The Search for Cheap Labor." In *Women's Work,* ed. Eleanor Leacock and Helen Safa, 58–73. South Hadley, Mass.: Bergin and Garvey, 1986.

Salaff, Janet. *Working Daughters of Hong Kong: Filial Piety or Power in the Family?* London: Cambridge University Press, 1981.

Salmerón Castro, Fernando I. *Intermediarios del progreso: Política y crecimiento económico en Aguascalientes.* Mexico City: Centro de Investigaciones y Estudios Superiores en Antropología Social, 1996.

Salzinger, Leslie. "From High Heels to Swathed Bodies: Gender Meanings under Production in Mexico's Export-Processing Industry." *Feminist Studies* 23, no. 3 (1997): 549–74.

Sassen, Saskia. *Globalization and Its Discontents: Essays on the New Mobility of People and Money.* New York: New Press, 1998.

Schneider, Jane. "Rumpelstiltskin's Bargain: Folklore and the Merchant Capitalist Intensification of Linen Manufacture in Early Modern Europe." In *Cloth and Human Experience,* ed. Annette B. Weiner and Jane Schneider, 177–213. Washington, D.C.: Smithsonian Institution Press, 1989.

Schulman, Michael D., and Cynthia Anderson. "The Dark Side of the Force: A Case Study of Restructuring and Social Capital." *Rural Sociology* 64, no. 3 (1999): 351–72.

Scott, Allen J. *Metropolis: From the Division of Labor to Urban Form.* Berkeley: University of California Press, 1988.

Scott, James C. *The Moral Economy of the Peasant: Rebellion and Subsistence in Southeast Asia.* New Haven: Yale University Press, 1976.

Simon, Bryant. "'Choosing between the Ham and the Union': Paternalism in the Cone Mills of Greensboro, 1925–30." In Leiter, Schulman, and Zingraff (1991), 81–100.

Sklair, Leslie. *Assembling for Development: The Maquila Industry in Mexico and the United States.* Boston: Unwin Hyman, 1989.

Smith, Chris. "Flexible Specialization, Automation and Mass Production." *Work, Employment and Society* 3, no. 2 (1989): 203–20.

Smith, Joan, and Immanuel Wallerstein. "Households as an Institution of the World Economy." In *Creating and Transforming Households,* ed. Joan Smith and Immanuel Wallerstein, 3–23. New York: Cambridge University Press, 1992.

Smith, Neil. *Uneven Development: Nature, Capital and the Production of Space.* London: Blackwell, 1990.

Smith, Robert Sidney. *Mill on the Dan: A History of the Dan River Mills, 1882–1950.* Durham, N.C.: Duke University Press, 1960.

Soros, George. *George Soros on Globalization.* New York: Public Affairs, 2002.

Spivak, Gayatri. "Can the Subaltern Speak?" In *Marxism and the Interpretation of Culture,* ed. Cary Nelson and Lawrence Grossberg, 271–313. Urbana: University of Illinois Press, 1988.

Stoney, George, Judith Helfand, and Susanne Rostock. *Uprising of '34* (film). Point of View, Public Broadcasting Services, 1995.

Su, Julie. "El Monte Thai Garment Workers: Slave Sweatshops." In *No Sweat: Fashion, Free Trade and the Rights of Garment Workers,* ed. Andrew Ross, 143–50. New York: Verso, 1997.

Tannenbaum, Frank. *Darker Phases of the South.* New York: G. P. Putnam, 1924.

Taylor, Frederick Winslow. *The Principles of Scientific Management.* New York: Norton, 1967. (Originally published 1911.)

Thompson, Edward P. The Moral Economy of the English Crowd in the 18th Century. *Past and Present* 50 (1971): 76–136.

Thompson, Holland. *From the Cotton Field to the Cotton Mill: A Study of the Industrial Transition in North Carolina.* New York: Macmillan, 1906.

Tiano, Susan. *Patriarchy on the Line: Labor, Gender and Ideology in the Mexican Maquila Industry.* Philadelphia: Temple University Press, 1994.

Tomaney, John. "A New Paradigm of Work Organization and Technology?" In Amin (1994), 157–94.

Waldinger, Roger, D. *Through the Eye of the Needle: Immigrants and Enterprise in New York's Garment Trades.* New York: New York University Press, 1986.

Wertheimer, Barbara. *We Were There: The Story of Working Women in America.* New York: Pantheon Books, 1977.

Wieneck, Henry. *The Hairstons: An American Family in Black and White.* New York: St. Martin's Press, 1999.

Williams, Karel. "From Shareholder Value to Present-Day Capitalism." *Economy and Society* 29, no. 1 (2000): 1–12.

Willis, Susan. *A Primer for Daily Life.* New York: Routledge, 1991.

Wolf, Diane. *Factory Daughters: Gender, Household Dynamics and Rural Industrialization in Java.* Berkeley: University of California Press, 1992.

Wolf, Eric. *Europe and the People without History.* Berkeley: University of California Press, 1982.

Wright, Melissa Webb. "Third World Women and the Geography of Skill." Ph.D. diss., Johns Hopkins University, 1996.

———. "Crossing the Factory Frontier: Gender, Place and Power in the Mexican *Maquiladora.*" *Antipode* 29, no. 3 (1997): 278–302.

Zeitlin, Jonathan, and Peter Totterdill. "Markets, Technology and Local Intervention: The Case of Clothing." In *Reversing Industrial Decline? Industrial Structure and Policy in Britain and Her Competitors,* ed. Paul Hirst and Jonathan Zeitlin, 155–90. New York: St. Martin's Press, 1989.

Magazines, Newspapers, and Trade Publications

AAFA [American Association of Footwear and Apparel Manufacturers]. *Trends: A Quarterly Compilation of Statistical Information on the Apparel and Footwear Industries.* Arlington, Va.: AAFA, 2000.

Abend, Jules. "The Out-Sourcing Revolution." *Bobbin,* May 2001, 38–44.

Aguascalientes State Council for Economic and Trade Development. *Mexico OnLine,* 2000. www.mexonline.com/aguacal.htm.

Apparel Industry Magazine. "With a Name Like Tultex, You've Got to Be Good." December 1997.

———. "Women's Wear Makers Look Ahead to 2005." November 1999.

———. "Apparel's 'Big Six' Retailers Grab a 90% Share." Industry News, June 1999.

———. "Parity Bill Still Afloat." November 1999.

Baker, Bernard. "Clower: Lessons of Tultex Must Never Be Forgotten." *Martinsville Bulletin,* December 3, 1999.

Bello, Walden. "No Logo: A Brilliant but Flawed Portrait of Contemporary Capitalism." *Z Magazine,* April 2001.

Blum, Justin. "Laid Off and Left Behind." *Washington Post,* February 28, 2000, B1.

Bow, Josephine. "Made in Merida: The Next Hot Mexican Label." *Women's Wear Daily Global,* August 1999, 8.

Breslin, Jimmy. "In Sweatshops, Plundered Lives." *Newsday,* April 11, 2001, A2.

Business Week. "Brave New Factory." July 23, 2001, 75–78.

CANAIVE [Camara Nacional de la Industria del Vestido]. "Higiene y seguridad laboral." *Informe: Delegación Aguacaliente* 2, no. 1 (2000): 4–5.

Cawley, Jon. "Tultex Head Fields Questions from Rowdy Crowd." *Roanoke Times,* January 12, 2000, A1.

Conrad, Andree. "Scaling the Heights in a Discount World." *Apparel Industry Magazine,* June 1999.

Cortázar, Mercedes. "El pulso de la industria: Alianzas progresistas en Aguascalientes." *La Bobina,* August 2001.

DesMarteau, Kathleen. "Liz Launches Global Quality Coup." *Bobbin,* July 1999, 34–38.

———. "TDA Implementation: The Clock Is Ticking." *Bobbin,* November 2000, 6–14.

Drucker, Peter. "Will the Corporation Survive?" *Economist,* November 3, 2001, 14–18.

Economist. "Couture Ordinaire." October 14, 1995, 79–82.

———. "America Bubbles Over." April 18, 1998.

———. "The Case for Brands." September 8, 2001, 11.

Ellis, Kristi. "Producer Prices for Apparel Fall below October 2000." *Women's Wear Daily,* November 12, 2001, 19.

Ellis, Kristi, and Kristin Young. "Who Pays? Liability Debate Rages On." *Women's Wear Daily,* January 29, 2001, 18–19.

Fairchilds. *Textile and Apparel Financial Directory.* New York: Fairchild's Books and Visuals, 1991, 1999.

Forbes. "Ready to Ware: Software and Hardware That Is." April 15, 1999, 30–32.

———. "The Great Quota Hustle." March 6, 2000, 119–25.

Friedhoff, Eric. "Clower Says Tultex Move Will Be Widely Felt Here." *Martinsville Bulletin,* December 3, 1999.

Friedman, Thomas L. "Protesting for Whom?" *New York Times,* April 24, 2001, A19.

Fung, Shirley. "Vendors Play the Margin Game." *Women's Wear Daily,* December 13, 2000.

Gereffi, Gary. "Global Shifts, Regional Response: Can North America Meet the Full-Package Challenge?" *Bobbin,* November 1997, 16–31.

Gladwell, Malcolm. "Annals of Retail: Clicks and Mortar." *New Yorker,* December 6, 1999.

Greenhouse, Steven. "Union Criticizes Plant Closing in Guatemala." *New York Times,* February 28. 1999.

Greider, William. "The Right and U.S. Trade Law: Invalidating the Twentieth Century." *Nation* 273, no. 11 (2001): 21–29.

Hale, John. "Tultex Gives Up." *Martinsville Bulletin,* February 10, 2000.

———. "Tultex Pensioners Stunned by Payout." *Martinsville Bulletin,* April 1, 2001.

Hayden, Tom, and Charles Kernaghan. "Pennies an Hour, and No Way Up." *New York Times,* July 7, 2002, A27.

Heisler, Eric. "Textile Turmoil: Sweeping Changes in the Apparel and Textile Industries Leave Workers and Community Leaders Struggling to Cope with an Uncertain Future." *Greensboro News and Record,* May 23, 1999, A1.

Heisler, Eric, and Michelle Cater. "Tultex Issues Layoffs." *Depot.Com,* December 4, 1999.

Hirschfield, Stuart. "Industry Factors Challenging Apparel Manufacturers and Suppliers." *Apparel Industry Magazine,* August, 1998.

Jacobs, Brenda. "Mexico Promises to Remain Number One for Production Sharing." *Bobbin,* March 1998.

———. "Duty Measures Spark Concern." *Bobbin,* February 2001, 64–68.

Kegley, Dan. "Tough Luck for Tultex Employees?" *Smyth County News and Messenger,* January 21, 1998.

Kegley, George. "Tultex Blacks Told to Vote against Union." *Roanoke Times,* September 11, 1990.

———. "Anti-union Speaker Disclaimed." *Roanoke Times,* September 13, 1990.

———. "Tultex Outgrows Fleecewear." *Roanoke Times,* March 26, 1993.

Kegley, George, and Patricia Lopez Baden. "Union Defeated Again at Tultex." *Roanoke Times,* September 21, 1990.

Kelly, Sandra Bown. "In This Mill Town, Its as Much about Respect as Pay." *Roanoke Times,* July 17, 1994.

Kilborn, Peter T. "Prosperity Builds Mounds of Cast-off Clothes." *New York Times,* July 19, 1999, A1.

Krishnamurty, Kiran. "As Holidays Near, Tultex Layoffs Hit Hard for Southside Workers." *Charlottesville Daily Progress,* December 7, 1999.

Kristof, Nicholas D., and Sheryl WuDinn. "Two Cheers for Sweatshops." *New York Times Magazine,* September 24, 2000, 6–7.

Krugman, Paul. "Hearts and Heads." *New York Times,* April 22, 2001.

Labick, Kenneth. "Benetton Takes on the World." *Fortune,* June 13, 1983, 192.

Lardner, James. "Annals of Business: The Sweater Trade I." *New Yorker,* January 11, 1988, 39–73.

———. "Annals of Business: The Sweater Trade II." *New Yorker,* January 18, 1988, 57–73.

Larson, Kristin. "Sourcing's New Dynamic." *Women's Wear Daily.* May 30, 2001.

Levine, Joshua. "A Lifestyle in a Label." *Forbes,* November 1, 1996, 155–57.

Lockwood, Lisa. "Charron's Catharsis." *Women's Wear Daily,* June 13, 2001, 14.

Malone, Scott. "Cut It Out: Vendors and Merchants Keep Finding New Ways to Slash Time from the Production Cycle." *Women's Wear Daily,* March 24, 1999, 24–25.

———. "Mills Move to Sewing Machines." *Women's Wear Daily* April 6, 1999, 12.

———. "Flying South? It's Time to Go." *Women's Wear Daily,* November 9, 1999, 8.

———. "Dramatic Departure: U.S. Advocate Milliken Quits ATMI over CBI." *Women's Wear Daily,* October 4, 2000, 1, 14.

Maquila Solidarity Network Update. "Will Fox Allow Independent Unions in Mexico's Maquilas?" December 2001. Maquilasolidarity.org/resources/maquilas/fox - dec2001.htm.

Martinsville Bulletin. "Union Vows to Explore Aid for Ousted Workers." December 3, 1999.

———. "Ex-Worker Now Works at Job Hunt." December 5, 1999.

———. "Franck: Tultex Hurt by NAFTA, Quickly Changing Industry." December 6, 1999.

———. "Safety Net Gives Help to Newly Jobless." December 19, 1999.

———. "Workers to File Claims." January 12, 2000.

———. "Executive Pay Questioned." January 12, 2000.

———. "Judge Cuts CEO's Request for Severance." February 10, 2000.

———. "Tultex Says Assets Won't Pay Creditors." March 29, 2000.

———. "Tultex Checks Slowed." August 10, 2000.

Melton, Page Boinest. "How Global Trade and NAFTA Hit a Vital Virginia Business." *Virginia Business,* August 2000.

Mexican Labor News and Analysis. Slower Growth in Maquilas 6 (May 2001). Accessed online.

———. Landmark Study Shows Mexican Maquila Workers Not Able to Meet Basic Needs on Sweatshop Wages. 6 (August 2001). Accessed online.

Mexico Investment Board. *The Textile Industry in Mexico.* Mexico City: Mexico Investment Board, 1993.

Prescott, Lee Ann. "Tultex Is Leaving Chilhowie." *Smyth County News and Messenger,* January 10, 1998.

Rabon, Lisa. "Navigating New Terrain." *Bobbin,* August 1999, 34–37.

———. "Season of the Consumer." *Bobbin,* December 2000, 1.

Ramey, Joanna. "More Industry Job Losses in May." *Women's Wear Daily,* June 10, 2002, 3.

Ramey, Joanna, and Scott Malone. "House to Get CBI Parity Bill Again." *Women's Wear Daily,* March 2, 1999.

La Reforma. "Adelanta PAN en Aguascalientes." August 5, 2001.

Rolnick, Alan. "Labor Law Liability: Where Does the Buck Stop? Lopez Case Shakes U.S. Manufacturer-Contractor Paradigm." *Bobbin,* April 1999, 64.

Ryan, Thomas J. "M&A: The Rush to the Altar: Efficient = Big." *Women's Wear Daily,* November 10, 1999.

———. "Analyst Tells Vendors: Be 'Naughty.'" *Women's Wear Daily,* April 3, 2000.

———. "Small Firms Need Size to Survive." *Women's Wear Daily,* November 13, 2000.

Southern Exposure. "News Roundup: Workers Win Biggest Victory since Stevens." 22, no. 3 (1994): 3.

Sturgeon, Jeff. "The Tultex Tale." *Roanoke Times,* February 4, 1996.

———. "New Leader Has Earned His Stripes." *Roanoke Times,* February 4, 1996.

———. "Third Quarter Profits at Tultex Hurt by Problems with Contract Work." *Roanoke Times,* October 24, 1997.

———. "Tultex Reports First Yearly Loss." *Roanoke Times,* February 18, 1998.

———. "Tultex Posts Dramatic $36.5 Million Loss." *Roanoke Times,* February 26, 1999.

———. "Martinsville, Virginia Apparel Company Dissolving amid Financial, Policy Woes." *Roanoke Times,* March 6, 2000.

Swoboda, Frank. "Labor's Day in Martinsville." *Washington Post,* September 5, 1994, section F1.

Thompson, Ginger. "Mexican Labor Protest Gets Results." *New York Times,* October 8, 2001.

Union of Needletrades, Industrial and Textile Employees (UNITE), Local 1994. *Union Chit Chat!* 1, nos. 1–3 (1996).

———. *Union News* 1, nos. 1–4 (1998–99).

Winger, Rocío María. "The E-Zone." *Apparel Industry Magazine,* November 1998. Accessed online.

Women's Wear Daily. "August Apparel Job Loss Is Worst in Six Months." September 7, 1999.

———. "Fashion's Wheel of Fortune." September 7, 1999.

———. "A Changing of the Guard at UNITE." June 26, 2001.

Wray, Ginny. "Tultex Stock on Hold." *Martinsville Bulletin,* December 6, 1999.

———. "Rollins to Reshape Tultex into Different Company." *Martinsville Bulletin,* December 7, 1999.

———. "Ousted Workers Sound Off." *Martinsville Bulletin,* January 12. 2000.

———. "Textile Aid Bill Is Rejected." *Martinsville Bulletin,* February 11, 2000.

Young, Vicki M. "Making the Most of the Midmarket." *Women's Wear Daily,* May 15, 2000.

Documents

ACTWU. Agreement between Amalgamated Clothing and Textile Workers Union (ACTWU) and Tultex Corporation, Martinsville, Virginia, April 3, 1995.

Bronfenbrenner, Kate. "Uneasy Terrain: The Impact of Capital Mobility on Workers, Wages and Union Organizing." Report submitted to the U.S. Trade Deficit Review Commission. September 6, 2000.

Instituto Nacional de Estadística, Geografía e Informática [INEGI-National Statistical, Geographic and Information Institute], *Aguascalientes hoy.* Aguascalientes: INEGI, 1993.

New York State, Office of the Attorney General. Press Release: Garment Manufacturers Cited under "Hot Goods Law." July 19, 1998.

New York State, Office of the Governor. Press Release: Governor Signs Law Adding Another Tool to Fight Sweatshops. August 10, 1998.

Patrick Henry Development Council. Community Profile. Martinsville, Virginia, 2000.

Tultex Corporation. Press Release: Tultex Corporation Announces Record Fourth Quarter and Annual. February 6, 1997.

———. *Operations.* 1998.

———. *Facilities.* 1999.

———. *The Manufacturing Process.* 1999.

———. *Qualifications Book.* 1999.

———. Press Release: Tultex Elects New President with Extensive Marketing Experience. May 25, 1999.

———. Press Release: Tultex Plans to Sell or Seeks Alternative Uses of Its Consumer Service Center. September 9, 1999.

———. Press Release: Tultex Announces Plant Closing in Bastian, Virginia. September 28, 1999.

————. Press Release: Tultex Files Chapter 11. December 3, 1999.

————. Notes, Shareholder's Meeting. May 27, 1999.

United States Census Bureau. *Provisional Estimates of Population for Virginia Counties and Cities.* Washington, D.C.: Government Printing Office, 1988.

United States Department of Labor. *"No Sweat" Initiative Fact Sheet.* 1996. www.dol. gov/dol/esa/public/forum/fact.htm.

United States Department of Labor, Bureau of Labor Statistics. *Employment Hours and Earnings, U.S. 1990–94.* Vol. 1. Bulletin 2445. Washington, D.C.: Government Printing Office, 1994.

United States Department of Labor, Employment Standards Administration. Press Release USDL-112. August 25, 2000.

————. Press Release NY-206. October 26, 2000.

United States General Accounting Office. *Garment Industry: Efforts to Address the Prevalence and Conditions of Sweatshops.* GAO HEHS-95–29, November 1994.

INDEX
